Fatal
Victories

For Anne

Contents

MORE PEOPLE, MORE POWER

FATAL

VICTORIES

William Weir

ARCHON BOOKS
1993

First published in 1993 as an Archon Book, an imprint of
The Shoe String Press, Inc., Hamden, Connecticut 06514

Printed in the United States of America

The paper used in this publication meets
the minimum requirements of American National Standard
for Information Sciences—Permanence of Paper
for Printed Library Materials.
ANSI Z39.48—1984   ∞

Library of Congress Cataloging-in-Publication Data

Weir, William, 1928–
Fatal victories / William Weir.
p.   cm.
Includes bibliographical references.
1. Military history.   2. Battles.   I. Title.
D25.9W45   92-38210   909—dc20
ISBN 0-208-02361-5 (alk. paper)

Acknowledgments

THE AUTHOR OF A BOOK LIKE THIS, WHICH AIMS TO PRESENT NEW INSIGHTS rather than new facts, is indebted to hordes of other people, most of whom he does not know. In this case, *Fatal Victories* could not have been attempted without all the writers, many of them anonymous, who recorded all the facts about all of the conflicts listed here. I am also indebted to all those who have analyzed sets of these facts and theorized about them.

All those facts and theories, though, would have been useless if I couldn't find them. Another group whose help was absolutely essential are all the people of the Connecticut state library system, particularly those in the Guilford and Wallingford libraries, who seemed able to find any book ever published.

The people at The Shoe String Press were enormously helpful. That's especially true of my editor, Shoe String's president, James Thorpe III. Jim's comments as the work went forward, invariably insightful and encouraging, stimulated thinking and led to the exploration of new aspects of subjects under consideration.

My thanks, too, to C. Brian Kelly, editor of *Military History* magazine, which first published my Majuba Hill chapter.

My wife, Anne, was always supportive and inspiring, although I spent a good part of each day monopolizing a computer that she also had important uses for.

As is customary, I want to point out that whatever good may be found in this book is there because of the help of others, but the errors are my own. Actually, that's pretty obvious, but authors always make the statement. So I do, too—just to emphasize how much help I've had and how much I appreciate it.

GUILFORD, CONNECTICUT
DECEMBER 11, 1992

Introduction

KING PYRRHUS KNEW THAT THE BARBARIANS WERE NOT TO BE TRIFLED with. He had beaten them once before, but only after his own army had suffered tremendous casualties: about 16 percent of his force had been killed. He had a larger army now, reinforced with troops from both the Greek cities in southern Italy and from the local Italian tribes who also feared the northern barbarians—Romans, they were called—who had begun expanding their territory.

The Romans had attacked in a checkerboard formation. Companies of Roman infantry were separated by open space, which was covered by companies in a similar formation in the second line. The checkerboard let the northerners extend their line to outflank his, and they had done so when Pyrrhus fought them near Heraclea. Only because Pyrrhus had managed to outflank the outflankers with his elephants and Thessalian cavalry had the Romans been defeated. To avoid being flanked again, the king of Epirus had rearranged his phalanx so the line would be longer and thinner in combat formation.

Pyrrhus had not achieved his reputation for military skill in the Hellenistic world by underrating his opponents. It's true that the Roman losses had been almost twice his, but they were in their own country and better able to make them up. His most reliable troops came from mainland Greece, across the Adriatic. The Italian allies were typical undisciplined barbarians, and the indolent Hellenes from the Greek cities in Italy were not much better.

Pyrrhus had tried to make peace with the Romans so he could go to Sicily, where the Greeks on that island had asked him to help them against the Carthaginians. Civilized, wealthy Sicily certainly promised richer booty than the small farms and unimpressive cities of central Italy. The Romans, though, had rejected his peace offer, saying it would be dishonorable to make peace after a defeat.

So Pyrrhus planned his campaign carefully. He recruited more allies in southern Italy, especially the Samnites, tough hillmen who had troubled the Romans for generations. He marched up the Adriatic coast, where the

Samnites could protect his communications. He didn't turn left until he was well north of Rome. With luck, he would be able to march south to the city, catching the Romans by surprise.

Pyrrhus had never been particularly lucky. His family had been driven from the throne of Epirus by usurpers; he had regained it only through a combination of cunning and hard fighting. Now, after turning east, Pyrrhus found his luck running true to form. Waiting for him was a Roman army twice the size of the one he had beaten at Heraclea.

At Asculum, on the Aufidus River, 40,000 Romans stood with their backs to the river and their flanks protected by two marshes. The country was rough and wooded—difficult terrain for a phalanx, which relied on a straight line and close order for maximum shock.

Pyrrhus drew up his new long phalanx formation, extended its line farther with Greek and Italian allies and attacked.

The Romans fought as they had at Heraclea, hurling spears from beyond the points of the Epirots' 18-foot pikes. The Roman spear heads were mounted on iron rods a yard long, so they could not be cut off when they stuck in the phalangites' shields and weighed them down.

After throwing their missiles, the Roman infantry charged, using their enormous shields to slide under the points of the pikes and attack the phalangites with their short swords.

The phalangites, trained in the tradition of the great Alexander, were not taken so easily. They had swords of their own, and the Romans had to withdraw. As they followed the retreating Romans, though, the advantages of the checkerboard formation became obvious. The Epirots tended to follow the groups nearest them, with the result that the phalanx bent and gaps appeared in the line. The Roman companies in the second line drove straight for those gaps.

The armies fought until it became too dark. Then both withdrew to their camps to count their losses.

The next day, Pyrrhus sent his light infantry to occupy the marshes the Romans had used to protect their flanks. He intended to compress that too-mobile Roman line and attack with his 10 war elephants. When the Romans attacked the next morning, Pyrrhus sent his elephants, escorted by light infantry, through the marshes and around the Roman rear. The Romans had arrayed chariots carrying long spears as a defense against such a maneuver. The rough ground that had hindered the phalanx, however, was even worse for chariots. The elephants broke through, routed the Roman cavalry, and the Romans fled to their camp.

About 6,000 Romans were killed at Asculum. But Pyrrhus lost 3,500, including most of his generals, his best friends and the flower of his army. He himself was severely wounded.

"One more such victory," said the Epirot King, "and I am undone."

While the Romans were recruiting new legions, Pyrrhus put the Roman war on hold and departed for Sicily, where in two years, he drove the Carthaginians out of all the island except the city of Lilybaeum. He was less successful politically than militarily, though, and he returned from Sicily little richer than before.

Back in Italy, Pyrrhus made one of his few military mistakes. Attempting a predawn attack on a Roman camp at Beneventum, he sent his phalangites through a dense wood. He did not try to march in battle formation, something the greenest rookie could see was impossible. But he did not realize how much time it would take for even single files to move through the forest at night carrying 18-foot pikes. The Epirots' did not emerge from the woods until well after the sun had risen, and the Romans chopped them up while they were trying to form a line. Somehow, Pyrrhus again brought up his elephants through another path in the forest. A Roman reserve force suddenly appeared however. The Romans killed two elephants and captured the other eight. Pyrrhus left Italy for good, having won every battle but the last.

A brilliant general, but an unlucky one, Pyrrhus was riding through the streets of Epirus three years later when an old woman emptying a chamber pot into the street lost her grip on the vessel. The pot hit King Pyrrhus on the head, killing him. In spite of all his victories, Pyrrhus, called "a second Alexander" by both friends and foes, left little but a phrase that entered most European languages—Pyrrhic victory, a victory won at excessive cost.

Although he gave his name to this sort of triumph, Pyrrhus's victories were not as Pyrrhic as many others. In spite of his losses at Heraclea and Asculum, Pyrrhus was able to go on to Sicily, clobber the Carthaginians and come back to Italy for another go at the Romans. It was his defeat at Beneventum, not his previous victories, that finished his Italian adventure.

There have, though, been victories that have totally or almost totally undone the victor. Many of them have been caused by the victor exhausting his resources. The armies of Justinian, for example, reconquered most of the Western Roman Empire, but they used up the empire's resources to such an extent that the western provinces were soon overrun by new sets of barbarians.

Most of the fatal victories in this book are not the result of simple exhaustion. In most cases, the victor won a tactical victory that destroyed him on the strategic, grand strategic or war policy levels.

Tactics is the art of handling troops in battle. Strategy is the art of approaching battle in the most advantageous way. Grand strategy is the art of concentrating forces where they will do the most harm to the enemy with the least harm to yourself. War policy is arranging for the forces needed to carry out grand strategic, strategic and tactical aims. In the Seven Years War, for instance, the French and Indian ambush of Braddock's column was tactical. The British intention of having Braddock take Fort Duquesne, then sweep north to Fort Niagara, was strategic. The British decision to leave most of the land fighting in Europe to Prussia while sending troops to fight the French in America was grand strategy. The French decision to place heavy reliance on their Indian allies was war policy.

In most of the battles here, the victorious general miscalculated the effect his victory would have on one or more of the interested parties. The effect of Cannae on Rome's allies was precisely the opposite of what Hannibal expected. Aëtius had no idea the effect his defeat of the Huns would have on the barbarian world. Marlborough never calculated what effect the cost of his victories would have on his own people.

Sometimes the victories dazzled the victors, to their undoing. The Moslem infatuation with the horse archer as the ultimate military force after Hattin led to disaster in some 300 years. The Afrikaner infatuation with the irregular rifleman led to disaster in less than 20 years.

Sometimes the victors were dazzling. Gustavus Adolphus and Wallenstein were both geniuses. Gustavus's death, during his victorious battle at Lützen, and Wallenstein's the next year, after his victory over the Swedes led by Thurn, doomed each of their causes. There's no substitute for genius. But both leaders had miscalculated the effects of their victories. Gustavus failed to notice the growing spirit of nationalism in Germany, which, among other things, led the Saxons to think of defecting and which made him follow Wallenstein into Saxony. Wallenstein failed to grasp the depth of Emperor Ferdinand's bigotry and jealousy, which caused the emperor to murder him after his victory over Thurn.

Down through the centuries, these same kinds of miscalculations have occurred again and again. The human mind worked the same way in 200 B.C. as it will in 2200 A.D. Weapons, of course, have steadily improved, and tactics have changed as armies adapted themselves to the new equipment. The adaptations, though, usually occur only after armies learn painfully that yesterday's tactics can't oppose today's weapons. The American Civil War and World War I are two particularly vivid examples. Occasionally, troops trained in one tactical tradition meet troops trained in another. When this happens on the home ground of one antagonist, the home team, whose tactics are adapted to the environment, usually wins. Examples are Braddock versus the Indians, the Redcoats opposing the colonists at Concord and the British fighting the Afrikaners in the First Boer War. Loosely disciplined irregulars may be more effective than highly-trained regulars, if the regulars are drilled in the wrong tactics. Irregular leaders, however, are just as susceptible to miscalculation as career generals and just as likely to suffer fatal victories.

The battles recounted in this book tend strongly to be from the Western European/American tradition. That's because (a) the author is an American of European descent brought up in that tradition and (b) it's one way to cut down what could have been an exhaustingly long list of grand strategical defeats stemming from strategic and tactical victories. Unfortunately, that aim meant leaving out some of the most decisive fatal victories in world history.

The victory of the founders of China's Ming dynasty over the Mongols is a good example. At the time of the Mongol conquest, China's was the most technologically advanced society in the world. Gunpowder, movable type, paper and the compass were all in use there. The Mongol conquest spread these ideas to the West—to Islam and then to Europe. The Mongols also picked up ideas in the West and brought them back to China, where cross-fertilization produced still more ideas. China became a sea power, with its ships making conquests from the East Indies to Arabia and Africa. In its effort to eradicate all traces of Mongol rule, though, the Ming dynasty threw out all new ideas—all ideas not found in the teachings of Confucius. With the return of native rule came the traditional Confucian contempt for the military life and commerce. China, which was equipped to do what the Europeans did do a couple of centuries later, went back to sleep.

The sort of negative victories described here have not been emphasized in popular works on military history. One reason, of course, is most battle histories are written by the victors; losers seldom like to dwell on their goofs. And it usually doesn't take too long for a fatal victory to be seen as a goof. (As we'll see, there are exceptions to that statement.) Occasionally— usually if the author is attempting to prove that no good ever came of war— everything is presented as sordid and horrible idiocy. The truth is that fatally victorious armies and leaders can display great skill and even brilliance as well as heroism and nobility. In fact, one of the greatest of fatal victories has been called the absolute masterpiece of military tactics.

AFFAIRS

OF

EMPIRE

1

216 B.C., CANNAE (SECOND PUNIC WAR)

The Absolute
Masterpiece

HE WAS A YOUNGISH MAN WITH A SHORT, CURLING BLACK BEARD. HE WORE the modeled bronze cuirass and ornate helmet of a high-ranking Carthaginian officer, and he straddled a magnificent bay mare. He was gazing intently down the hill at the Roman army facing him. He had never seen so many soldiers before.

The Roman line, spread out across the plain in front of the low, V-shaped ridge where the officer sat on his horse, was more than a mile long, sparkling with the gleam of polished iron armor. On the young officer's left, there were horsemen standing by the bank of the river. Beside them were infantry. At the end of the line, there were tiny figures of more horsemen.

The officer saw more than that. The horsemen on his left were heavy cavalry, Roman citizens in full armor. On the far right, the Romans had their light cavalry, composed of troops from Roman allies. The solid glint of iron between the bodies of horsemen showed the officer that the Roman commander of the day, Gaius Tarentius Varro, had ordered his centurions to close the intervals between their maniples, or companies. He had also arranged the maniples so that each had a narrower front and more depth than usual. The Roman infantry would not advance in its customary checkerboard formation today. The Romans would charge in three successive phalanxes. Varro was aiming for a quick knockout.

Neither of the Roman cavalry wings had numbers to equal its Carthaginian counterpart. That seemed to worry Varro. He'd jammed his heavy cavalry tightly against the river, probably to reduce the chance of the superior Carthaginian horse flanking his army. But the Roman cavalry troopers had no room to maneuver: they could only charge straight ahead.

Infantry was the decisive arm, though, and here the Romans were

3

frighteningly formidable. The Carthaginians had 10,000 horsemen to the Romans' 6,000, but the Romans had 80,000 infantrymen to the Carthaginians' 30,000.

And the Roman were better armed. All the men in the front ranks wore iron scale armor, and the men behind them had iron ring armor or bronze breastplates. Men in the first wave carried the *pilum*, a small spearhead forged to a long iron shank which fitted into a wooden shaft—in effect, an enormous needle with a wooden handle. Each man carried two pila, a light one to throw at twenty paces and a heavy one to throw at ten paces. Either could pierce the stoutest shield. Romans in the second and third waves carried the long spear, or *hasta*.

All of the Romans were experienced soldiers; all were fighting for their homes. Half of the troops in the Carthaginian army were half-savage Gauls and Spaniards or wild Italian hill tribesmen. Most of what armor they had came from the bodies of Romans killed in the two previous battles. Almost all of the "Carthaginian" troops were mercenaries.

The officer trotted over to a group of other officers who were also examining the enemy army. One of them looked particularly unhappy.

"What's the matter, Gisco?" he asked the mournful-looking officer. "You look worried."

"I am worried, son of Hamilcar. I didn't think there were that many Romans in the world."

"Amazing, isn't it? But I'll tell you something even more amazing."

"What's that, Hannibal?"

"In all that vast array of men, there is not one Gisco."

The knot of men roared at the jest. Perhaps they laughed a little too loudly, but at least they had stopped staring at the Romans with that horrified fascination. Hannibal smiled and nudged his horse into motion again.

He inspected his own forces. On the left, by the river bank, the Gaulish and Spanish heavy cavalry waited. They were heavy cavalry only in the sense that the men themselves—and their horses—were huge. Aside from helmets and shields, they wore little armor. A few chiefs had tunics covered with metal rings, but some of the Gauls were naked from the waist up. The troopers used a heavy javelin, like the Roman pilum, and a sword. The Gaulish sword was a long, almost pointless slashing tool, crudely forged from wrought iron. Their fellow Celts, the Spanish, however, carried a short, pointed, two-edged weapon made of the finest steel in Europe.

Next to the Celtic horse was the first detachment of Libyan heavy infantry. The Libyans wore Roman-style armor—some of it actual Roman armor taken from Romans. They carried long spears like the Roman hastae and fought in phalanx formation. In the center of the infantry line were Gauls and Spaniards, some of them, like their cavalry, shirtless. Some of the Gauls didn't even have metal helmets or spears. They relied on their shields and their long swords alone. Another unit of African heavy foot formed the far end of the infantry line. Beyond them, milling around impatiently, was the Numidian light cavalry, wearing long robes and mounted on small, agile horses. The Numidians used no bridles; they guided their mounts with their knees and threw their short iron javelins with both hands. All the Spanish and Gaulish cavalry, unlike the Roman, were used to fighting on horseback. But the Numidians, Berber nomads from North Africa, were practically centaurs. In front of the army were Balearian slingers, wearing only short tunics, with three lengths of slings draped around their bodies. The Balearians could throw lead sling bullets that outranged any arrow. In back of the main line were other formations of Libyan heavy infantry.

Hannibal noted with pleasure that a brisk wind was blowing from behind his army. Any dust would blow in the eyes of the enemy. Further, the Romans were facing the southeast, so the sun would be in their eyes. Hannibal reached the center of the line and called to his brother, Mago, who would help him command this sector. As Mago trotted over, Hannibal looked again at the Roman army. He wondered what Varro was doing right now.

2

Gaius Tarentius Varro was a popular politician and a commoner. Because of this, he was despised by aristocratic Romans. According to Livy, Varro was "a demagogue," "arrogant," "reckless and passionate," and "superstitious." The reason, aside from the fact that he was a leader of the common people, was that Varro had the temerity to criticize Quintus Fabius Maximus for following Hannibal with a Roman army and watching him devastate Italy at will.

Fabius, "the Delayer," had been elected dictator after Hannibal arrived in Italy and began destroying Roman armies. He held that his nibbling strategy would eventually weaken Hannibal so that he could easily be beaten. To Fabius and men of his class, Hannibal's operations could only mean the loss of a few slaves. But to Varro's followers, Hannibal was Death and Famine incarnate. To save their lives, they had to flee to the city, where they sold their land at a loss in order to survive. The buyers were senators like Fabius.

To Varro, Hannibal was the man who was killing his people. If the Romans continued to delay, Hannibal might possibly weaken (Varro doubted it), but by that time, many more Roman citizens and allies would be cut down or made homeless.

Varro could not understand the aristocratic party's fear of Hannibal. It was true that the Carthaginians had defeated a Roman force at the Ticinus River, routed a Roman army on the Trebia River and annihilated a third Roman army on the shore of Lake Trasimene in Eturia. But the first fight was little more than a cavalry skirmish; in the second, the Roman army had been sent into action the day it arrived from Sicily, marched through an icy river without breakfast and surprised by an ambuscaded party of Carthaginians after the battle began. Even so, it had fought its way out of the trap and retired in good order. At Lake Trasimene, the Romans had marched blindly into a fog and into the greatest ambush in history. Hannibal had won his victories through trickery. Or maybe just luck.

Romans had nothing to fear in an open, stand-up fight with Hannibal's troops, Varro knew. The Romans could field more soldiers than Hannibal could ever hope for. Better ones, too. Hannibal's troops were largely barbarians—Gauls, Samnites, Bruttians, Lucanians and Spaniards. Rome's legions had beaten such men time after time. And this time, the barbarians were not even fighting for their homes—for just money and loot.

The Carthaginians, a race of money-grubbers, had never been able to raise an army of their own, Varro knew. All their troops were mercenaries. And the Carthaginians couldn't keep either mercenaries or allies. After the last war, the mercenaries in the army of Carthage mutinied because the Carthaginians tried to cheat them out of their full pay. Other Punic cities, furious over the exactions of the Carthaginian tax collectors during the war, joined the revolt. Only by hiring a new batch of mercenaries and putting them under the command of Hannibal's father, Hamilcar Barca, had the Carthaginians saved themselves.

Varro had denounced the aristocratic generals as fools and cowards for letting Hannibal destroy Italy unmolested. And the common people elected him consul at the end of Fabius's term as dictator. The Senate, though, made sure Varro would not have untrammeled command of an army. Instead, his army and that of the other consul were combined. The consuls alternated the command each day. The other consul, an aging gentleman named Lucius Aemilius Paulus, was an experienced but cautious soldier of the senatorial class. The Senate could have devised no better way to prevent Varro from taking his troops into action.

Varro, though, would stand for no delay. It was not just a question of emotion, but of grand strategy. The butcher's son who had become Rome's leading politician saw the situation from a different angle than the aristocrats.

So far, Rome's civilized dependencies had remained loyal, even those only recently subdued. But they were loyal to Rome, Varro believed, because Rome had been loyal to them. The Romans protected the Etruscans from the Gauls, the Greeks from the Samnites, and the Latins from both groups of barbarians. If Rome did not protect its allies from Hannibal, it had better be prepared to see them defect. And if Hannibal could lead the disciplined, well-equipped troops of the Etruscan, Greek and Latin cities, Rome was doomed.

Today, near the village of Cannae on the banks of the Aufidus River, Hannibal had finally led his army out on a day when Varro was in command. Today, there would be a battle.

From his position on the left of the Roman line, where he had direct command of the light cavalry, Varro saw the infantry in Hannibal's center advance. They marched a short distance into the plain and stopped. Their line described a bow, with the center of the curve closest to the Romans.

3

The Carthaginians had taken a very peculiar position. As with the Roman army, both flanks were covered by cavalry, although the Gauls and Spaniards on the Carthaginian left had more room to maneuver than the heavy horsemen on the Roman right. The African heavy infantry held the two tips of the V-shaped ridge just inside the cavalry wings—again quite orthodox. But the Celtic infantry now formed a thin line that bowed out, with its center closest to the center of the Roman line. The infantry center was far ahead of the Carthaginian cavalry and far from any support the horsemen could give it.

Hannibal knew that the unorthodox position of his lightly armed Celtic center would puzzle the Romans, but he didn't think it would discourage them. The apparent vulnerability of that barbarian infantry, flung out ahead of support from either the heavy infantry or the cavalry, would probably provoke the Romans.

Looking over his motley army, Hannibal must have thought that his optimism would seem insane to his friends back in Spain. But the whole invasion seemed insane to them. The invasion had succeeded only because he had been able to out-think the Romans. The Romans had expected him to fight them in Spain, where he had settled with his father after Carthage's defeat in the First Punic War.

That war began in Sicily, where the two expanding Mediterranean superpowers collided. It lasted almost a generation, and it was the bloodiest war in the Mediterranean world up to that time. It ended with Carthage losing all its territory outside of Africa.

Hannibal's father, Hamilcar Barca, was Carthage's greatest hero in the war. After putting down a mutiny of Carthage's mercenaries at the end of the war with Rome, Hamilcar would not accept the role of one of the leaders of an exhausted republic. He went to Spain, recruited a new army and conquered a new empire for his city. He took Hannibal with him. When he died, Hannibal inherited his army at the age of 29.

The Romans trumped up an excuse for another war. Hannibal didn't wait for them. He went to Italy. Anyone who invaded Italy would come by sea, the Romans thought; he marched across Gaul. When the Romans thought he was crossing the Ebro in Spain, he was about to cross the Rhone in Gaul. The Alps and the wild Gauls who inhabited them would stop any army, the Romans thought. Hannibal not only crossed the Alps, he crossed them with 37 elephants and enlisted the mountain barbarians into his army. Although the elephants later succumbed to wounds, exhaustion, lack of food and the rigors of the north Italian climate, Hannibal quickly proved that he had a formidable fighting force. At least, as long as he was directing it. His secret was to never do what the Romans expected.

In Italy, at the Trebia, he had concealed part of his army and struck the Romans from ambush. The next spring, two new Roman consuls lined up their armies to command the eastern and western roads to Rome. Hannibal took neither road. Instead, he made a terrifying march through a swamp, wading through water for four days and three nights. He caught a fever which killed the sight of one eye, but he made one of the Roman armies follow him to ground of his own choosing—the foggy shore of Lake Trasimene. The Romans, strung out along the road in the fog, were struck down by javelins and sling bullets hurled by troops Hannibal had stationed above the fog. Hannibal armed his heavy infantry with the weapons and armor of the defunct Roman army.

After his victory, the Romans expected Hannibal to dash to Rome. But he knew it would be suicide for his small army to attempt to invest that enormous city set in a populous and hostile countryside. Rome and its Latin allies had more than 6,000,000 people; Carthage and all the territory it controlled in Africa had less than 700,000. Hannibal knew his 40,000 mercenaries could no more besiege Rome than a cat could swallow an elephant. The Carthaginian's real aim was at once more subtle and more naive.

He had come to Italy as the deliverer of the Italians from Roman oppression. From his boyhood in his father's camp in Sicily, Hannibal saw Rome as an insatiable, power-mad aggressor. He was sure that no one knew this better than the peoples of Italy. His army would be the catalyst of a great Italian revolt.

So far, his only support had come from a few unimportant towns and some barbarian tribes. He had hoped that by now his army would contain Greeks, Etruscans and Latins as well as these barbarians. Rome had subdued the Etruscans only a short time before the now-revolted Italian Gauls. The Latins were still restive: after the last war with Carthage, Rome had to put down a revolt by the Faliscans. As for the Greeks, they called the Romans barbarians, and old men could still remember Pyrrhus of Epirus, who almost established Greek supremacy in Italy. Hannibal had not given up hope of civilized allies. One signal victory might bring them in. Roman overconfidence would help. The Romans were sure of themselves because they were more numerous, better armed and knew there was no place on this field to conceal an ambush party. Still, Hannibal was sure he could give them a surprise or two.

Suddenly, Hannibal heard a sound he'd heard once before, on the banks of the Trebia—the Roman battle cry and the clash of thousands of spears on shields. The horde of Romans had started to move.

4

The Romans advanced at a walk, as slow, inexorable and deadly as a lava flow. A bank of dust rose behind the gleaming iron mass. Then the velites, the Roman light infantry, and archers and slingers from Syracuse ran ahead. They wore leather or quilted linen corselets and jogged ahead of the main body. With a shout, Hannibal's Balearians came to life. They fitted lead bullets to their longest slings and opened fire. The Romans raised their shields and kept on coming.

A chorus of shrill shrieks exploded from both flanks of the Carthaginian line. The cavalry wings charged at full speed. The Numidians, under Maharbal, swept up to Varro's light cavalry, hurled their darts and wheeled away. The Romans tried to pursue, only to be caught in the flank by more of the agile African nomads.

The battle on the Carthaginian right swirled back and forth. Maharbal's men were trained to move on signal; they led the Romans such a dizzying dance neither Varro nor any other Roman officer could have controlled his light cavalry. Then a party of Numidians managed to get surrounded. They threw down their javelins. Varro detailed a detachment to take the prisoners to the rear.

The Romans didn't fare so well on the left side of the Carthaginian line. Hannibal's shrieking Celtic horsemen charged straight at the Roman cavalry, hurling their pila as soon as they came into range. The big iron needles skewered the Romans through their shields and scale armor. The Roman heavy cavalry used the lance instead of the pilum. As no cavalry at the time had stirrups, a powerful lance thrust was a good trick under the best of circumstances, especially for a man unbalanced by body armor. A trooper struggling with a shying horse and dodging gigantic Gaulish berserkers on proportionately gigantic horses was not in the best of circumstances. And the Romans didn't have room to dodge and weren't even good riders. The Gauls and Spaniards caught the lance thrusts on their shields and drew their swords for close combat.

At the beginning of the battle, a sling bullet struck Consul Aemilius Paulus on the arm, broke his arm and drove the jagged end of the bone through his flesh. Weakened by loss of blood, Paulus slipped off his horse. His troops, too, had begun to dismount. They couldn't cope with the Celts on horseback and tried to fight as infantry. But they were confused and without the organization that made Roman infantry so formidable. The Gauls and Spaniards kept riding up and tossing their pila. As the Romans grew weaker, the Celts, too, dismounted. They were stronger, more numerous and fighting the kind of battle they were used to—a confused, swirling brawl.

By this time, Paulus couldn't even stand. While he had the strength, he tried to direct the fight. Growing weaker, he shouted to his men to sell their lives dearly. There was little else they could do. A tribune named Lentulus offered Paulus his horse, but the old consul shook his head.

"You don't have much time," he told the younger man. "Don't waste it on useless pity. Go to Rome. Tell the Senate what happened. Tell them to fortify the city as well as they can before the Carthaginians get there."

A few minutes later, Lucius Aemilius Paulus, a timid general but a brave man, was dead. So was most of the Roman heavy cavalry.

The consul's pessimism would have been incomprehensible to the Roman infantry. The legionaries were making their first contact with the Celts of Hannibal's bowed-out center at the same time their heavy cavalry was being chopped up. The Celtic footmen were not faring as well as their mounted kinsmen. The Gauls swung their swords with all the strength of their long, brawny arms, but clubs would have been as effective against the iron scale armor of the Romans. The Spaniards crouched and charged like bulls, covering their heads with their shields and trying to drive the needle-sharp points of their short swords through the Roman corselets. Some did, but the pila of the Roman first wave punched through the Spanish shields. Even when it didn't reach the man behind the shield, the heavy Roman spear made a shield impossible to manage, giving the Romans a chance to use their own swords effectively.

Hannibal and Mago were everywhere, striking with their swords and directing their men to retire slowly. As the line straightened, it became denser. The Roman drive slowed momentarily, but the legionaries shouted their battle cry again and pressed on. The Celts gave ground. Inch by inch at first, then foot by foot. They wavered as their line bent back. It was all Hannibal and his brother could do to prevent them from bolting. The line curved farther and farther to the rear, but the heavily armored African infantry formations at either end of the Carthaginian line stood as firm as twin mountains. The Romans sideslipped around the Africans, toward the center, to pursue the fleeing Celts. The Roman infantry became somewhat disorganized, but it was advancing rapidly.

The Celts retreated up the ridge to their rear. As gaps opened in their line, new phalanxes of heavy infantry appeared in the gaps. The Gaulish and Spanish resistance suddenly increased. The Romans crowded up and attacked the Celts and Hannibal's African infantry reserve with redoubled fury. By this time, they had lost their cohesion: centurions found themselves surrounded by strange soldiers; legionaries didn't know their comrades. All that really counted, though, was getting at the Carthaginians. Crowded and jostled from the side, they pressed straight on, trying to break through the Carthaginian center. At first, they didn't notice that they were being squeezed together. Before long, they had no room to throw their pila or to change the direction of their long spears.

The Africans at the ends of the Carthaginian line had pivoted inward and pressed against the Roman flanks. The citizen-soldiers of Rome, still disorganized by the pursuit, were forced back as the iron-clad Libyans thrust their long spears like the complete professionals they were. In effect, the Romans were being crowded into a sack with the African heavy infantry pulling the drawstring. The Romans were crowded too tightly to change front. And Hannibal, commanding the Carthaginian center, was performing the most difficult tactical maneuver in the book—controlling a retreat under pressure, then turning it into an attack.

Meanwhile, the 500 Numidians who had surrendered to Varro on the Roman left flank suddenly whipped concealed swords from under their cloaks and cut down their captors. Their mates massed on signal and charged, yipping their war cry and throwing darts with both hands. And then the Celtic heavy cavalry struck the Roman light cavalry like a thunderbolt. The Celts' commander, Hasdrubal, having annihilated the Roman heavy cavalry on Varro's right flank led his troops around the rear of the Roman infantry and fell on the Roman cavalry opposing the Numidians on the Roman left. The cavalry fight was all over. The Roman survivors, including Varro himself, were swept from the field.

Hasdrubal left pursuit to the fleeter Numidians and massed his Gauls and Spaniards. He checked quickly to make sure each man had weapons. Then he launched his horsemen straight into the struggling mass of Roman infantry from the rear. The Celts hurled their pila and leaped off their horses swords in hand, screaming with barbaric fury. They slashed the Romans across the backs of their knees, drove the deadly short Spanish swords through the scale armor corselets, dragged the Roman spearmen down from behind and cut their throats. The Libyans continued to close in from the flanks, and as the cramped, confused Romans squirmed helplessly, the Celtic swordsmen in front had their revenge.

Of the 86,000 Romans who took the field that morning, 70,000 were dead and 4,500 were prisoners by afternoon. Hannibal had lost 5,700 men. The Carthaginian had created the absolute masterpiece of military tactics.

Hannibal's feat of mass jujutsu at Cannae has been studied by generals from Scipio Africanus to Erwin Rommel, but most of them didn't get it. Most soldiers noticed only the double envelopment Hannibal used to trap the Roman infantry. Double envelopment has often been an effective tactic. It's often failed, too. During World War I the Russians attempted a double envelopment at Tannenberg. They lost two field armies.

The Schlieffen Plan used in World War I could have approached Cannae. Count Alfred von Schlieffen knew that Hannibal's secret at Cannae was unbalancing the Romans by letting them exert their strength in the wrong place. Under Schlieffen's plan, the Germans would let the French drive into Germany against gradually increasing resistance, then, when they had become unbalanced with the pursuit, flank them with a German right wing attacking through Belgium. Helmut von Moltke the Younger, the German chief of staff, however, was afraid to weaken his left wing and let the French penetrate *der Vaterland.*

In the next war, the French and British were ready for another Schlieffen Plan, with their strength concentrated in the north. Erich von Manstein aimed his panzers at the northern end of the Maginot Line, the hinge of the Allied left wing. This time, the Allies *were* unbalanced. The result was Dunkirk and the French surrender.

"My men still have plenty of energy," Maharbal, commander of the Numidians, told Hannibal when the fighting was over. "Let us go ahead of you to attack Rome and keep the enemy from organizing their defenses before you bring up the main army."

"And after the main army got there, what would it do?" the general asked. "We couldn't capture a city like that."

The cavalryman spat in disgust. "Truly, Hannibal, the gods don't bestow all their gifts on one man. You know how to win victories, but you don't know what to do with them."

Hannibal smiled. "After this victory, my friend, we won't have to do anything. Wait and see. Rome's allies will become our allies, and we will have destroyed Rome's power without the need to put a single ladder against her walls."

That night, Roman troops left to guard the camps of Aemilius Paulus and Varro joined each other. A young officer named Publius Cornelius Scipio led them home. Varro had already taken back the fugitives from the battle. Senators welcomed the defeated consul outside the walls of Rome and congratulated him on not having despaired of the Republic.

The Romans consulted their sacred books, then performed a human sacrifice by burying alive four foreigners, two Greeks and two Gauls. They freed 8,000 slaves and put them in the army. And they called up more troops. There were plenty: every Roman between 18 and 45 was eligible for military service.

Meanwhile, Hannibal waited in his camp. A delegation from the Greek city of Capua arrived and said their city was cutting its ties with Rome. Hannibal moved his army to Capua for the winter and waited for more Roman allies to come to him. He waited in vain. No other important town joined him.

Hannibal had demonstrated at Cannae that he was the supreme master of tactics. His march from Spain had shown that he was also a master strategist. But his plan to detach Rome's allies was on a third plane of war—grand strategy. It involved not the minds of opposing generals, but the psychology and morale of a whole nation. Nothing in Hannibal's experience prepared him for what followed Cannae.

By spring, Rome had nine new legions in the field, with an equal number of troops from allied cities. The next year, the Romans had 20 legions to carry on the war. Capua gave Hannibal virtually no reinforcements, and as "liberator" he could not compel the Capuans to give him any. The big, pleasure-loving southern city was an albatross around the Carthaginian's neck. He used up most of his time and energy defending Capua from the Romans. Hannibal destroyed four more Roman armies and killed five more Roman commanders, but he steadily grew weaker. A Carthaginian army sent to reinforce him was destroyed farther north in Italy. Finally, his miniscule army could no longer defend Capua. After that, Hannibal could do no more than hold his own in the extreme south until he was recalled to Africa.

Meanwhile, the Romans were learning. Six years after Cannae, it became apparent that they had produced a genius of their own, the same Publius Cornelius Scipio who had led the troops from the Roman camps after Cannae. In 210, he was appointed Roman commander in Spain, where he showed leadership and tactical gifts almost equal to Hannibal's and a grasp of strategy superior to the Carthaginian's.

Scipio also took advantage of Rome's superior political situation. The Carthaginians, unlike the Romans, didn't make firm friends. Scipio picked up powerful Numidian allies in Africa when he invaded the Carthaginian homeland, and he used them to cause Hannibal's first defeat and the end of the war.

5

At Cannae, Hannibal had created a masterpiece, but a military victory was not the answer. The problem was political. Carthage had done nothing for its allies but tax them, while Rome protected its allies and earned their loyalty. And nothing had demonstrated Rome's loyalty to its allies as much as Cannae, where it sacrificed the flower of Roman youth to help its friends.

Most modern historians list the Battle of the Metaurus, where Caius Claudius Nero defeated the reinforcing army of Hannibal's brother Hasdrubal as the decisive battle of the Second Punic War. But Hasdrubal's army would not have solved the problem of gaining Italian allies, nor would it have given Hannibal the strength to invest Rome.

Hannibal lost the war with his victory at Cannae.

And in spite of the aristocratic historians of ancient Rome, and most historians since, Gaius Tarentius Varro, the despised butcher's son, had been right.

2

451 A.D., ATTILA'S INVASION OF GAUL

Who's Afraid of the Big Bad Hun?

THE TROUBLE BEGAN WHEN THE EMPEROR FOUND HIS SISTER IN BED WITH her personal steward. The steward was, apparently, far more personal than the emperor had suspected. His sister's conduct was a most unpleasant surprise to Emperor Valentinian, lord of the Western Roman Empire.

Valentinian wasn't greatly offended by his sister's dalliance. He, himself, was a world-class lecher. Nor did it bother him that much that she was sleeping with a servant. He hadn't confined his own sexual conquests to noble ladies. What bothered him was it was this servant, the bedazzled Eugenius. Eugenius would do whatever the Augusta Honoria wanted him to do. What Honoria probably wanted was something her brother didn't like to think about.

Valentinian and Honoria were children of a Roman princess named Galla Placidia, who had been Queen of the Goths and then Empress of Rome. A strong-willed woman, as well as a ravishing beauty, she had ruled both the king and the emperor. Valentinian, as a boy emperor, had chafed under his mother's regency. Whenever Valentinian looked at his sister, he saw the young Placidia. And Honoria made no secret of her contempt for both her brother's brains and his character. If anything happened to Valentinian, Honoria's husband would become emperor. That husband might be Eugenius, or it might be anyone else she fancied.

Valentinian had Eugenius executed and immediately betrothed his sister to a safe and stolid senator named Flavius Bassus Herculanus. Honoria turned to the only monarch in Europe powerful enough to save her.

Attila the Hun.

15

2

The Huns were not only a powerful nation, they evoked a kind of superstitious dread among the Romans. They had appeared suddenly just beyond the empire, and, with the exception of a handful of black Africans, they were different from any other people the Romans had ever seen. All the neighbors of the empire—Celts, Germans, Slavs, Alans, Arabs and Persians—were Caucasians. The Huns were a Mongolian people.

The historian Priscus, describing how the Huns defeated the Alans—the most formidable cavalrymen the Romans had hitherto encountered—says:

"Those men [the Alans], whom they perhaps in no wise surpassed in war, they put to flight by the terror of their looks, inspiring them with no little horror by their awful aspect and by their horribly swarthy appearance. They have a sort of shapeless lump, if I may say so, not a face, and pinholes rather than eyes."

He adds that the Huns were trained in cruelty from the time they were born and "in short, live in the form of humans with the savagery of beasts."

This sort of reaction is understandable from a Roman surprised by the appearance of strange people who, for all he knew, could have dropped from the moon. It is exasperating, though, to find twentieth century writers reflecting the superstition and prejudice of the fifth century.

The Huns did not, for example, rout the Alans and Goths because of their horrible appearance and their sheer ferocity. They beat the other barbarians because they had a better military system—incomparably better when compared to that of the Goths and other Germans. Nor did they, as is still being written, start to move west because the Chinese built the Great Wall. The Chinese drove the Hsiung-nu into the desert and completed the Great Wall while Hannibal was campaigning in Italy, before the foundation of the Roman Empire. For centuries later, the Hsiung-nu, the people generally identified as the Huns, remained on the borders of China, collecting and giving tribute as the fortunes of war varied.

The Chinese eventually stirred up a civil war among the Huns. They helped one faction, and the other had to move west. The defeated Huns crossed the Altai Mountains then the T'ien Shan range. In 35 B.C., a Chinese general named Chen Teng sneaked an army over the T'ien Shan, fell on the camp of the Western Huns, defeated them and returned with the head of their khan. The Western Huns moved farther west and lost contact with their cousins in the Gobi.

In 304 A.D., the Huns in the Gobi took over China. The khan, who took the name Emperor Liu Yuen, died in 318. Immediately after his death,

Mongol, Turkish and Tibetan tribes invaded China. The weaker competitors, including the Hsiung-nu, fled for their lives. The westernmost of these Huns became known as the White Huns, after the color of the west in Chinese symbolism. They invaded Persia, Afghanistan and India. And their movement disturbed their cousins, the original Western Huns, who moved into Europe.

As they drifted west, the Huns encountered the Alans, one of the two great powers of the western steppes. The Alans were Iranian nomads who greatly impressed the Romans.

"Almost all the Halani are tall and handsome," wrote Ammianus Marcellinus, a Roman soldier and historian. "By the ferocity of their glance, they inspire dread, subdued though it is. They are light and active in the use of arms. In all respects they are like the Huns, but in their manner of life and their habits, they are less savage."

The Alans were anything but savage in their methods of war. They were the first heavy cavalry the Huns had ever seen. Alanic nobles wore mail and charged with long lances. With his feet securely planted in stirrups (a steppe invention that had not yet reached the settled peoples of the West) the Alan could put both his own weight and that of his horse behind the lance point. Less wealthy Alans fought as light-armed horse archers.

The Huns had stirrups, too. But their armor was hardened leather, and the bow was their chief weapon. The most important advantage they had was organization. From time beyond memory, the clans of the Gobi had used a decimal organization, with squads of ten and companies of a hundred. When they periodically united, they also had battalions of a thousand and divisions of ten thousand. Faced with the armored Alanic lancers, the Huns united. The Alans didn't. That was a mistake, because the Huns were cavalrymen such as the west had never seen before.

"They are almost glued to their horses," Ammianus Marcellinus wrote. "From their horses, everyone of that nation buys and sells, eats and drinks, and bowed over the narrow neck of the animal, relaxes into a sleep so deep as to be accompanied by many dreams."

Their flexible organization and their incredible horsemanship let the Huns scatter before the masses of Alanic lancers and press their attacks from the rear and flanks.

According to Ammianus Marcellinus, "They fight from a distance with missiles." After their archery had demoralized the enemy, they charged. "They gallop over the intervening spaces and fight hand-to-hand, reckless of their own lives; and while the enemy are guarding against wounds from saber thrusts, they throw strips of cloth plaited into nooses over their opponents and entangle them."

Before long, all of the Alanic clans had been defeated. Most were incorporated into the Hunnish nation; some fled to the west and went freelancing across the steppe and into Europe.

The defeat of the Alans brought the Huns into contact with the Ostrogoths, the second great power of the western steppes. The Ostrogoths, under their king, Ermaneric, had unity. Their tactics, though, were primitive compared to those of the Huns or even the Alans. Their cavalry were all lancers. The only archers were infantry, who couldn't support the fast-moving horsemen. The Ostrogoths were defeated, and Ermaneric fell on his sword. The Goths fled west, but there was another fight, and most of the Ostrogoths ended up in the Hunnish horde. The rest joined their cousins, the Visigoths, and entered the Roman Empire for protection.

Through all this fighting, the Hunnish kings had been building up their power by gathering the only resource that counted—warriors. The best warriors were nomads, like themselves, the Alans and the Goths, the Huns believed—tough men, used to hardship, familiar with weapons, good riders and trained to teamwork.

When danger no longer threatened, the Hunnish nation broke up into the usual collection of squabbling clans. The Huns' Alan and Ostrogothic vassals did the same. Then two strong kings appeared, Rugila, then his nephew, Attila. The Huns may have sought strong leadership because they were now in contact with two huge empires—Persia and Rome.

3

Settled empires had immense power, Attila, now the Huns' khakhan or king of kings, believed. But, fortunately for nomads like the Huns, the empire-dwellers seldom understood that. If you asked a Roman emperor about the strength of his country, he would tell you about his miles of territory, the wealth of his cities, the size of the buildings in those cities and the strength of the fortifications that protected them. But Attila knew that the real strength of Rome, of China, of Persia, was none of those things. It was men. The empires could drown the nomads in manpower—millions of men, all responding to a single commander.

When Attila became his nation's supreme leader, he commanded most of the nomad warriors in Europe. He wanted the rest, most of whom had taken refuge in the Roman Empire. He had been negotiating with the Eastern Emperor for the return of fugitives hiding in his domain. But now Marcian, the new emperor, was resisting pressure.

The khan was considering what to do when the messenger from

Honoria appeared, bearing the princess's plea for her rescue and her ring, as a token of the genuineness of the message.

Attila took the message and the ring as a proposal of marriage. The proposal was a marvelous opportunity. Gaul, in the Western Empire, was filled with Goths, Vandals and Alans—the rest of the nomad warriors he coveted. It would make a fitting dowry for the Roman princess.

Attila looked at one of the guards at the door.

"Bring me Orestes," he said.

A tall man in the costume of a Hunnish noble entered.

"You called, my khan?" he asked in Latin-accented Hunnish. Orestes, Attila's secretary, years before had left the world of cities to live and fight with the nomads.

Attila asked Orestes to sit and told him about the message of Honoria. He enjoyed the look of amazement on the secretary's face—a look that grew when the khan said he wanted to send a letter to his brother, the Roman Emperor of the West, telling him he accepted Honoria's offer and claiming his bride and her dowry.

Honoria's messenger was not at all like the last Roman envoy, Orestes observed. That Roman said he had come to negotiate, but instead he brought gold to bribe a member of Attila's bodyguard to assassinate the khan.

When he discovered the plot against his life, Attila indulged in a little psychological warfare. He sent Orestes to Constantinople. Attila's Roman secretary appeared before the great men of the Empire with a bag around his neck—the bag that had carried the bribe. He cried that this dastardly attempt must be avenged. But Attila did not send out his army or even break off negotiations. He merely held the Roman ambassador for ransom. To Attila, statecraft was business, and business and emotion do not mix.

That was true now, too, after receiving Honoria's message. The attraction was not Honoria, however beautiful she might be. It was Gaul.

Attila and Orestes discussed the Western Empire as Orestes penned his master's message. The Roman Empire had become an eventful place after the Huns defeated the Ostrogoths.

4

After the Romans agreed to give them refuge, the Visigoths, with the remnants of the Ostrogoths and some Alans, crossed the border. The Romans tried to take advantage of the refugees. War broke out. Near the city of Adrianople, an army of Roman infantry was assaulting a Gothic wagon fort—a circle of wagons similar to those used in the American Wild West—

when a force of Alanic and Ostrogothic lancers appeared, led by the Alan kings Alatheus and Saphrax. The Romans had never before faced a mass charge of lancers equipped with stirrups. They had been attacking the fort and did not form a solid line to stop the cavalry, which they expected to repel with javelins. Roman cavalry tactics were basically javelin-throwing contests. The heavily armed lancers from the steppes rode right through them. The result was the worst Roman defeat since Cannae.

Adrianople was a decisive battle because it convinced the Romans that stirrup-equipped heavy cavalry was the ultimate weapon. Infantry, the "queen of battles" in European warfare since the invention of the Greek phalanx, was now of secondary importance. That notion would persist through most of the next thousand years of European history.

The importance of heavy cavalry spurred the Romans to enlist into their army as many of the mounted barbarians as possible. With the whole Visigothic nation in the empire now, the Romans took them into the army en masse, allowing them to serve under their own leaders. The empire, in effect, was subsidizing a nomadic nation, living under its own laws and owing only tenuous allegiance to the emperor. Although they were called barbarians, the average Goth was not much less civilized than the average Roman. The Goths were Christians and about as literate as the Romans—some of them in both Gothic and Latin. Jordanes, a Gothic writer, is one of the principal historians of this era. The Goths were far more civilized than the Gauls Caesar had conquered and who had been successfully Romanized.

Nevertheless, the Goths were a problem. For a generation, they were the problem of the Emperor of the East. Then the Eastern Emperor persuaded Alaric, the Gothic king, to move west and make trouble for the Western Emperor, now ruling in Ravenna instead of Rome. Alaric was checked by Stilicho, the Western Empire's master of soldiers, the army's top officer. Stilicho did not attempt to destroy Alaric's forces, because he saw the Gothic king as a Roman general, taking the traditional way of seeking redress of grievances. It was different with "foreign" barbarians. Stilicho wiped out two German war bands that had crossed the border to escape the Huns. To do it, though, he had to pull troops out of Gaul.

Then on the last day of 406, the Rhine froze from bank to bank. Over it, spearheaded by clans of Alans, rode the Vandals, Burgundians and Sueves, eastern Germans who fled west to get away from the Huns. The next day, warriors from the western confederations, the Franks and Alemanni, walked across the frozen river. Stilicho proposed to Alaric that he take his army to Gaul and drive out the invaders. Before that could happen, the Roman government, caught in a wave of religious and nationalistic chauvinism, arrested Stilicho and executed him for treason. The Roman officials suspected Stilicho of being soft on barbarians because he was a Vandal and an Arian Christian, like the Goths, instead of a mainstream Christian. Many other prominent Arians in the army, all, like Stilicho, of German descent, were killed. The government renounced all agreements with Alaric. In revenge, Alaric sacked Rome and established a puppet emperor, Attalus.

After that, the Western Empire plunged into chaos—a mind-boggling orgy of treachery, assassination and wholesale murder. In brief:

Alaric died soon after the sack, and his brother, Athaulf, became king. The Roman government, in the impregnable city of Ravenna, promised Athaulf grain if he would take his people to Gaul.

About this time, a Roman general named Constantine proclaimed himself emperor in Britain. He then invaded Gaul from the west, as the Visigoths came in from the east. Constantine fought inconclusively with the Goths in Gaul, then he invaded Spain, which had so far been untouched. The Spanish troops invited the Vandals into Spain to help them against Constantine. Their general, Gerontius, proclaimed his son, Maximus, emperor. That made six emperors in the year 410: Theodosius II in Constantinople; Honorius in Ravenna; Attalus, the Gothic puppet, in Rome; Constantine in Spain; Constantine's son, Constans, made co-emperor by Constantine, and Maximus, who was fighting father and son in Spain.

It got worse. Barbarian war bands and Roman mutineers continued to proclaim emperors. Honorius, the emperor in Ravenna, reached a kind of agreement with Athaulf, King of the Visigoths, and arranged to have his other rivals murdered as opportunities presented themselves.

As relations between Athaulf and Honorius improved, the Roman asked Athaulf to return his sister, Placidia, who had been taken hostage. Athaulf, though, had still not received the promised food. He told Honorius no grain, no girl. Instead of grain, Honorius sent an army under a general named Boniface, which whipped the Goths soundly. Instead of returning Placidia, Athaulf married her. Before long, Athaulf was saying, "I hope to be known to posterity as the initiator of a Roman restoration."

Then one of the Gothic king's slaves murdered him. He was succeeded by a family enemy named Sinerich, who ruled seven days. That was long enough, though, to kill all of Athaulf's children. A man named Wallia got rid of Sinerich and sent Placidia home.

Honorius married Placidia to a general named Constantius who died a short time later, reportedly of natural causes. Placidia and Honorius then scandalized the Roman court with their incestuous behavior. They quarreled, and Honorius banished Placidia to the east. Then he died. A man named Joannes seized the throne. He hardly had time to sit on it before the armies of the East arrived and knocked him off. Placidia then ruled as regent for her son, Valentinian.

Arriving too late to help the usurper was a man Attila knew well—Flavius Aëtius—leading 60,000 Huns.

As a child, Aëtius had been sent to the Hunnish court as a hostage. There he struck up a friendship with Attila. It was a lucky friendship. Aëtius, as a rising warlord, depended on Hunnish mercenaries to enforce his will. When he achieved power, he continued to rely on Huns to keep the turbulent Germans in line.

Aëtius, who has been sainted by historians as "the last of the Romans," decided to replace Boniface as the chief military supporter of Placidia, who now ruled the West. He wrote to Boniface, who was in Africa, that Placidia was planning to get rid of him. He advised Boniface that if the empress sent for him, his only chance of staying alive would be to refuse. Then he wrote to Placidia advising her that Boniface was planning to revolt. She summoned Boniface, and he revolted. He invited the Vandals over to Africa. The Vandals came, led by Gaiseric, a cripple with a lightning-fast mind. Gaiseric took over Africa, beating both Boniface and an Eastern army under Aspar the Alan.

Placidia recognized cleverness when she saw it, and she decided Aëtius had far too much of it. Instead of Aëtius, she appointed a man named Felix master of soldiers. Aëtius raised an army of Huns, marched into Gaul and racked up victories over the Visigoths and Franks, who were posing no more of a threat than usual. The victories earned him the admiration of the Roman nationalists, and he was able to force Placidia to execute Felix and make himself master of soldiers. Placidia invited Boniface to return. He did and defeated Aëtius, who fled to his friend, Attila. But Boniface died soon afterwards, and Aëtius returned and took over the top command of the Western Roman army.

Meanwhile, the Visigothic king found a way to end his dependence on Roman grain. He wrote to Gaiseric, who ruled Africa, the granary of the empire, proposing a marriage between his daughter and the Vandal's son.

Through letters and agents, Aëtius convinced Gaiseric that the girl was unworthy to be a member of his family. At the Roman's urging, the Vandal king had the girl's ears and nose cut off as a sign of repudiation and sent back to her father.

With tactics like this Aëtius managed to keep the Germans from becoming a threat. In time, the empire might assimilate them as it had once assimilated the Greeks.

Then Valentinian found his sister in bed with her steward.

5

When he heard of her dealings with Attila, Valentinian considered executing Honoria. But his mother, the formidable Placidia, and Marcian, the Eastern Emperor, would not hear of it. Valentinian had to get ready for the ultimate barbarian war—an invasion by the Huns themselves. He told Aëtius to begin gathering troops.

Attila had already begun gathering troops. The army he assembled looked very much like the one Aëtius was gathering.

The Huns hadn't had to fight an all-out war for generations—not since they crushed the Ostrogoths, and that victory was largely due to their Alanic vassals. As he looked over his army, it may have occurred to Attila that there was a flaw in his drive to acquire more and more nomad warriors. The real Huns in his army were greatly outnumbered by Goths, Gepids, Heruls, Slavs, Alans and other European barbarians. And except for the Alans, they all fought the same way—with mindless, bull-like lance charges. The Huns had entered Europe with one of the finest military machines in the world. They had assimilated the conquered nations into their army. They were too successful. The Huns could no longer use their horse archer tactics, because the bulk of Attila's army could only charge with the lance.

Attila's army was mostly German, but so was that of Aëtius. Most of the Roman regulars were of German descent, and Aëtius enlisted all the barbarians he could. He worked especially hard to enlist the most powerful barbarian nation, the Visigoths, under their king Theodoric. He also acquired a contingent of the ubiquitous Alans and a mass of Frankish footmen. Aëtius and the rest of his army didn't trust either group. The Alans had kinsmen in Attila's army. They also spoke a different language and had a different way of life than the familiar Germans. As for the Franks, there wasn't a horseman in the tribe, and Adrianople had convinced the Romans that infantry was useless.

6

On a plain identified as the Mauriac Place, probably near Troyes, Attila set up a wagon-ringed camp, a feature of both Hunnish and Gothic warfare. In the center, he built a funeral pyre where he could meet an honorable end if routed. That sort of forethought indicates that the King of the World, as he had begun calling himself, was experiencing something less than supreme confidence.

Aëtius, in turn, was hardly reckless. He selected a long, U-shaped range of hills near Attila's camp. Roman generals, of course, had all studied Hannibal's victory at Cannae. Aëtius placed his most reliable troops, the

Visigoths, under their king, Theodoric, and the Romans, under his personal command, on the projecting flanks. His doubtful units, the Alans and the Franks, were in the center. At Cannae, Hannibal let his center retreat before the Romans to suck them into a trap. Aëtius couldn't do that. His Frankish infantry wasn't mobile enough. The Franks, in fact, nailed the Roman army in place.

Aëtius didn't need a ruse to lure the Huns to attack the center of his army. Attila was already determined to strike there. If he had been leading a true Hunnish army, Attila would have circled the stiff Roman formation and shot it to pieces. That's what the Hunnish mercenaries under Aëtius did during the Roman general's campaigns against the Franks. But now Attila had a German army that could do nothing but charge. And the place to charge was the center, where the Frankish infantry stood. The Franks weren't mobile enough to contain Attila's cavalry.

Attila pointed to the center of the Roman line. "Seek swift victory in that spot," he told his lieutenants. "For when the sinews are cut, the limbs soon relax."

The Hunnish kettle drums rolled. From the center of Attila's line, where the khan commanded his best troops, the Huns and the Alans, a cloud of arrows whistled toward the Roman lines. A few arrows flew back from the Alans on the Roman side.

The Roman forces sat on their skittish horses and watched the Huns trot toward them. Then the whole Hunnish army broke into a ground-shaking gallop. Lances leveled, and the war cries of a dozen nations trilled above the hoofbeats. Dust blotted out all but the front ranks. The invaders were coming on like contestants in a monstrous horse race—Ostrogoths and Slavs on the right; Gepids, Lombards, Heruls and other eastern Germans on the left; Huns and Alans in the center.

To Attila, the enemy seemed frozen in place as his army started up the hill. Then the Germans on the Roman wings, both Visigoths and Roman regulars, lowered their lances and thundered down the hill. The war whoops changed to screams and curses, the drumming of hooves to the clang of sword on shield, as the German wings of each army crashed together.

Attila continued straight ahead, where the fur-clad Franks waited like statues. Suddenly, the statues swept their arms back and threw thousands of short, flashing objects. A second later, a shower of stubby, razor-sharp axes hit the Huns. Horses reared, screamed and tumbled end over end. Riders fell from the saddle, dropped their lances or just gazed dumbly at shields split by the deadly francisca, the Frankish national weapon. Thousands of Frankish infantry shouted simultaneously and rushed at the Huns, throwing heavy barbed spears and drawing long swords. The Huns and

Alans felt their horses shy and buck. Never before had the riders from the steppes had a chance to learn that no horse, unless rigorously trained, can be driven straight into a solid mass of armed men. (And even if trained horses are used, charging an unbroken line of spears is a recipe for disaster.) The nomads had never before encountered infantry that would stand up to them, let along charge them en masse. The horses milled around while the Huns hurled their lances like javelins and reached for their bows.

The Alans in the Roman army, stationed next to the Franks, had slipped their bows back into their cases. They leveled their lances and spurred forward. The ironclad Alans had invented this style of warfare.

The Huns weren't as big as the Alans, but they made up for their lack of weight with their courage and ferocity. But the Huns were fighting uphill, and the Frankish tactics had taken them by surprise.

The Germans on the Hunnish left were having troubles, too. Aëtius was making good use of his high ground.

On the Hunnish right, though, the Ostrogoths were pushing back Aëtius's Visigoths. Attila deftly slipped his Huns and Alans to his own right, away from the Roman Alans and the Franks. Suddenly, old Theodoric, the septuagenarian king of the Visigoths fell from his horse. Unnoticed in the thudding, clashing, screaming melee, he was trampled to death. Then one of his soldiers saw Theodoric's mangled body.

"They have killed the king!" he bellowed. Others took up the shout. "Revenge our king," they yelled. Hysterical, berserker fury seized the Visigoths. The Ostrogoths and Huns couldn't hold them back.

Hemmed in and giving ground on three sides, Attila told the drummers and standard bearers to signal retreat. The huge army galloped to the rear. The Huns and Hunnish Alans dropped back to discourage pursuit with volleys of arrows.

But the Roman forces didn't attempt pursuit. With Theodoric dead, the Visigoths had no leader; the Frankish footmen couldn't chase horsemen; and Aëtius positively forbade the Roman regulars to closely follow the Huns. Attila's troops retired peacefully to their ring of wagons. They had not been routed, and Attila felt no need to use his funeral pyre.

Attila in defeat was scarcely more frightened than Aëtius in victory. If the Romans destroyed the Huns, they'd destroy the only force Aëtius had to coerce the German tribes. He had been lucky: he'd beaten the Huns but left their army intact. They'd still be available as mercenaries. Aëtius's biggest worry now was the Visigoths, still mad for vengeance. As soon as the fighting was over, Aëtius sent for Theodoric's son, Thorismund. He suggested that Thorismund hurry home to secure his throne before a usurper could seize it. Usurpation being a Visigothic habit, the new king went back to his troops and ordered a departure the next morning.

Aëtius and the rest of the Romans watched Attila's camp for several days. Finally, the Huns hitched up their wagons and moved away. Aëtius followed them until they crossed the frontier. Then the Roman alliance broke up, each barbarian contingent going home.

7

The desperate fight that became known as the Battle of Chalons (although it happened closer to Troyes) was over. Tradition says that between 162,000 and 300,000 warriors lost their lives. That's far too high. The slaughter, though, was enormous.

The trouble was that Attila didn't act as if he'd been beaten. The next year, Attila, still pursuing Honoria and her "dowry," invaded Italy. The Germans in Gaul and Spain were too busy with their own affairs to save a neighboring country from the Huns. Aëtius could not induce them to help him. The master of soldiers could do no more than watch Attila ravage his way down the peninsula to the gates of Rome before turning back. Perhaps, as many historians believe, the Hunnish army was suffering from plague and hunger. Most contemporaries, though, credit the appearance of Pope Leo I, who confronted Attila outside Rome.

The legend of Leo and Attila hints at one of the things that made Attila's last two campaigns decisive. Whether or not Attila was awed by Leo is irrelevant. The truth is that by their treachery and cruelty, emperors, kings, generals and all the secular leaders had begun to lose the confidence of their people. Public opinion in the fifth century was not the force it became in the twentieth, but even then, there was a limit to what people would take. The last straw was the impotence of Aëtius after his victory. Church leaders like Leo had stayed with the people in the face of danger. The people put their confidence in the clerics, even believing that they could perform miracles. The Middle Ages had begun.

Aëtius had miscalculated the effect of the battle on Attila. That was a serious error. He also miscalculated its effects on Attila's people. That error was fatal.

The invasion of Italy was the last the Romans ever saw of Attila. The next year, he married a new wife, a beautiful German girl named Idilco, or Hilda. The celebration lasted far into the night, and the usually temperate Attila drank heavily. The next morning, he did not appear. Woozy-headed Hunnish nobles went to the palace to investigate. At the door to the khan's chambers, they heard a woman weeping. They entered, and a red-eyed

Idilco led them to the body of her husband. Attila had had a violent nosebleed during the night and had drowned in his own blood.

The Huns slashed their faces in mourning and buried the great khan with his wealth in an unmarked grave, leaving no memorial but the legends about him in the folklore of Central Europe.

Attila's empire died with him. With the charismatic khan gone, the Germans in his horde wondered why they deferred to the Huns. They were, after all, in the overwhelming majority. Chalons had showed that Germans could beat Huns, even Huns aided by other Germans. They rebelled. The resulting Battle of Nedao, a year after Attila's death, ended forever the Hunnish domination of non-Roman Europe.

Attila's empire died with a bang, but the Roman Empire of the West went out with a whimper. Nedao was a direct result of Aëtius's victory at Chalons, and Nedao guaranteed that Aëtius could no longer keep the Germans obedient with Hunnish mercenaries. Gaul and Spain went their own ways. Aëtius's great victory had lost half of the West.

A few years after Chalons, Aëtius and Valentinian were going over accounts when Valentinian suddenly drew his sword and killed the master of soldiers. A few days later, two of Aëtius's Hunnish body guards assassinated Valentinian. What was left of the Western Empire slipped back into the chaos that reigned before Aëtius became the strongman of the West. Never again would the Romans have the opportunity to assimilate the Germans as they had previously assimilated Greeks, Gauls and Egyptians. Roman nobles, military adventurers and barbarian chiefs all vied for power. Finally, Attila's former secretary, Orestes, led an army of eastern Germans, former vassals of the Huns, into Italy. He made his son, Romulus Augustulus, emperor.

In spite of his years as an amateur barbarian, Orestes was too Roman to let his troops settle on the sacred soil of Italy. They mutinied, killed him and deposed Romulus Augustulus, the last Roman Emperor of the West.

Historians call this coup the fall of the Western Empire. Actually, the Western Empire had already fallen as low as it could get. And for all practical purposes, it had died years before, when Aëtius won his fatal victory on the rolling plains around Troyes.

MATTERS

OF

RELIGION

3

What Happened
at Hattin

IT WAS NOVEMBER 27, 1095. THE POPE AND THE BISHOPS WHO ACKNOWL-
edged his authority—all in the Western, or Catholic, Church—had been
meeting for a week in Clermont in the heart of the French Massif Central.
Town life was reviving in Western Europe, and the great barbarian invasions,
a feature of life for the last half-millenium, had almost ceased.

In Germany, a century before this, Emperor Otto I had crushed the
Magyar horsemen from Central Asia and forced them to settle down. Now
Hungary was a Christian kingdom. In Ireland, 81 years before this, the
forces of King Brian Boru had smashed the last great effort of the Vikings—
pirates from Iceland, the northern islands, Norway and Denmark. There
had been a Norse invasion of England in 1066, but that was by the army of
Norway, led by King Harald Hardrada, not Viking freebooters. That invasion, too, had been defeated. But the descendants of Viking freebooters,
the Normans of Duke William, had invaded England at almost the same
time, and now William the Bastard was William the Conqueror. Normans
had also invaded Sicily and were nipping at the territory of the Eastern
Roman Empire.

There was still plenty of turmoil, but most of it was internal—barons
fighting barons and slaughtering each others' peasants. The decade of 1020
to 1030 has been called "perhaps the most unpleasant in French history,"
and conditions hadn't greatly improved. Turmoil extended to the very top of
the social order. The pope and the German emperor had quarreled over the
emperor's assumption that he could appoint bishops. The pope excommunicated the emperor, who, in turn, excommunicated the pope and appointed
an anti-pope. The King of France had put away his wife and married the

wife of the Count of Anjou. One of the items on the agenda of this council was the king's excommunication.

Before the council ended, the pope let it be known that he wanted to address the people on a matter of great importance. So on the morning of November 27, several hundred people were gathered around the papal throne set up in a field outside of Clermont.

"A grave report has come from the lands around Jerusalem and from the city of Constantinople," Pope Urban II said. "A people from the kingdom of the Persians, a foreign race, a race absolutely alien to God . . . has invaded the land of those Christians, has reduced the people with sword, rapine and flame and has carried off some as captives to its own land, has cut down others by pitiable murder and has either completely razed churches of God to the ground or has enslaved them to the practice of its own rites."

As Urban warmed up, he looked directly at the knights and barons in his audience.

"You oppressors of orphans, you robbers of widows, you homicides, you blasphemers, you plunderers of others' rights . . . if you want to take counsel for your souls you must either cast off as quickly as possible the belt of this sort of knighthood or go forward boldly as knights of Christ, hurrying swiftly to defend the Eastern Church."

In recent decades, a new race, Turks from the same steppes north and west of China that had bred the Huns, had replaced the Arabs as the sword arm of Islam. In 1071, the Eastern Roman Emperor, Romanus Diogenes, recklessly pursued the Turkish horse archers into a trap. He was captured, his army was destroyed, and Alp Arslan, the Turkish sultan, swept over all of Anatolia. The new emperor wrote to the pope asking for help and offering to reunite the Eastern Church with the Western.

That was a great inducement for Urban. So was the opportunity to channel the ferocity of the European barons into fighting the enemies of Christianity. So, too, was the chance to help restore to Europe the unity that was lost since the great days of the Roman Empire. A great, all-European movement led by the papacy would also get rid of the Western Emperor's annoying pseudo-pope.

Knowing there was no great love for Constantinople among his listeners, Pope Urban concentrated on Jerusalem. For centuries, pious Christians had made pilgrimages to Jerusalem and venerated relics from the Holy Land, even water from the Jordan. The Arabs, who had conquered Jerusalem when the followers of the Prophet first burst out of their desert peninsula, tolerated the pilgrims. The Christians, like the Jews, were also "people of the book." They worshipped God and honored most of the prophets, but they failed to recognize Mohammed, the last prophet. The Turks, though, were recent converts to Islam, enthusiastic and intolerant. Making a pilgrimage had become a dangerous enterprise.

Urban hit the bullseye with his audience. They chanted, "God wills it! God wills it!"

There was, in fact, too much enthusiasm for Urban's taste. The first army to take the field was a crowd of peasants, clerics, poor knights and a few nobles aroused by the preaching of a man known as Peter the Hermit. They swarmed through Europe, practically leaderless, often robbing the inhabitants, especially Jews. Jews were frequently killed—the flip side of religious enthusiasm. A German count named Dithmar reportedly said he would not leave Germany until he had killed a Jew. In the Rhineland town of Worms, crusaders following Count Emich of Leinengen murdered 800 Jews. When Peter the Hermit's crusaders reached Constantinople, Emperor Alexius ferried them over to Asia as quickly as possible. The Turks fell on the leaderless mob and annihilated it.

The next year, the expedition Alexius had been hoping for got under way. Sometimes called the Baron's Crusade, sometimes the First Crusade, it was composed of nobles from France, Normandy and the Norman holdings in Italy, all accompanied by highly trained solders—heavy cavalry, infantry spearmen and crossbowmen.

Attacks by the Avars, Vikings, Magyars and Moorish Moslems had caused the Franks to modify their military system. The infantry phalanx which had routed Huns and Lombards, Visigoths and Arabs was too slow to counter raids coming from all points of the compass. The trend got started under Charles Martel. In 732, Charles met the Moors near Poitiers. He formed his infantry into squares and refused to be lured out of position by the Moslem riders.

"The men from the North," wrote the Spanish historian Isadore, "stood immovable as a wall, or as if frozen into ice, but hewing down the Arabs with their swords."

Charles knew, though, that without cavalry, he was seldom likely to "get there first with the most." He began expanding the mounted palace guard. Charlemagne carried the process further. He ordered possessors of land to appear at the muster armed in a manner appropriate to the value of their estates. Richer men had to come mounted, wearing armor and carrying sword and spear. These men had leisure to practice the difficult art of fighting on horseback while weighed down with mail. And as the barbarian raids continued, they got plenty of practical experience. The Franks, though, did not immediately forget the art of infantry fighting in the two centuries after Charlemagne. At the start of the crusades, the French foot soldiers were probably the most formidable infantry west of China.

In spite of his earlier plea for help, Alexius greeted the crusaders coolly. He was not particularly happy that one of the leaders was Bohemond of Taranto, a Norman baron who had conquered some of the emperor's land in Italy and had been attacking his possessions in Greece. Further, the situation had changed. The East Roman armies had cornered and wiped out the Pechenegs, a pagan Turkish tribe that had invaded their territory, and the Moslem Seljuk Turks were plagued with internal revolts. The Fatimid caliphs of Egypt had declared war on the Seljuks and taken Jerusalem from them. To Alexius, the crude and illiterate crusaders were the latest wave of northern barbarians, descendants of Goths, Vikings and Franks, once again threatening civilization. But they could be useful.

He would give them supplies and ferry them to Asia if they would swear fealty to him and give him the territory they conquered. Most of the crusaders resisted but had to eventually agree. Bohemond, though, had the soul of his pirate ancestors. He readily agreed, mentally reserving for himself the right to change his mind.

For years, historians took Bohemond to be a typical crusader. They held that the men who took the cross were adventurers who hoped to better themselves financially or to increase their personal power. Recently, historians have begun to examine more closely the letters crusaders wrote and the mortgages on their property they agreed to. They'd be away from home for at least two years. They'd lose the income from their crops; their wives and children would be thousands of miles away; the cost of outfitting themselves and traveling across the continent was enormous. What made them do it is hard for people in later ages to understand. The simple fact is that most crusaders seriously wanted to fight for God and gain eternal salvation. Their motives were much easier for their enemies to understand than their descendants.

2

Their enemies, the Turks, had the same sort of single-minded religiosity. They had entered the lands of Islam first as slaves, then as soldiers. Like the Germans in the Roman empire, they first took over the army of Persia, then the empire. Then they spread all over the Middle and Near East. The process was peaceful enough to allow the Turks to acquire both the religion and the culture of the Persians and Arabs, imperfectly in both cases.

The Koran exhorted the faithful to fight the enemies of God and kill them if they refused to adopt Islam. The newly converted Turks didn't understand why exceptions should be made for Jews and Christians. They, like the European barbarians—and their descendants—enjoyed fighting and killing.

Persian culture was ancient and many faceted. The Persians had picked up from the Indians, and passed on to the Arabs, modern arithmetic, including the flexible "Arabic" numerals and the zero. Persian painting picked up elements from the Chinese but was an exquisite and distinctive national style. Persian poets were among the world's greatest. The Arabs learned much from the Persians, but also contributed ideas they had picked up from the Greeks and the Jews and enriched through their own efforts. In all the arts and sciences, from architecture to zoology, the lands of Islam were light years ahead of western Christendom.

After the great invasions, Western Europe was rebuilding from almost zero. The Middle and Near East had had invasions, too, but they weren't as long-lasting and destructive. The Turks were exposed to, and gradually absorbed, the arts and sciences of the world from Spain to China and India.

One contribution the Turks made was military. They reintroduced the horse-archer tactics of the steppes. As long ago as the Roman triumvirate of Caesar, Pompey and Crassus, the Parthians had used horse-archers to annihilate Crassus's army. As time went on, the settled powers of the Middle East increased their reliance on heavy cavalry lancers. The Turks changed that. And they did not, like the Huns, allow their military system to deteriorate by adopting the tactics of the losers.

The one weakness in the Turkish military system was the Turks' own machismo. They liked to fight hand-to-hand. As soon as their arrow fire began to disorganize an enemy, they couldn't resist casing their bows and charging with swords. Such charges had scattered their enemies from Tashkent to Tripoli.

When Peter the Hermit's army landed in Asia Minor, the Turks attacked in the usual manner—a storm of arrows followed by a charge with sabers. They had never, they agreed later, met such a feeble foe. There was no sense of alarm, then, when they saw a second army of western barbarians about to cross over from Constantinople. Sultan Kilij Arslan was off in the east fighting a rebel emir.

The Franks, as the Turks called them (all had come from France or Norman-occupied Italy) surrounded Nicea, the capital of Anatolia. When Kilij heard that his capital was under siege, he returned, expecting to deal with these Franks as he had with the first group. Christian infantry and engineers were working on the walls. Another line of infantry far behind them was guarding against a relief column. Between the two lines of infantry was the Franks' heavy cavalry. The Turks rode closer and began shooting. The Franks responded with crossbows, a new weapon to Kilij, which could shoot farther than the Turkish bows and pierce more armor. Most of the Turks wore a light helmet and a skimpy corselet made of small metal plates laced together. The Franks wore heavy riveted mail over thick felt shirts. The arrows didn't seem to bother them.

"I have seen soldiers with up to 21 arrows stuck on their bodies marching no less easily for that," wrote a Moslem official, Beha ed-Din Ibn Shedad. The spear carriers stood in front of the crossbowmen, trying to protect them from charging cavalry.

There was nothing to do but charge. It took only one charge to eliminate the last army of Westerners. The Turks charged, but the Franks didn't move. Like their ancestors facing the Huns, the spearmen stood solidly. The Turkish horses skidded, reared and tried to turn while the Frankish crossbowmen picked off their riders. The Turks ran. Kilij rallied them and charged again. Same result. Another charge began. The Frankish infantry opened gaps in their lines, and the cavalry rode through the gaps and charged—a straight line of iron-clad men on leather-barded horses, holding lances longer than any in the Turkish army. The Turks fled, and the siege went on.

A little later, as the crusaders were marching through a mountain pass near a place called Dorylaeum, the sultan tried again. He attacked the crusaders' advance guard camp at dawn.

"The Turks came upon us from all sides, throwing darts and javelins and shooting arrows from an astonishing range," wrote one of Bohemond's knights. There was no charge this time. The Turks rode around, shooting and trying to get the knights to break formation and charge. Bohemond held firm, and the main body of crusaders came up and joined him. Then Bishop Adhemar of Le Puy, the pope's representative, led one division over a path that bypassed the pass. He appeared in the Turks' rear. Both lines of knights charged the Turks caught between them.

"We pursued them, killing them for a whole day," wrote Bohemond's follower.

The crusaders besieged the great city of Antioch. After fighting off several relief expeditions, the crusaders entered the city after Bohemond talked a traitor into lowering a rope ladder. They had no sooner secured the city when a large Turkish army under an emir named Kerbogha besieged them.

The size of the Moslem army discouraged the crusaders from trying to break out. Their food ran low, their horses began dying and the sick multiplied. Then a man named Peter Bartholomew went to Adhemar and told him he had a vision in which St. Andrew showed him where the lance used to stab Jesus Christ on the cross could be found. The crusaders dug a deep hole in the floor of a church where Peter said the lance was hidden. Suddenly Peter Bartholomew leaped into the ditch and came up holding a rusty lance head. It sounds suspicious, even though Bohemond's chronicler wrote that he touched the lance head when it was still embedded in earth. At any rate, the crusaders believed. They were convinced the forces of heaven would be with them if they boldly attacked the Turks.

Morale in the Turkish army was quite different from that in the crusader camp. Kerbogha was, at best, first emir among equals. The other Moslem officers were grumbling that this victory over the infidels would give him too much power.

The gates of Antioch opened and the crusaders marched out. Many knights had no horses. According to some accounts some knights were riding cattle, although that seems doubtful. Kerbogha tried to flank the Christians, but Bohemond and the horsemen he had charged the Turks and drove them back. Kerbogha feigned a retreat to draw the crusaders farther from their walls and into a trap. Some Moslems saw the movement and drew the wrong conclusions. A few of the Moslem emirs began to leave the field. Kerbogha's army panicked. What began as the orderly withdrawal of some princes and their contingents became a rout.

"The Battle of the Lance," as it came to be called, is a proof of Napoleon's dictum that "The *moral* is to the physical as three is to one." The morale of the Moslems had been crushed. The crusaders prepared to leave on what turned out to be a fairly easy march to Jerusalem.

Before they left Antioch, Bohemond successfully argued that because the emperor had not come to their aid during the sieges of Antioch, he had forfeited their allegiance. Anything they captured now would be theirs, and they had no obligation to turn it over to the emperor. When the crusaders started for Jerusalem, Bohemond stayed behind and organized his new domain, the Principality of Antioch.

The emperor began negotiations with the Fatimid caliph in Cairo, who had taken Jerusalem from the Turks. The Egyptians sent emissaries to the crusaders, offering them free passage to the Christian holy places if they would renounce their intention of capturing Jerusalem. The crusaders rejected the offer. They besieged and captured Jerusalem, massacred everyone they found inside its walls and set up the Kingdom of Jerusalem. The kingdom, which included a number of fiefdoms ruled by crusader nobles, stretched from the Red Sea to Bohemond's Principality of Antioch. Most of the crusaders then went home. A few stayed in the "Latin" states.

Almost a century later, they were still there.

3

One reason was that the Moslems seemed unable to unite. They even allied themselves with the Christians against other Moslems. Then in 1174, a young man born Yusef Ibn Ayub—Joseph, son of Job—seized power in Egypt after his uncle's death, took a new title, El Malik en Nasr Salah ed-Din—the Conquering King Sword of the Faith. He lived up to his title. He quickly conquered all the squabbling Moslem factions in Syria and Mesopotamia. Then he turned to the Christians.

The man the crusaders called Saladin was a complex personality. He hated war, never fought in the front lines and was inept with weapons, but he proved to be a master strategist. His Christian foes honored him as a gallant and chivalrous enemy, but he slaughtered captured knights for the entertainment of his dinner guests, and it seems likely that he poisoned his uncle. One thing was certain about him: he loved God and Islam. So he had vowed to fight all his life until the last Christian was converted or dead. He would make truces when he had to, and he would never break his word or sully his honor, but he would make no permanent peace until God's enemies were wiped out.

Just as Saladin was completing the conquest of his empire, King Amalric of Jerusalem died. Amalric, a general of uncommon gifts, had more than held his own against Moslem forces that greatly outnumbered him. At least he did until Saladin appeared. Now he was gone and was succeeded by his 16-year-old son, Baldwin. The boy was dying of leprosy.

For the next eight years, Baldwin the Leper, one of the most underrated generals in history, outmaneuvered, frustrated and defeated the great Saladin. In his last battle, Baldwin, lacking fingers and toes, so weak he couldn't sit up, gave his orders from a litter. But he forced Saladin to make a truce.

Then he died. The crown of Jerusalem passed to Baldwin's brother-in-law, a healthy, handsome fool named Guy de Lusignan. He was no man to lead the willful, independent crusader barons. There was, for example, Reynald de Chatillon, who believed he was not bound by any pact the King of Jerusalem signed with infidels. There was Count Raymond of Tripoli, a self-centered opportunist. And there were the grand masters of the military monks, the Templars and the Hospitalers, who recognized the authority of no one but the pope.

Reynald broke the truce, something he did regularly. A robber and a pirate (he once put galleys on the Red Sea to raid the Moslem pilgrim ships to Mecca), he attacked and robbed a Moslem caravan.

The Kingdom of Jerusalem, on the verge of anarchy under Guy's blundering rule, reunited. The holy war was on again. By stripping castles of their garrisons and using all available cash to hire soldiers in Europe, Guy assembled 1,200 knights, 1,000 of the light horsemen called Turcopoles because they fought like Turks, and 10,000 infantry. Guy also announced that he was taking along a piece of the True Cross, which he would keep in his tent.

On his side, Saladin had gathered troops from Persia to Egypt's western desert and from the Caucasus to Aden. There is no record of Moslem numbers, but Saladin's army was many times the size of Guy's.

Sultan Saladin picked his first target carefully. It was the town of Tiberias. Commanding its garrison was Lady Eschiva, the wife of a man known to Christian and Moslem alike for his devotion to his own interests, Count Raymond of Tripoli. Eschiva got a message through to her husband, who was with the royal army at Acre. At a council of war, Raymond spoke against attempting to relieve Tiberias. Many gallant Crusaders had died before Eschiva, he said, and the army's first consideration must be the safety of the kingdom and the holy places. It was the middle of summer; the Moslems would find no fodder for their horses and little water. They couldn't forage very far, and such a large army would soon run out of supplies. The Christian army, camped near a well-watered spot, would be able to discourage small raiding parties.

The trouble with Raymond's suggestion was nobody trusted him. He'd once made a separate truce with Saladin. Opposing him was the Grand Master of the Temple, who had his own shame to live down. A few months before, he had run away from a fight that killed almost all his brother monks. Also opposed was the fanatical Reynald de Chatillon. Right now, they said, they had the strongest crusader army anyone could remember. The Christians might wait out Saladin and force him to retreat, but he'd be back again. On the other hand, if they attacked now, they could deal all the powers of Islam a crushing blow.

The council decided to advance to Sephoria, a place with both wells and pastures and close to Tiberias. Then it would decide what to do next.

Another council was held July 2, after the army reached Sephoria. Sephoria was a strong position, and the council agreed that if Saladin attacked, he'd probably be beaten. But that night, the Grand Master of the Temple called on Guy privately and shamed him into attempting to relieve Tiberias.

The attack planned was the sort of thing the crusaders had been doing for generations. They would drive directly at Saladin's water supply—the Sea of Galilee—relying on their steady infantry and heavily armed cavalry to cut through the Moslem light horse. With the water under their control,

Saladin would have to either retreat or fight at close quarters. The first course of action would hurt his prestige—and his ability to attract soldiers—much more than if he'd retreated on his own initiative—as he would with Raymond's plan. The second would destroy his army.

4

Agonizingly climbing the ridge between Sephoria and Tiberias, the Christian soldiers began to see the flaw in the Grand Master's plan: before they could control the Moslem's water supply, they'd have to reach it. The summer sun was high now, and it turned the Franks' armor searing hot anywhere it was not shielded by their surcoats. Infantrymen, encased in their stifling layers of mail and felt, sweated profusely. Some had already drained their water bags. And now the Moslems had come.

The crusaders had never seen so many infidels at one time. They churned up dust clouds that covered the horizon. Small groups of riders dashed out of clumps of brush or from behind hillocks, shot their arrows and ran away before the crossbowmen could cock their bows. The circle of horse archers drew closer. Larger and larger groups attacked the Christian army, riding in from all directions. Each time, the crossbowmen had to stop to cock their bows, using a cord and pulley. When the crossbowmen stopped, the spearmen and heavy cavalry stopped, too, because the crusader military system depended on each component protecting the others. So the whole army waited when any group of crossbowmen stopped to cock their bows, fit bolt to string and aim at the rapidly moving horse archers. The Christian Turcopoles were also horse archers, but the number of the Turks simply overwhelmed them. They, too, were now sheltering behind the infantry.

Now the Turks were dashing up in waves. More and more arrows struck the Christians. Some of the the Turks were shooting at a high angle to get extreme range. It was a method that hardly produced pinpoint accuracy, but it decreased the danger from the crossbows, and they didn't need pinpoint accuracy to hit a target the size of the crusader army.

All the time, the sun grew hotter; the dust grew thicker; and the Christians grew thirstier. The Sea of Galilee was only a few miles away across the ridge, and the Moslem horsemen could ride back and refresh themselves whenever they felt the need. By mid-afternoon, the panting Franks were still west of the ridge. Because the Christians had to stop to shoot, the clouds of horse archers held them in place as effectively as a solid phalanx.

From time to time, the Moslems came too close. Then the knights put on their great helms and charged. Usually, though, the nimble Turks managed to avoid the thundering iron-covered mass. The arrows the Moslems shot as they fled did less harm than the knights' own armor. The great helm, a recent invention, covered the head completely: the occupant looked through a slit and breathed through tiny perforations in the padded iron bucket over his head. Heated to a searing temperature by the sun, the helm became an instrument of torture. Men literally suffocated in their own helmets and died without receiving a single wound. Most knights eventually discarded their helms and fought bareheaded. Even so, each of their charges became weaker than the last. They were running out of water for the horses as well as for themselves.

The Templars in the rear sent word to Guy that their horses could go no farther. Guy noticed houses just below the ridge. Where there are houses, there must be water. He ordered an advance to the little village of Hattin. The host should march steadily, he ordered, without stopping to shoot or charge, and they'd spend the night at the village well.

Nobody told Guy that the well of Hattin had run dry, and the village had been abandoned.

Once the army stopped, nobody could get the dead-beat men and horses moving again. Guy didn't try very hard. Count Raymond did, but the soldiers could no longer be moved by mere shouting.

During the night, Saladin moved his army in closer, distributed more arrows and kept 70 arrow-laden camels deployed around the circle. He had had his tent set up where he had a good view of the village and the ridge behind it. Saladin was a strategist, not a fighter: he directed his battles from behind the lines.

The next day, the clouds of horse archers returned to the attack. The parched crossbowmen shot back. And the sun rose higher. The crusader knights could manage little more than a half-hearted charge or two. Soldiers were collapsing from heat and thirst. Some crossbowmen no longer had the strength to cock their bows.

The ridge was just ahead of the Christian position, and from there it was only three miles, all downhill, to the Sea of Galilee, hundreds of square miles of cool, fresh water. Suddenly, the footmen bolted from their position and ran for the ridge. Saladin concentrated most of his army against them. The once rock-steady infantry was half-destroyed by thirst. The men couldn't push through the masses of Moslem horsemen.

Next, the Turks concentrated their arrows on the crusader cavalry. The knights were no longer shielded by the infantry, and the horse armor—which few retained—was not really arrow-proof. Most of the horses were destroyed. The cavalry had no hope of rejoining the infantry. The crusaders' coordination of infantry and cavalry, their greatest tactical strength, was gone. Raymond of Tripoli, his followers and a few other knights were able to cut their way out of the trap, but they didn't stop to help the footmen.

Next, the Moslems set fire to the brush upwind of the Christian position. The crusaders went on fighting as the fire swept through them, but they had reached the end of their rope. The infantry surrendered. Some were too exhausted to stand. One witness saw a single Moslem lead away 30 bound Christians.

The cavalry fought on. Finally, reported Saladin's son, Afdal, only Guy and 150 of his bravest knights held out on a hill near the village.

"I was beside my father when the King of the Franks retreated to the hill; the brave men who were round him fell on us and pushed the Moslems to the bottom of the hill," he wrote. "I looked at my father and saw the sadness on his face. 'Give the devil the lie!' he shouted, tugging at his beard. At those words, our army hurled itself on the enemy and forced him to the summit of the hill. . . . but the Franks returned again to the charge and advanced once again to the bottom of the hill, where they were again repulsed; and again I cried, 'They flee! They flee!' Then my father looked at me and said, 'Be silent; they will not be truly defeated until the King's tent falls.' Now, he had barely finished speaking when the tent collapsed. My father immediately got down from his horse and prostrated himself before God and gave thanks to Him, weeping tears of joy."

Guy's remaining knights were unhorsed and exhausted, too weak, most of them, to even stand when the last Moslem wave swept over them, knocked down the king's tent and carried off the piece of the True Cross.

After the battle, Saladin received Guy and some of the leading Crusaders in his tent. He gave Guy a cup of chilled rose water. The king drank only a part and offered the goblet to Reynald de Chatillon.

"Remind the king," Saladin said to his interpreter, "that it is not I, but he, who gives drink to this man." Saladin had adopted the Bedouin custom of granting safety to any prisoner to whom he gave food or drink. Later, after the leading prisoners had washed and eaten, he sent for Reynald again and asked if he would embrace Islam. As the sultan expected, Reynald contemptuously refused.

Saladin drew his sword and struck at Reynald, cutting off his arm. Embarrassed by their sultan's swordsmanship, Saladin's servants immediately cut off the crusader's head.

The Christian commoners were sold into slavery. The Templars and Hospitalers, those implacable foes, were all beheaded. Saladin held the nobles for ransom. They brought him little revenue, however. Saladin released the captives he liked, including King Guy, if they promised to leave the Holy Land. If the ransom were not promptly paid on the others, he had them slaughtered, one by one, for the amusement of his court.

But such entertainment came later. As soon as the battle was over, Saladin swept down on the Crusader-held cities and gobbled them up. On October 2, he took Jerusalem.

5

A handful of crusaders held out in Tyre. Guy de Lusignan, who had promised to leave for Europe, arrived before Tyre with his followers, but was refused admittance. He then took his followers to Acre and besieged it. Saladin had dismissed his levies. Before he could raise a new army, fighting men had begun arriving from Europe to help with the siege. The Third Crusade had begun.

The Holy Roman Emperor and the kings of France and England all took the Cross. The emperor drowned on the overland route, and his army disintegrated. The English and French monarchs arrived, and Richard the Lionhearted of England quickly dominated the Crusade. Unlike Saladin, he was a matchless fighting man, and his feats of arms made "el Malik Rik" a name to frighten Moslem children for generations. But though he marched to within sight of Jerusalem, he did not try to take the city. He knew the horse archers could isolate and starve out the garrison by stopping the movement of anything smaller than a full field army. Richard made a truce with Saladin, and the reconquest of Jerusalem was secure, although the Christians would retain a foothold on the coast for generations to come, and there would be crusades for another century.

6

The Christians took back with them a taste for the products of the Orient. All of those exotic goods from India and China had to pass through Moslem hands, as did the gold the Europeans paid for them. The lands of Islam fattened at the expense of the Christians.

That, from the Moslem point of view, was the good side of Hattin. There was another, much darker side.

The triumph of the horse archer was too complete. The Moslems were convinced that the mounted bowman was the ultimate weapon, at least in their arid homeland. It was absurd to think of anything that could unseat the horse archer. So no one tried.

About 50 years after Hattin, Moslem savants were writing about a substance they called "the snow from China." It was salt petre (potassium nitrate), the basic ingredient of gunpowder. The Chinese had been using it to produce a mild explosive almost two centuries before that, and they had already given it serious military use in both bombs and rockets. The Moslems thought it had some value in medicine, but they made almost no attempt to develop its potential in weaponry. How, after all, could such an exotic item be integrated into a military system based on the invincible horse archer?

A few years later, Roger Bacon, an Englishman, and Albertus Magnus, a German, wrote treatises on the substance and its explosive properties, using sources published in Moslem Spain. Before the century was over, Europeans were using guns in war. Even after the gun had been invented in Europe, the Moslems largely ignored it as a weapon. They contributed nothing to its development. What could cumbersome cannons and clumsy, inaccurate muskets do against the mobile, fast-shooting horse archer?

Even the Ottoman Turks, the most progressive of the Islamic peoples, barely tolerated the gun. They hired renegade Christians to manufacture and operate their artillery. Bowmen long outnumbered musketeers in their famous Janissaries. Incidentally, the Janissaries, the most efficient infantry ever raised by a Moslem power, were all slaves, born of Christian parents. That indicates the esteem in which infantry was held by the Moslems. Free-born warriors fought as horse archers.

While the world of Islam grew in wealth, it let technological progress slip away in its infatuation with the horse archer. The poison fruit of Hattin stunted more than military progress. The Moslem lands, once the most receptive in the world to new ideas and the most ingenious in adapting them, now turned away from any ideas from the West. After Hattin, the Moslem hatred of European Christians congealed into contempt. What could the clumsy and inept Franks contribute?

It took more than three centuries for this intellectual stagnation to catch up with Islam. And the occasion of the showdown was also a result of Hattin. Moslem control of the trade routes drove the Christians to a desperate measure—sailing on the ocean. To do that, they had to develop a new type of ship—one powered entirely by sail, because no ship on a long voyage could carry enough food for a horde of rowers. It could not maneuver like a galley. It had to have a high freeboard to survive ocean storms, so it wasn't much good for boarding galleys, even if it could carry (and it couldn't) as many soldiers as a galley.

The crusaders had failed because they tried to fight the Turks in their natural element, the arid, scorching steppes of Asia. Now these denizens of the foggy, stormy Atlantic coast were moving into an element familiar to them, but as strange to the Turks and Arabs as the desert had been to the Europeans.

Perhaps significantly, this innovation began on the Iberian Peninsula, where Portugal and Spain were finishing their centuries-long war against Moslem invaders. The Portuguese began sailing down the African coast. When they reached India, Moslem rulers became disturbed. The European sailors were cutting into their profits.

The Sultan of Egypt sent a fleet of galleys and 15,000 marines to the Indian Ocean to take care of the Portuguese problem. The galleys searched for months. Eventually, they cornered a Portuguese convoy off the Indian port of Diu.

And the Portuguese blew them out of the water.

The 15,000 marines never got a chance to board. To protect their clumsy, undermanned vessels, the Portuguese had lined their sides with cannons. They kept their distance from the galleys and sank them with shot.

Diu was followed by several more similar battles, all with the same result. This series of sea fights was far more significant than the celebrated engagement at Lepanto. Islam had been outflanked globally. The Moslems' disaster had been long in the making, and it was too late to ever undo it.

The Portuguese victory was not the true cause of the Islamic decline that followed it. Diu merely confirmed an existing situation: the Moslem world had fallen hopelessly behind Christendom in technology—a situation that began after Saladin's victory at Hattin.

Islam's chance of catching up became even more remote as a result of Spain's ventures on the open sea. While the Portuguese were blasting open the eastern sea route to the Orient, their Spanish rivals tried to beat them by sailing west. The Spanish hoped that by sailing directly to China, they could also contact the Great Khan, the Mongol emperor. Europeans had been trying to enlist his aid in another crusade before contact with China and Mongolia was broken two centuries earlier. Columbus didn't reach the Orient, but the New World he found unbalanced the scales in favor of Christendom more than all the wealth of the East.

In the long run, Saladin's victory at Hattin brought not the salvation, but the ruin, of his people.

4

1205, CONSTANTINOPLE (FOURTH CRUSADE)

The Blind Leading
the Blind

THE PEOPLE OF CONSTANTINOPLE HAD NEVER SEEN SO MANY SHIPS.
Crowded on the battlements of their city's walls, they watched sleek galleys
with heavy bronze rams, warships with high wooden "castles" above their
bows and sterns for archers and engines, merchant ships carrying supplies,
fat passenger ships crowded with mail-clad soldiers, and shallow-draft
transports carrying bridges that could be lowered to let mounted men ride
ashore.

It was a sight to inspire awe—and terror. For these ships had come to
attack the capital of the Empire. Constantinople, the New Rome, would
have to defend itself from a new horde of barbarians.

That was an old story. In the past, Goths and Huns, Avars and Slavs,
Bulgars and Magyars had found the double land walls impregnable. The
harbor had seen other ships, too, from the longboats of the Russians to the
galleys of the Arabs, and it had seen them all leave, shattered and defeated.
Wave after wave of pagans and infidels had broken against the walls of
Constantinople as if the city had been the very rock on which Christ founded
His church. But this wave was different.

The attackers were Christians.

Aboard the fleet, the soldiers gazed at the walls and felt the same
emotions as the watchers on the wall.

> I can assure you that all those who had never seen Constantinople before
> gazed very intently at the city, having never imagined there could be so
> fine a place in all the world. . . . There was indeed no man so brave and
> daring that his flesh did not shudder at the sight.

So wrote Geoffroy de Villehardouin, marshal of Champaign, one of the
leaders of the expedition and author of an insider's history of this strange

46

campaign. The men on the ships had another reason to shudder besides the fear of assaulting so strong a city. The red crosses they wore reminded them that they had vowed to fight the Saracens and recover the holy city of Jerusalem. They were permitted to fight Christians only in self defense or to prevent a great injustice.

To be sure, relations between the Latins, or Roman Catholics, and the Greeks, or members of the Orthodox Church, had seldom been happy. The Greek emperor had tried to use the First Crusade to recover his lands, and he abandoned the crusaders to their (apparently dire) fate when they took an independent course. The Normans had pushed the Greeks out of Sicily and southern Italy, and they had attempted to take Constantinople, as well. The Greeks of Cyprus, under the rebel emperor, Isaac Comenus, had plundered the ships of Richard the Lionhearted and kidnapped the king's sister. And Reynald de Chatillon had plundered Cyprus between raids on Moslem pilgrims. When a pretender named Andronicus seized power in Constantinople, he murdered all the Italian merchants. And when Saladin captured Jerusalem, Emperor Isaac Angelus sent his congratulations.

None of these incidents would have induced this host of French soldiers to attack Constantinople. They had left their homes and families for a far greater project. Only an appeal to religion, a desire to do God's work, could have brought out all the soldiers who appeared before Constantinople in June of 1205.

What had happened?

2

In 1197, the five-year truce Richard the Lionhearted had signed with Saladin ended, and the Moslems resumed their reconquest. Neither Saladin nor Richard were present. The sickly Saladin, worn out from decades of war, had died within a year of the peace, revered for both his conquests and his charity to his Islamic brethren.

"He who had possessed so much and such great riches," wrote Beha ed-Din, "did not leave in dying more than forty-seven dirhems and a single piece of Syrian gold."

Richard, at the same time, was languishing in the dungeon of a feudal enemy. Finally ransomed, he was killed fighting a continental war in 1199.

Richard had been as much a French lord as an English king. He had many supporters among the French nobility in his struggle with his nominal overlord, King Philip of France. Richard's French followers saw little chance that the late king's brother, John Lackland, could help them against Philip. To reduce tensions in France, they proposed a new crusade. Crusades were no longer the novelty they were in 1096. The great nobles of France, more worldly than their followers, saw a crusade as more than an exercise of militant piety.

The barons organizing the expedition decided to strike first at Egypt, which King Richard called the most vulnerable part of Islam. To lead it, they settled on Boniface of Montferrat, a cousin of both the King of France and Philip of Swabia, the strong man of the Holy Roman Empire. They chose six envoys, one of them Geoffroy de Villehardouin, to arrange passage to Egypt. The envoys went to Venice.

Venice was a city-state and a republic. At the base of the government was the Great Council, composed of members of 200 aristocratic families. The Great Council elected almost all officials, from minor magistrates through senators and cabinet officers. At the top of the pyramid was the duke, or doge. Theoretically, he had few political powers, but the doge had lifetime tenure, while the other officials held office for only a few months. A doge with a strong personality could often run the city-state as he saw fit.

The current doge was Enrico Dandolo, a man of 80, who had spent his life serving his city-state as well as himself. Dandolo was a type of man never seen north of the Alps at this time. He was a north Italian noble—a spiritual heir of the Caesars and a spiritual ancestor of the Borgias. He had helped make his canal-laced town one of the foremost naval powers in the Mediterranean. He had fought the Pisans, the Genoese and the Byzantines. In one of his battles with the Greeks, he had suffered a blow on the head which killed his vision.

Losing the use of his eyes affected neither Dandolo's hindsight nor his foresight. Looking back, he could see Andronicus's massacre of the Italian merchants and the Greek attempts to keep the Venetians from their markets. Looking ahead, he could envision a Venetian thalassocracy based on Crete, Rhodes, Cyprus and the Greek islands.

When the French envoys arrived to rent a fleet, Dandolo asked for a week to discuss the matter with his council. To take an army to Egypt would mean attacking Venice's leading trading partner. A lesser man would have resigned himself to losing either the ferry contract or the Egyptian trade. Dandolo saw a way to keep both and gain a lot more besides. The European renaissance began in northern Italy, and Dandolo was a child of his environment. Cynical, Machiavellian before Machiavelli, but intensely patriotic, he saw a way to use the fanaticism of his medieval guests. He sent an envoy to Saphadin, Saladin's brother and now Sultan of Egypt, telling him not to worry. Then he outlined his plan to the council.

When Dandolo met the envoys, they agreed that the Venetians would supply transports to carry 4,500 horses, 4,500 knights, 9,000 squires and

20,000 well-equipped soldiers called sergeants. They would also supply 50 warships with their crews and nine months rations and fodder for the army. The contract would last for one year from the day the fleet sailed. In return, the French would pay 85,000 silver marks and share everything they conquered evenly with the Venetians. The price in silver was calculated as two marks for each man and four marks for each horse.

As the crusaders arrived, the Venetians put them up on the Island of St. Nicholas of Lido, located several miles from shore. They had no desire to have an army of armed and aggressive foreigners interfering with the life of the city. There was a lot of work to be done—building a fleet, for example. According to Robert of Clari, the doge commanded "that no Venetian should be so bold as to engage in any business, but rather that they should all help build the navy, and they did so." Clari wrote the other important history of this crusade. Where Villehardouin gives the leadership point of view, Clari describes the war as it appeared to an ordinary knight.

Villehardouin and his fellow envoys borrowed 5,000 marks from the Venetian bankers for a down payment and promised to pay the rest when the fleet was completed. Most of the money would come from the "pilgrims" as the crusaders called themselves. While the fleet was under construction, problems developed.

They revolved around the crusaders' destination. Strategists might see that the easiest way to Jerusalem was through Egypt—rich, populous but militarily soft Egypt, the breadbasket of the region. Most of the crusaders weren't strategists, though. They were simple farmers and country gentlemen, accustomed to fighting for their liege lord, but unacquainted with international politics or grand strategy. They had vowed to fight for Jerusalem, and they were not going to take any detours. They began leaving for Syria in small parties from other ports. That not only cut down the size of the crusading army, it cut back the money available to pay the Venetians.

When the fleet was ready, Dandolo asked for his money. The crusaders came up short. Dandolo protested that his people had lost a great deal of their own money by concentrating on the construction of the fleet. He added: "You shall not depart from the island until we are paid."

The doge knew that the French had no way of raising the money, and he knew several other interesting facts. He knew that Alexius Angelus, son of the former East Roman emperor and brother-in-law of Philip of Swabia, had met some of the leading crusaders. Alexius was now staying with Philip, whose cousin, Boniface, was the leader of the expedition.

Alexius's father, Isaac, had been overthrown by his brother, also named Alexius, in a palace coup. Alexius the usurper had Isaac blinded and put both him and his son in prison. But the young man escaped and fled to Germany.

After joining Philip, Alexius sent envoys to the leaders of the crusade. They discussed the events in Constantinople and promised to help young Alexius regain his throne if the prince would aid their crusade. Philip and Boniface saw a chance to use the religious enthusiasm of their simple followers to gain the kind of influence in the East Roman Empire that they now exercised in the Holy Roman Empire.

Dandolo cared little about the politics of the Holy Roman Empire as long as it left Venice alone. The East Roman Empire was something else. If Venice could make it a client state, the city of canals would be the sole link between Europe and the Orient.

At this moment, the doge had under his control the largest navy in the world and the most powerful army in Europe. Alexius had enhanced his opportunity to eliminate his country's greatest rival. All he had to do was use this enormous military power to put Prince Alexius on a throne in exchange for certain concessions.

But would the crusaders attack the Christians of Constantinople? It was hard enough to get them to go to Egypt instead of Syria. (Not that he intended to take them to Egypt.) The pope would be furious at an attack on Constantinople by men who had taken the Cross, and the crusaders feared excommunication.

The doge talked things over with the council and went to the crusaders with a proposal. The King of the Hungarians, he told them, had stolen the city of Zara from Venice. (Actually, Venice never held it. Zara was a Hungarian city.) If the crusaders would retake the city for Venice, he would remit the debt and take the Cross himself.

The barons knew that if they didn't do something, the best that could happen would be that the army would disintegrate. They were permitted to fight Christians in self defense or to right a great wrong. Surely, this would fit the second condition.

Not all the crusaders agreed. More of them deserted. Others, after their leaders had agreed to Dandolo's proposal, went to Zara but refused to fight. Still others, like Simon de Montfort, negotiated with the King of Hungary and set out for the Holy Land across his territory.

Enough crusaders remained, though, to besiege Zara. After five days, the city surrendered on the condition that the lives of the citizens be spared. Dandolo had acquired new territory for Venice. And he had accomplished something more important. He had tarred the crusaders with the guilt of having attacked Christians.

As soon as he heard the news, Pope Innocent III pronounced excommunication against all who had taken part in the attack. The crusaders sent envoys to beg the pope's pardon and to explain their side of the story. The pontiff sized up the situation: this crowd of northern bumpkins had been taken in by his wily Italian compatriots. He sent back word that they were forgiven because they had been misled, but he warned them not to attack Christians again, at least, not until they had fulfilled their vows.

Pope Innocent was anything but innocent of the ways of the world. While warning the crusaders against shedding more Christian blood, but forgiving them, he was threatening, very subtly, the East Roman Emperor with this uncontrollable horde of wild Franks. If the emperor would bring his people back into communion with Rome, acknowledging the ecclesiastical supremacy of the Bishop of Rome, they would be safe from the fanatical followers of the Latin rite.

Meanwhile, having taken Zara, the crusaders were eager to get the holy war under way. They went to Dandolo and demanded to be taken to Egypt.

The doge pointed out that it was already November—a bad time to begin campaigning. They were late, he said, because they had not paid their debt on time. He couldn't take them to Egypt, because winter storms would now make sailing impossible, and he would not be able to supply their army. The supplies they had with them, he added, were almost exhausted. There was really no choice, Dandolo continued, but to sit out the winter in Zara. They were in the middle of a rich country where all necessities could be taken care of.

By no coincidence at all, Prince Alexius appeared on the scene. At the first of the year, Philip of Swabia sent messengers to petition the crusaders on behalf of Alexius. They offered, Villehardouin records:

> Firstly, if God permits you to restore his inheritance to him, he will place his whole empire under the authority of Rome, from which he has long been estranged. Secondly, since he is well aware that you have spent all your money and now have nothing, he will give you 200,000 silver marks, and provisions for every man in your army, officers and men alike. Moreover, he himself will go in your company to Egypt with ten thousand men, or if you prefer it, send the same number of men with you; and furthermore, so long as he lives, he will maintain, at his expense, five thousand knights to keep guard in the land overseas.

Not surprisingly, Boniface of Montferrat proved to be the most ardent advocate of Alexius's offer. He and a number of other barons announced that they would accept the offer. Only twelve of them actually signed the agreement to help Alexius, but most of the others went along. It seemed to them there was nothing else they could do.

Alexius himself joined the crusade in April. He repeated the promises in person. On Easter, the expedition sailed for Constantinople.

3

The crusaders sailed past the great city and landed at Scutari, on the Asian side of the Bosphorus. Alexius III sent a herald to offer the crusaders supplies and money if they would proceed to Egypt. The barons, however, said they had come to restore Prince Alexius to his rightful throne. If the emperor would agree to step down, they would see to it that the former Alexius III would be allowed to live as a wealthy man. But unless the emperor would agree to this, they told his messenger, he should send no more envoys. The next day, the crusaders put young Alexius on a boat and took him up under the city walls.

"Here is your natural lord," they shouted to the people on the walls. "We have not come to harm you, but to return your lord to the place that was treacherously taken from him by the tyrant who now rules you. Rally to his side, and no harm will come to you."

There was absolutely no sign that the people on the walls wanted, or even recognized, young Alexius.

The next day, the Franco-Venetian force prepared to assault the city. Soldiers trooped aboard the transports in full armor; knights and squires packed horses, all saddled and caparisoned, aboard the big freighters; some knights rode aboard the drawbridge-equipped assault boats. Venetian sailors attached lines from the galleys to the transports, so rowers could tug the big sailing ships across the strait.

Other sailors tightened the skeins of rope that powered the mangonels and ballistae and made sure the rocks and javelins those engines threw were in place. Both engines used rope skeins as torsion springs. On the mangonel, engineers drew back a long arm against the tension of the skein around the bottom of the arm and loaded rocks in a spoon or a sling at the top of the arm. When released, the arm snapped back, shooting the rock at or over a city wall. The ballista used two skeins and two shorter arms which snapped out horizontally. It was, in effect, a giant crossbow.

Before the ships could start, the Byzantine army—cavalry and infantry—filed out of the city and lined the shore. When they saw the enemy army, the crusaders hesitated. Dandolo told the barons his sailors would clear the way for them. He called up the crews of warships not towing transports and sent them straight at the city. As they neared shore, the Venetian ships turned broadside. From engines on their fore and stern castles, head-size boulders and short, heavy spears shot into the ranks of the Greeks. Showers of arrows and crossbow bolts came from loopholes in the seagoing castles, from fighting tops—perches among the masts—and from the shield-lined gunwales. The enemy ranks broke and the Byzantine soldiers stumbled back.

Behind the screen of missiles, brawny oarsmen were dragging transports across a strait boiling with clashing wakes. Knights and sergeants jumped off in water up to their waists, a dangerous practice for armored men on an unknown shore, and struggled through the water to close with the Greeks. The assault boats dropped their drawbridges, and mounted knights rode ashore with lowered lances. The Greeks hesitated a few moments, then they fled along the edge of the harbor, known to the ancients as the Golden Horn. They crossed a bridge that led into Constantinople, broke down the bridge and dashed into the city.

The harbor was still in Greek hands, however. Between the city walls and the fort of Galata, the Byzantines had stretched a heavy chain. The French, now on the Galata side of the harbor, besieged the fort. The garrison sallied out, but the crusaders pushed the Greeks back, pursuing so closely they couldn't close the gate. In a short time, the French owned the fort. Meanwhile, the Venetians sent galley after galley crashing into the chain. With the barrier stretched taut on the ramming beaks of several galleys, one more huge ship struck it at full speed. The chain snapped.

The allies held a council of war. The Venetians wanted to attack the sea wall of the city: it was only a single wall. Once across, they'd be in. The land wall, on the other hand, was a double wall. If they captured the outer wall, they'd still be exposed to fire from the higher inner wall. And the space between the walls was so constricted that either getting over or breaking through the inner wall would be most difficult. The French granted the difficulties of the land approach. However, they pointed out, they were landsmen. They needed good horses between their knees or solid land beneath their feet to fight at all. So the council adopted both approaches: the Venetians would attack the sea wall, while the Franks assaulted the land wall near the harbor. It was a decision that defied all the theoretical dicta about dividing forces. But the Franks would not fight from ships. And Dandolo, a sea fighter of vast experience, would not waste his powerful navy or the advantage of assaulting a single wall. Though 80 years old and blind, Dandolo had the solid support of his Venetians. He could not be swayed.

The crusaders drove the Greeks who were guarding the bridge away, repaired the bridge and built a palisaded camp outside the wall near the Blachernae Palace, which guarded the city gates. They camped for ten days, while the Greeks sallied out almost daily.

At last, the crusaders had all their missile engines and scaling apparatus in order. They attacked a tower guarding the gate, and, after hard fighting, managed to get 15 men on the tower. The tower was held by the Varangian Guard, English and Danish mercenaries who fought with battle axes, as had their ancestors when the unit was formed. It was axe against sword, and the axe proved to be a better armor-cutter. The French suffered heavy casualties, and the Varangians took two captives alive.

Meanwhile, the Venetians built more scaling towers and bridges on the decks of their galleys. Protected by plaited rope and hides, the towers would allow three soldiers to pass abreast over drawbridges from the ships to the tops of the walls. When everything was ready, the galleys swept up to the walls of the city. Mangonels banged; crossbows snapped, and missiles flew. But the defenders shot back, and the galleys didn't get close enough to use the drawbridges.

Finally, Enrico Dandolo had a crewman bring him the ensign of St. Mark. Holding it before him, he screamed at the sailors he could not see, "Put me ashore, you craven dogs!"

The ship pulled as close to wall as it could, and a dozen men leaped out at the foot of the wall to shield their doge. Up on the towers, the drawbridges thumped down and sword-swinging soldiers raced to the wall. The men at the wall's base put scaling ladders against the rampart and started up. The rest of the ships came up to the wall, and all the Venetians scrambled for the fortifications.

By the end of the day, the Venetians held 25 towers, each a bowshot from its nearest neighbors. The emperor called back the troops that were fighting the Franks and hurled them against the Venetians, who were advancing through the city. The Italians retreated, and, as the wind was at their backs, set fire to the houses between them and the imperial army. The Greeks retreated before the inferno, and the Venetians went back to their towers.

Next, the emperor led his army out on the plain where the French troops were camped.

"It looked as if the whole plain was covered with troops, advancing and in good order," Villehardouin recalled. "We were, it seemed, in a pretty desperate situation, since we had no more than six divisions while the Greeks had close on sixty, and not one of them but was larger than ours. However, our troops were drawn up in such a way that they could not be attacked except from the front."

In this emergency, Robert of Clari recalled, the crusaders armed their cooks and horse boys with clubs and large pestles, wrapped them in quilts and saddle blankets for armor and put copper kettles on their heads. So armed, they augmented the seventh division, which held the palisade around the camp.

The crusaders could not advance, or the huge Greek army would envelop both of their flanks. The Greeks, on the other hand, hesitated to meet the Franks on a narrow front where numbers would make no difference. Finally, the emperor slowly withdrew his army into the city.

That night, Alexius III and his immediate household sneaked out of the city. The citizens, finding themselves without an emperor, dug old Isaac out of his dungeon and proclaimed him emperor again. Then they opened the gates to the crusaders. They might say they did this of their own free will, but the fact remained that Constantinople had been taken by force for the first time since Constantine the Great had founded it some 900 years before.

4

Isaac Angelus, Prince Alexius, the crusader barons and Enrico Dandolo met that day. Prince Alexius joined his father as the co-emperor, Alexius IV. Actually, he was the emperor. Isaac was broken in spirit as well as in body. But Dandolo, far older than Isaac and just as blind, was the real power in Constantinople.

Their mission for young Alexius completed, the crusaders asked the new emperor for the money and men he had promised. Alexius replied, with Dandolo's backing, that although the capital had been freed, the usurper still held most of the empire. As soon as he had restored order, Alexius would fulfill his commitments to the letter.

Actually both Alexius and Dandolo knew that there was no way the Byzantine could ever keep his promises. There simply were not 200,000 silver marks available. Nor, as the Greek army was composed of mercenaries and salaried regulars, was there any way he could afford to send 10,000 men on crusade.

Some of the crusaders suspected as much. They came to Dandolo and asked to be taken to Egypt. The doge said there were only two months left to his contract. He could take them to Egypt, but there was no way he could supply them, protect their sea flank or evacuate them if it became necessary. He pointed out that Alexius had already paid them 100,000 marks (half of which, by the original agreement, went to the Venetians). If the new emperor could settle his empire, he would surely pay the rest. Dandolo suggested that the crusaders might want to stay and speed that happy day. If they would, he continued, he'd keep the Venetian fleet with them for another year without extra charge.

Awed by this generosity, the main body of crusaders agreed to stay.

And Dandolo was sure that with an army of Franks in a Greek city, the natural course of events would not only preclude the Egyptian expedition but would make Venice mistress of the Mediterranean.

Meanwhile, the pope had learned that the crusaders had disobeyed his prohibition against attacking any more Christians. The only thing that prevented him from excommunicating them was that the papal legate he had sent with the crusaders had already absolved them from guilt. The legate, in fact, had even praised them for bringing the schismatics back into the fold. As the deed was done, Innocent tried to make the best of it and take advantage of Alexius's promise to put the Orthodox Church under the authority of Rome.

Opportunities for both the pope and Dandolo improved very soon. Late in 1203, a brawl between some Greeks and Franks turned into a riot. Then the riot turned into a revolt against Alexius IV, whom the Greeks had begun to regard as a tax collector for the Latins. Another large section of the city was burned before the riot was stopped. Helping to put down the disturbance was the emperor's palace guard, commanded by one Alexius Ducas, son-in-law of Alexius III. He was nicknamed Murzuphlus because of his thick eyebrows.

The riot took place while Alexius IV was away putting the empire in order. When he returned, the crusaders again asked him to meet his commitments. They asked again and again. Each time, he put them off. Finally, the barons named a commission, including Villehardouin, to demand payment. If he didn't pay up, they told him, they would take what was due them by force.

In response, the emperor attacked the Latins. Well coordinated, the attack drove the French and Venetians from the city. The Greeks even tried to destroy the Venetian fleet with fire ships.

Then, feeling that Alexius IV could not provide the kind of leadership the empire needed, Murzuphlus led a new coup. He put both emperors back in the dungeon. When poison failed to dispatch Alexius IV, Murzuphlus strangled him. As for Isaac, he died of natural causes a few days after he entered the dungeon.

The crusaders, driven out of the city, now had a new war against a hostile empire and a hostile emperor. For a few weeks, they campaigned outside of Constantinople, then they again closed in on the city. The clergy assured the men that as they were fighting to bring the Orthodox inhabitants of the empire under Rome, they were due the same indulgences they would earn on crusade against the infidels.

The crusaders began their assault on a Friday, attacking the sea wall from the Venetian ships. The attack was just short of a disaster. "We were in very grave danger at that time," Villehardouin admitted. Masses of crusaders were cut down and accomplished nothing.

The allies spent the weekend repairing and strengthening the ships. On Monday, they renewed the assault. This time, the ships carrying towers and drawbridges were tied together. The previous assault showed that defenders of a tower could outnumber soldiers attacking from one ship. Now, two ships could attack simultaneously.

Once again, the Venetians moved their ships up to the sea wall. Once again, stones and arrows forced them back. The assault had been going on fruitlessly for some time when a gust of wind drove a pair of ships, *Pilgrim* and *Paradise*, into the wall. The tower on *Pilgrim* bumped against the wall. Instantly, two soldiers, a Frenchman and a Venetian, jumped onto the battlements. Other troops followed. While defenders crowded around the threatened spot, the other ships moved up and more soldiers clambered onto the wall.

They took three more towers, and the defenders fled. The rest of the Franco-Venetian army swarmed along the shore and broke down three of the undefended gates. Knights on horseback charged the Greeks in the streets of Constantinople. Murzuphlus fled with his army, while the Franks and Venetians sacked the city and slaughtered citizens.

For the second time in two years, the crusaders and Venetians had taken the strongest city in the world. No army would take it again until 1452.

5

The French and Venetians didn't delay organizing things in Constantinople. First, a commission composed of representatives of both groups chose a new emperor. They chose neither of the strongmen—both Boniface and Dandolo preferred to be out of the New Rome—but Baudouin of Flanders, a valiant knight of no great ambition.

The French took half of the wealth turned up in the sack; the Venetians took the other half. The conquerors gave half of the city to the new emperor and split the other half between themselves.

Because there was still a lot of fighting to be done in the rest of the empire, an expedition to liberate the holy places was shelved indefinitely. French knights established fiefs on the Greek mainland and forgot about crusading entirely. Less worldly knights went home in disgust. And the very worldly Venetians took over the Aegean islands and made Dandolo's dream of a Venetian thalassocracy a reality.

The Latin Empire of Constantinople lasted a couple of generations—long enough to irreparably damage the institutions and infrastructure that made the Eastern Empire strong—but it never succeeded in uniting the Catholic and Orthodox churches. The French in Greece and the Venetians on the islands remained until the Ottoman Turks pushed them out. The East Roman Empire was eventually resurrected. It staggered through another two centuries as the real "sick man of Europe," before Turkey inherited the description.

And Enrico Dandolo, the brave, ruthless, devious and unscrupulous ancient who was responsible for the incredible double capture of Constantinople, ultimately brought death, destruction and slavery into Southeastern Europe. It came within a millimeter of his beloved Venice.

For centuries, the Eastern Empire and especially Constantinople had been Europe's bulwark against conquerors from Asia. Dandolo's victory weakened both the morale and institutions of the empire so that it became less a bulwark than a prize to be taken. The Turks isolated Constantinople and pounded its walls with the world's heaviest artillery. In 1452, the city fell and the Moslems flooded into Southeastern Europe up to the gates of Vienna. The Venetian empire was swept away. For centuries, Turkish, not Venetian, ships dominated the eastern Mediterranean.

The eventual fall of Constantinople was perhaps inevitable, but Dandolo's victory had an effect that was far more disastrous. The pope continued to go along with the *faits accomplis*, recognizing the new Latin Empire and attempting to use its existence for the church's profit. Perhaps there was little wrong in this in itself, but it legitimized the crusade against Constantinople as a kind of precedent: it was now possible to have a crusade against Christians. Later in Innocent's reign, the Albigensian heresy in southern France began to spread. It occurred to the pontiff that a crusade against the Albigensians might solve the problem.

The crusade got rid of the Albigensians, but it created a new problem. It changed the character of the church's authority. Instead of relying on moral suasion and an appeal to conscience, the church had adopted naked force. From there on, all Christian groups—supporters of the papacy and dissenters from its authority—relied on military means to enforce their will. The Hussites, a century and a half after the Albigensians and a century before Martin Luther, developed an almost invincible military machine. With the Protestant Reformation, warfare of Christian against Christian reached its peak, but it began when the Fourth Crusade turned against Constantinople.

And so the fruit of Dandolo's fatal victory was the religious wars of the sixteenth and seventeenth century—wars which by any reckoning were, collectively, the most disastrous event in the history of western civilization, climaxing in the incredibly bloody Thirty Years War.

5

Mephistopheles and the Snow King

THE SUN GLINTED OFF THE HELMETS, CORSELETS, THIGH PIECES AND swords of the soldiers slogging northward over the muddy Saxon road. The men dragged the butts of their long pikes, and they did not march in step. Route step was less exhausting for men carrying armor and heavy equipment on a long march.

Between the blocks of pikemen came musketeers, unarmored and wearing broad-brimmed hats, with swords and bandoliers hanging from their shoulders. Dangling from the bandoliers and rattling with each step, were small wooden cylinders, each holding enough gunpowder for one musket shot. Each soldier rested a 20-pound musket on his shoulder with one hand and held a thick musket rest with the other.

Barely keeping up with the heavily burdened infantry were the cannons. No artillery team had fewer than 16 horses. On some guns, 36 horses strained to drag them through the mud. But they continually got stuck, and each time, the road became a pandemonium of cursing, flailing drivers, straining, blaspheming gunners and infantrymen, and struggling, neighing horses. The whole army slowed down.

Horsemen, some in full armor, some armored only from the head to the knees, trotted through the countryside along the road. Each trooper carried a sword at his waist and two, four or six wheel lock pistols slung across his saddle. Every now and then, a horseman galloped over to a carriage near the head of the column. He'd poke his head through the window and confer with the man inside—a dark, lean, craggy-faced individual doubled up on the carriage seat with one leg extended. The dark man had the gout, and traveling in the bumpy carriage was torture almost beyond endurance. But endure it he would, because he was on his way to an appointment that could make him the most powerful man in Europe.

2

Farther south and also moving north, another army was headed for the same appointment.

This army was moving faster. The heaviest armor anybody wore was a helmet and a corselet. Only pikemen and some of the cavalrymen wore that much. Most of the horsemen were content with a leather "buff coat." The pikes were shorter than those in the first army; the muskets were lighter, and few of the musketeers carried musket rests.

The infantry, both pikemen and "shot," marched in much smaller, more numerous formations. The cavalry, riding wiry, agile horses, cantered along in small groups. For weapons, each trooper had only a pair of pistols and a sword.

Riding at the head of the first cavalry unit in the main body was a man who obviously commanded the entire army. He was tall and fair, with broad shoulders, a big belly and a small, pointed yellow beard.

He, too, was looking forward to the meeting. If successful, he would change the world.

3

The world had already changed radically since the time of the Fourth Crusade. Feudalism had continued to grow after the sackers of Constantinople went home, and knights gained so much prestige that infantry was almost ignored in France and Germany. In England, too, for a time, but the English campaigns in Wales demonstrated the value of archery. The English adopted the bow, and English infantry archers became the terror of Western Europe for a century. About the same time, the Swiss developed an infantry phalanx that overthrew any knights who opposed them.

Meanwhile, the results of the crusader defeat at Hattin were becoming apparent. The Portuguese had opened the way to the Indies and the Spanish to the New World. The Dutch, English and French followed them. Colonies were established in the Americas, Africa and Asia. Though no one could see it at the time, Europe was starting to establish a world hegemony. One component of this hegemony was ocean-going ships; the other was guns.

Less than 50 years after the Fourth Crusade, Roger Bacon, an English monk, recorded the formula for gunpowder. In 1326, Walter de Milimete gave Edward III, the future victor at Crecy, the first picture of a cannon. By the late 14th century, cannons were starting to demolish castles all over

Europe. Feudalism was dead. But in seventeenth century Germany, nothing had appeared to take its place. Baronial fighting forces had disappeared, and there were no national armies.

There was still fighting, of course. And after the Protestant Reformation, fighting greatly intensified. The place of feudal forces, which had disappeared, and national armies, which had not been born, was taken by mercenaries who raised, trained and equipped private armies and rented them out to rulers. At this time, there were several private armies in the field. Their leaders, Ernst von Mansfeld, Gottfried von Pappenheim, Bernard of Saxe-Weimar, Ottavio Piccolomini and others, were entrepreneurs. If a ruler stopped paying rent, the mercenary chief took his troops around the country like a swarm of locusts, killing and robbing peasants and burghers until he found a new employer. The only difference between mercenaries and brigands was that brigands had more sympathy for their victims. To many of the mercenaries, the victims weren't even countrymen. The mercenary chieftains had filled their armies with the scum of Europe. Besides Germans, there were Flemings, Croats, Scots, Italians, Irish and English. Protestants, Catholics and atheists fought beside genuine religious fanatics on both sides.

A technological advance and a sociological lag were responsible for the rise of the mercenary.

The technological advance was the musket, the only hand weapon that could pierce good plate armor at a reasonable distance. The longbow was faster and the crossbow more accurate, but neither could compete with the musket in perforating armor.

The musket required more than training in individual marksmanship. It required a new organization. The reason was the gun's slowness in loading. Enemy cavalry could easily ride down the musketeer while he was charging his clumsy piece. To prevent that, the infantry "shot," or musketeers, and the pikemen were drilled to work together. The shot would fire, the pikes would cover them while they loaded, then the musketeers would emerge and fire another volley. That took some rather sophisticated maneuvering. No longer could a prince rely on feudal levies who, like the English bowmen in the previous century, got their training by shooting at targets on a Sunday afternoon.

The sociological lag was the inability of sovereigns and subjects to get out of feudal habits of mind. There was, for example, no regular taxation in all of Central Europe. Rulers were expected to live on the revenue from their lands. If a war began, the people would allow themselves to be taxed so the prince could raise an army. But most princes had no money for a standing army in peacetime, so there were no experienced soldiers to train recruits, even if there were time to train them.

The mercenary seemed like the answer to a prince's prayer, offering instant power for a little gold each month. There was quite a bit of competition in the mercenary business, so the price often seemed reasonable. But the mercenary captain usually kept his costs down—and his bid low—by stealing everything his army needed. The costs of a mercenary army, then, were much higher than its quoted price.

4

The tall, dark man with the first army had already changed his own world. Albrecht Eusebius Wenzeslaus von Waldstein, the orphaned son of a small Czech landowner, was now Count Wallenstein and the Duke of Friedland. Baptized a Lutheran, he had changed his religion while growing up in the family of a Catholic uncle. Now he was leading a Catholic army in Europe's greatest war of religion.

Not that he was a religious fanatic. Personally, Wallenstein followed the teachings of the Catholic Church, but he had no use for the intolerance of his master, Emperor Ferdinand, or for Ferdinand's Edict of Restitution. In lands under Wallenstein's control, enforcement of the edict, which would return to the Catholic Church property it had owned before the Reformation, was slow, indeed.

"Give the peasantry plenty of time," he advised Ferdinand. "Do not press the lower orders too hard about religion."

Wallenstein placed his greatest faith in astrology, but to him and thousands of others at that time, that had nothing to do with religion. Astrology was a science, he believed. To prove it, he could point to the success he had had following the stars. Some of Ferdinand's courtiers, though, attributed the Czech's rise to more sinister forces than any to be found in the zodiac. A few of them even compared Emperor Ferdinand to a savant of Württemberg who had died less than a century before, a certain Dr. Johann Faust.

And, in fact, Ferdinand had made a Faustian bargain with the saturnine soldier. Wallenstein had promised the emperor what he most desired. In return, he had asked for, if not Ferdinand's soul, just about everything else.

Wallenstein, however, got the power to deliver what Ferdinand wanted not by dickering with the Evil One, but through the application of an icily brilliant intelligence.

Years before, he began trying to advance in the world by joining the Imperial Army to fight the Turks. He quickly learned that opportunities were limited for members of the minor gentry, like himself. So he left the army and married, at the age of 23, a very rich and very old widow. Not unexpectedly, the lady died in a short time, leaving him extensive estates.

Wallenstein familiarized himself with all the details of his holdings. He planned the agriculture, built storehouses for surplus crops and sold his produce far and near. In his villages, he established industries and schools. For his tenants, he organized medical services, poor relief and provision for times of famine. In the early seventeenth century, these were revolutionary innovations. Wallenstein's reforms improved the efficiency and profitability of his estates. He soon became one of the richest men in Moravia.

<h1 style="text-align:center">5</h1>

In 1618, what future generations would call the Thirty Years War broke out. The Thirty Years War was the greatest of the wars of religion, but it was much more than that. Its origins are immensely complicated for a number of reasons. Not the least of these is Germany itself, or to give this strange ghost of the Western Roman Empire and the domains of Charlemagne and Otto the Great its proper name, the Holy Roman Empire of the German Nation. The empire consisted of some 2,000 principalities. At the head of this conglomeration was an emperor who had only as much power as he could bluff the other rulers into giving him. The emperor, moreover, was elected, by the seven princes called electors, from the royalty of Europe, a process that produced some rather spectacular electioneering.

While the last emperor, Matthias, was dying, the campaigning was especially frenzied, because the emperor was also the King of Bohemia, and the Bohemian crown, too, was elective. The successful candidate for both thrones was Archduke Ferdinand von Hapsburg, who combined great personal charm with the most narrow bigotry.

Matthias, the old emperor and Bohemian king, demonstrated his own bigotry just before his death. The Bohemian nobles who had elected him king showed their displeasure by throwing his ministers out of a window (an event known ever after as the Defenestration of Prague). Their leader was Heinrich Matthias, Count Thurn, a noble who would play an important, though not heroic, part in the years to come. As for Ferdinand, emperor-elect and king-elect, the nobles took back the crown and gave it to Frederick, the Elector Palatinate, son-in-law of James I of England.

Ferdinand's reaction was to declare war. He was joined, verbally at least, by most of the Catholic princes. Frederick got less support from the Protestant princes. Although a Protestant, he was also a rebel—something divinely ordained monarchs, whether Lutheran or Catholic, regarded with total abhorrence. Complicating the situation was Ferdinand's cousin, the Catholic King of Spain who was interested in helping German Catholics only if it didn't interfere with his war against the Protestant Dutch. Then there was the Catholic King of France, who would help Protestants, Moslems or Devil-worshippers if it would discomfit the Spaniards. Still another complication was Frederick himself. The new King of Bohemia, a Calvinist bigot, accomplished the seemingly impossible feat of alienating *both* his Catholic and his Lutheran subjects.

Then there were the mercenaries, who rode across Central Europe like the Four Horsemen of the Apocalypse. The mercenary business was a good way for a captain to make money, something Wallenstein quickly appreciated. Early in the war, though, the Czech saw an even better way.

After some initial successes, Frederick stopped paying his mercenary leader, Ernst von Mansfeld. Mansfeld stopped fighting. On the other side, Maximilian of Bavaria sent his personal general, a Fleming named Johan Tzerclaes Tilly, with his army to help the emperor. Frederick fled, and the Protestant nobles fled with him. Emperor Ferdinand confiscated their estates and sold them at auction. The biggest purchaser was the wealthy Moravian noble, Count Wallenstein. Before long, the Czech controlled a quarter of all the land in Bohemia.

Wallenstein got his estates at bargain prices, but the money was all clear profit for Ferdinand. Everything seemed to be going the emperor's way. The Spanish took advantage of Frederick's status as a rebel to invade his homeland, the Palatine States, and bluff the other Protestant princes out of any effort to help the fugitive King of Bohemia.

Then Count Mansfeld found a new home, teaming up with Christian of Brunswick. The two Protestant armies tried to drive away those of Tilly and Spain but accomplished little. About the only thing that happened was that all four armies ravaged hundreds of square miles of countryside.

The war threatened to spread beyond the borders of Germany. The powerful kings of Denmark and Sweden began to worry about the possibility of a united and militantly Catholic Holy Roman Empire. Then France suddenly declared war on the empire and invaded the Val Telline, a vital link between the Hapsburg possessions on the Rhine and in Italy.

Just about that time, Ferdinand realized he was running out of money. He couldn't hire a new army to meet the French threat. As it was, he had for several years depended on loans from Wallenstein. The saturnine count had given his Bohemian estates the same treatment he introduced in Moravia. He was now one of the richest men in Europe. He had thrived even though Ferdinand had given him titles instead of repaying the loans. In 1623, when he was forty, Wallenstein married Isabella von Harrach, the daughter of one of the emperor's closest advisors, and Ferdinand made him Duke of Friedland.

With France now in the field against him, Ferdinand could only hope that Wallenstein would produce enough money to hire a new mercenary force.

The dark duke did better than that. He arrived in Vienna and offered to raise and equip a new army of 50,000 men. It would cost the emperor nothing but their monthly pay. Wallenstein would also lead the army. So far, the Duke of Friedland had demonstrated early in the war only that he was a good subordinate general. His real genius seemed to be in making money. But 50,000 men was 50,000 men, and the price was low. Or so it seemed to Ferdinand.

A Huguenot revolt forced France to drop out of the war, but Denmark, urged on by James I, entered it. Wallenstein took his new army north.

In his first major battle, Wallenstein found himself pitted against the old professional mercenary, Count Ernst von Mansfeld. Mansfeld did not worry. Ferdinand's own courtiers were calling the new general the Bohemian Blowhard. Mansfeld expected that the mere sight of his experienced troops would rout the adolescent farm boys who made up Wallenstein's army. But Wallenstein had given his farm boys the best artillery in Germany and had seen to their training with the same care he lavished on his estates. By nightfall, a third of Mansfeld's army was dead.

Wallenstein detached some troops to help Tilly, then hounded Mansfeld all across Germany and into Dalmatia, where the old mercenary died and what remained of his army disintegrated. The Czech then turned north and threw his full strength against Denmark. He invaded Jutland, and Christian, considered the strongest king in Northern Europe, fled to the Danish islands. Christian was glad to sign a treaty that took from him all the German lands he was holding. "The Friedlander," as Wallenstein's admirers now called him, turned east and began securing the Baltic coast. Everywhere he went, Wallenstein had crowds of men applying to join his army. He took only the best, but he soon had the largest army in Europe under his personal command.

The Spanish wanted Wallenstein to move west, instead of east, to help them in the Netherlands. Olivarez, the Spanish prime minister, was not fond of military adventurers who ignored the interests of His Most Catholic Majesty. The Catholic German rulers were frankly terrified of the Czech upstart who controlled the largest army on the continent. Ferdinand himself was afraid of Wallenstein and afraid of trying to remove him. But Spain threatened to cut off the flow of its American gold and silver to Ferdinand.

Worse, the German princes said they'd refuse to recognize Ferdinand's son as his heir and successor.

Ferdinand summoned all his courage and ordered Wallenstein into retirement. To everyone's relief, he went.

6

Then a new threat to the empire and the Catholic cause appeared in the north. Gustavus Adolphus, the King of Sweden, had entered the war.

Before Gustavus joined the fight, the Protestant cause had appeared doomed. There was no Protestant force left to oppose the armies of the Empire and the Catholic League, both commanded by Tilly since Wallenstein's retirement. Tilly was a man of impeccable personal character and dogged loyalty, but he had never been more than a good journeyman general. Now he was over seventy and losing control of his troops.

Gustavus, on the other hand, was 36 and the idol of his men. Born to the throne of the only major kingdom in Europe with a real standing army, he began campaigning with his father at the age of six. At 16, he had an independent command in the war against the Danes. At 17, he was king. From that time on, Gustavus's life had been one long war. Sometimes he was fighting the Danes, sometimes the Russians, sometimes the Poles. And the fighting always ended with a truce, not a treaty. As C. V. Wedgwood put it in her *The Thirty Years War,* "Gustavus was one of those born conquerors to whom peace is an ideal state, always for excellent reasons unattainable."

He had, in fact, signed a truce with the King of Poland so he could enter this war. Inducing Gustavus to change the scene of his operations were the offer of a large amount of French gold and the fear of a reinvigorated and Catholic Holy Roman Empire facing him across the Baltic.

The Thirty Years War was a war of religion. It was also a war between the dynasties of Bourbon, in France, and Hapsburg, in Spain and the empire, and a war for the personal advancement of adventurers from all over Europe. But because it was a war of religion, and because most of the sources used by those who write English were Protestant, in some writings, Gustavus acquires something like a halo. At the same time, the reader wonders if Wallenstein's floppy hat concealed a pair of horns. The truth is that in enemy territory, the armies of both commanders made "Sherman's bummers" look like lovable kids at a kindergarten outing. Both Gustavus and Wallenstein maintained stricter discipline than any of the other generals, and both had better means of supply. But each used plunder, massacre and arson as instruments of policy. Wallenstein laid waste to

Saxony to persuade its sovereign to join him. Gustavus vowed to burn Bavaria from end to end and almost did. His troops routinely tortured to death any Catholic priests and nuns they caught. Any peasant who protested the burning of his house, or who merely failed to get out of the way, was lucky if his end was swift. Before the first battle in Germany, Gustavus told his troops, "Now you have in front of you, for the first time, a camp filled with precious booty, afterwards a road which passes the sumptuous villages and fertile lands of the Catholics. All that is the price of a single victory."

Even in friendly territory, both Wallenstein and Gustavus brought destruction. Among the Catholic nobles pressing most strongly for Wallenstein's retirement were those whose lands his armies had devastated. Writing home from Protestant territory to his chancellor, Axel Oxenstierna, Gustavus said, "We have been obliged to carry on the war *ex rapto*, with great injury and damage to our neighbors. . . . We have nothing to satisfy the soldiers except what we have taken by pillage and brigandage." The lack of supplies from Sweden was not simply an unfortunate lapse. Before Sweden entered the Thirty Years War, the army absorbed five-sixths of the government's total revenues. During the war, with Gustavus leading a vastly larger force, the army took one-sixth of the revenues. Gustavus became as adept as any mercenary captain at making war pay for war.

The Thirty Years War was more than a religious war or a religious and dynastic war. It was also, as we'll see, one of the first nationalistic wars. Most important, though, it was also—thanks to the mercenary influence— a war for the sake of war.

When Gustavus landed in Germany, Catholic wits had predicted that the "Snow King" would melt as he approached the southern sun. But they hadn't seen his army.

In the operation and equipment of his army, Gustavus had given his genius full rein. The Swedish army was completely different from anything else in the world.

All other European armies had copied the system developed by the Spanish. The infantry was divided equally between pikemen and musketeers. The musketeers fired at the enemy until he was within range of edged weapons. Then they retired behind or into the formations of their armored colleagues, the pikemen, who usually decided the conflict.

First the Swiss, then the Spanish, had retaught the cavalry of Europe that horsemen can't break a line of disciplined infantry pikemen. So the cavalry abandoned the lance and put its faith in pistols. The technique was to charge the pikemen in column. Just before he came within reach of the pikes, a horseman would fire his right and left pistols at the infantry, wheel out of the way and ride back to the rear of the column. Most troopers carried several pistols. If he were unfortunate enough to have only two pistols, a horseman could reload as he trotted back to the front. This maneuver, called the caracole, was possible only because cavalrymen carried expensive wheel lock pistols, rather than matchlocks, with their ever-smoldering cords, or "matches". Even so, the caracole could not be done at a gallop. Consequently, these trotting horsemen were an excellent target for the musketeers, whose weapons had far more range and penetrating power than any pistol.

Artillery, used as a siege weapon for centuries, was now beginning to be used in the field. It was, however, enormously heavy, cumbersome to move, difficult to aim, and slow to reload. Because of this, it was usually lined up in front of the infantry well before a battle.

Gustavus changed all that. He believed that the most mobile army could decide when and where to fight. He drastically cut back the armor of pikemen and cavalrymen. He lightened the muskets so they didn't have to be placed on a rest before firing. And he developed guns that could be pulled by one or two horses instead of 16 or 36. Two of the one-horse guns, which fired a three-pound cannon ball, accompanied each infantry regiment.

The Swedish army could outrun any army on the continent. And when it chose to hit, it could hit harder than any army in the world. The Swedish King's musketeers could fire faster than any other musketeers, because Gustavus had replaced his matchlocks with wheel locks, and because his troops used paper cartridges.

When loading a matchlock, the musketeer first had to remove the smoldering match to a safe place. Then, after he finished loading, he put the match back on the clamp of the "serpentine" which dropped it into the priming powder. With a wheel lock, none of these movements were necessary.

The paper cartridge replaced the wooden powder containers and the bullet pouch hanging on the bandolier. Both powder and bullet were contained in a roll of paper. To load, the soldier bit the end of the cartridge, put a little powder in the priming pan, dumped the rest through the muzzle, then rammed the bullet and the wadded-up paper after it. In addition to speeding up the loading process, the paper cartridge contributed to the troops' safety. It was not unknown for powder in the wooden charge cups to ignite from shock or friction while on the soldier's bandolier.

Fast as his musketeers could fire, Gustavus's artillerymen could fire even faster. Gustavus had introduced a thin wooden cartridge to hold the powder for his light field guns. The projectile could be solid shot. More often, it was canister—a flimsy metal cylinder full of musket balls. Using artillery cartridges, the cannoneers could fire eight shots to the musketeers' six.

In addition to these ultra-light infantry guns, Gustavus also had six- and 12-pounder field guns. Three of these guns supported every 1,000 men. For sieges, there were guns firing 16- and 30-pound balls. All told, the Swedish army had the firepower of a couple of normal armies.

In his cavalry, Gustavus got away from firepower. Only the first rank of his horsemen even fired their pistols, and they fired only once before meeting the enemy with the sword. Gustavus knew, of course, that cavalry can't *break through* a line of good infantry. It could, *break up* an infantry formation already shaken by artillery fire or starting to retreat. It could, that is, if it relied on shock and momentum instead of firepower.

The trick was to use the cavalry in a way that didn't get horsemen hung up on a row of pike points. The troopers had confidence that Gustavus wouldn't let that happen: he usually led the cavalry himself.

An enemy that tried to charge Gustavus's cavalry received a surprise. When the Swedish cavalry was on the defensive, companies of musketeers were interspersed in their formation. Charging horsemen were cut down by volleys of musketry long before they expected to come under fire.

With this fighting machine, Gustavus had confronted the troops of "Father Tilly."

Tilly's army had been in Mecklenburg, a duchy Ferdinand had given to Wallenstein. For once, Tilly's veteran plunderers found nothing to plunder. In retirement, Wallenstein had kept part of the army he'd raised. That gave him enough strength to deny any supplies to the Catholic League troops, many of whom had once served under him. When Wallenstein retired from active soldiering, the troops he did not keep went to either Tilly or to Hans Georg von Arnim, a Saxon Lutheran who had been Wallenstein's lieutenant and who now served John George, the Elector of Saxony.

Unable to get supplies from Wallenstein, Tilly took his army to Magdeburg. He hoped to get what he needed at that wealthy Protestant town. But before he could begin a proper siege, Gottfried von Pappenheim, his fiery subordinate, launched a storm without orders. His troops blew in a gate, while others swarmed over the walls. They had just begun to sack the town when fires appeared almost simultaneously in some 20 different places. The fires spread quickly, driving the conquerors beyond the walls. Then the fires developed what in World War II was called a fire storm—a furnace-like blaze fed by a wind storm it created. Most of the inhabitants of Magdeburg burned to death. And Tilly, of course, got no supplies. The "Sack of Magdeburg" became the most famous atrocity in a war filled with genuine atrocities. Although it's often cited to show the cruelty of Tilly's troops, the evidence indicates that the fires were deliberately set by agents of Dietrich von Falkenburg, commander of Magdeburg's Protestant garrison.

Tilly still needed supplies. The nearest source he could think of was Saxony, which, though largely Lutheran, had remained neutral. The appearance of Tilly's wasters over his borders drove Elector John George into alliance with Gustavus.

And so, Tilly had to meet the combined armies of Saxony and Sweden at a place called Breitenfeld. Tilly had taken up a strong position near Leipzig, but the restless Pappenheim urged him to go out and meet the Swedes. Tilly had 13 or 17—sources differ—solid squares of pikemen and musketeers, each containing 1,500 to 2,000 men ten ranks deep. On the left, Pappenheim commanded his personal army, the Black Cuirassiers, and on the right, Fuerstenburg and Isolani led the rest of the 10,000 cavalry. Opposing the 35,000 Imperialists were 26,000 Swedes and 16,000 Saxons.

The Saxon commander, von Arnim, was a gifted general, but his troops were the rawest recruits. When Tilly's Croatian light horse swept down on their flank, screaming wildly as their red cloaks streamed behind them, the unsophisticated Saxon militia thought they were meeting the forces of Hell in person. They turned their horses and dashed for safety. When the Saxon footmen saw what their cavalry was doing, they ran, too. That left the Swedes alone, outnumbered by some 10,000 men.

In spite of Tilly's numerical superiority, the Swedish musketeers could hold their own. The Swedes could fire faster. Also, the Swedish musketeers were drawn up in a line three ranks deep. Tilly's "shot" was ten ranks deep. In each case, the front rank fired while the others loaded. At any one time, a third of the Swedish musketeers were firing, but only a tenth of the Imperialists were. The Swedes' overwhelming musket fire would have been enough to insure victory for Gustavus. But Lennart Torstenson's Swedish artillery also kept pouring in deadly fire, while most of Tilly's artillery had not been able to keep up with the infantry in the fast-moving battle.

Gustavus's infantry-reinforced cavalry routed Pappenheim's cavalry. The king then led his horsemen against the flank of Tilly's infantry. Gustavus was pioneering what was to become standard tactics for the next three centuries. Cavalry could not break up a tight infantry formation, but artillery could devastate a mass of standing infantry. An infantry formation could avoid damage from projectiles by dispersing and taking cover, but that gave the enemy cavalry the chance it was looking for. Every time Tilly's infantry sought cover from the Swedish fire, Gustavus charged.

The slaughter went on until darkness made further action impossible. In the end, Tilly, wounded in the neck and chest, his right arm shattered, lost 12,000 of his 35,000 soldiers. The rest were so scattered that he and

Pappenheim between them could round up only about 2,000 on the first day of retreat.

The road to Vienna lay open to Gustavus. It would be weeks before Tilly could regroup enough to oppose the Swedes. Presuming, that is, that he could induce his troops to face Gustavus again. Gustavus's lieutenants urged him to march on the enemy capital. Gustavus, though, chose to reward his troops by letting them rob, rape and kill their way through Catholic Franconia. He may have hoped to terrify Ferdinand's allies into submission. He certainly terrified Ferdinand, who began thinking of the only man who seemed capable of meeting the Lion of the North—Count Wallenstein.

7

In Bohemia, Wallenstein was writing to his friend, Arnim, urging him to convince John George of Saxony that all German princes, Protestant and Catholic, must make an acceptable peace and get rid of the foreign invader.

Arnim was of the same mind. "Should the war last longer," he replied to Wallenstein, "the Empire will be utterly destroyed. He who has an upright, honest mind must be touched to the heart: when he sees the Empire so afflicted, he must yearn after peace. So it is with me. Therefore, I have let no opportunity escape . . . but have urged peace on friend and foe . . . our beloved Germany will fall a prey to foreign people and be a pitiable example to all the world."

Other notable Germans were coming to the same conclusion. Frederick, the ex-King of Bohemia and former Elector Palatine, refused Gustavus's offer to return him to the Palatinate as a Swedish vassal. "The King of Sweden is hard to content," he confided to a Brandenburg noble.

In a verbal slip to the ex-Duke of Mecklenburg, Gustavus himself had said, "If I become emperor . . ." a prospect no German anticipated with pleasure.

The German Protestants were starting to think of Gustavus not as a liberator, but as a conqueror. There was a new spirit in Central Europe, one totally alien to a German of the previous century but which would easily have been understood by Enrico Dandolo. Later ages would call it nationalism. To nobles of the empire, it meant that many of them were now thinking of themselves as Germans first and Catholics or Protestants second.

With the next spring, Gustavus prepared to march into Bavaria. Maximilian wrote frantically to Ferdinand, begging him to reinstate Wallenstein. Gustavus crossed the Danube and began laying waste to Bavaria so thoroughly his troops even uprooted the wheat sprouting in the fields. Tilly and

Maximilian tried to stop him, but a cannon ball took Tilly's leg off early in the battle—the final, fatal wound suffered by that oft-wounded veteran of decades of warfare. Maximilian ordered an immediate retreat, leaving guns and baggage on the field.

About the same time, in Austria, Wallenstein agreed to come back into the war. He dictated conditions to Ferdinand. The written agreement has never been found, but the evidence indicates that the emperor agreed to give his general full and total control over the army; absolute control of all peace negotiations, with the right to conclude treaties; the exclusion of the emperor's son from any part of the command, and of Spain from any influence on the conduct of the war. Rumor had it that Wallenstein would receive part of the Hapsburg lands and the title of elector.

The principal commanders were now laws unto themselves. Gustavus, absolute monarch as well as commanding general, dictated policy, strategy and tactics. Wallenstein, the adventurer, now did the same. Each commander was going to use the utmost ruthlessness to bring the protracted bloodletting to a victorious conclusion.

While Wallenstein was negotiating with the emperor, Arnim invaded Bohemia. It was a curiously bloodless campaign. Wallenstein returned and simply withdrew his troops before the Saxons, while Arnim held the traditional pillage and rapine to the minimum. With his new commission in his pocket, Wallenstein pushed the Saxons out in the same bloodless manner. At the same time, he begged John George, through Arnim, to throw his prestige behind a new all-German league, pledged to religious toleration and home rule.

John George, though, had a real and justifiable fear of the King of Sweden. Gustavus had replaced Wallenstein as the Dragon of Central Europe. Even with the Friedlander at his side, the elector was afraid to cross Gustavus.

Wallenstein replied in the only way he could think of: all-out war against Saxony. While Gustavus was burning out Bavaria, Wallenstein was burning out Saxony. With his base in Bohemia, the center of Central Europe, Wallenstein needed neither Bavaria nor Austria. If Saxony turned against Gustavus, though, the King of Sweden could be stranded at the foot of the Alps and starved to death. Gustavus turned back to meet the Czech. In the battle of master strategists, Wallenstein won the first round.

At Schwabach, Wallenstein joined his army with that of Maximilian. And the Archduke Max, most powerful of the old Catholic princes, was happy to put his army under Count Wallenstein, the Czech adventurer. Gustavus failed to block this consolidation of forces, so he fell back on Furth, on the outskirts of Nuremburg. Wallenstein followed, located the Swedish camp and built a camp nearby.

The Friedlander knew that Gustavus's success rested on his mobility and firepower. He couldn't do anything about the firepower, but he could neutralize the Swede's mobility. Wallenstein refused to leave his fortified position. Gustavus would have to come to him.

He did. Gustavus had ravaged the country so thoroughly that he could find no supplies. Wallenstein could bring supplies in from Bohemia, but Gustavus would starve until he either defeated Wallenstein or left the field. If he retreated without a fight, his prestige would be destroyed—and so would much of his power.

Gustavus chose to fight. Outnumbered, he attacked the strong Imperialist position and was defeated. Gustavus, his mystique damaged, went back to Bavaria in an attempt to draw Wallenstein after him. Wallenstein continued moving into Saxony. It was the Snow King who had to turn around and follow.

8

The Saxons were wavering, but the Swede caught up with Wallenstein near Leipzig before they could change sides. This time, Gustavus entrenched. Wallenstein had no intention of attacking the entrenched Swedish army with its enormous firepower.

Wallenstein may have thought he could intimidate the Saxons in spite of Gustavus. Or perhaps Pappenheim, who had impulsively attacked Magdeburg was restless again. At any rate, Wallenstein let Pappenheim attack Moritzburg, while he waited in camp at Lützen. That left Wallenstein with only 8,000 foot and 4,000 horse.

Gustavus was not the general to let such an opportunity pass. He led his 14,000 infantry and 5,000 cavalry out against the Imperialists. Learning of the movement, Wallenstein immediately sent a messenger to Pappenheim, a day's march away.

Wallenstein lined up his infantry in five huge blocks, called "battles," each ten ranks deep. Four of them formed a kind of cross behind a sunken road. The fifth sheltered behind three windmills on a hill. Most of his cavalry covered his left flank. The rest connected his fifth battle with the main body and with the village of Lützen, on the extreme right flank.

The Swedes lined up in their usual open formation, infantry in the center and musket-supported cavalry on the flanks. They had 40 light cannon divided between each wing, with 20 heavy guns lined up in front of their center. Darkness was falling when the two armies made their final dispositions.

The next morning, November 16, 1632, heavy fog shrouded the scene. It began to lift about 11 o'clock, and Gustavus ordered his artillery to commence firing. Then he drew his sword and ordered a general advance. On his right, the momentum of the Swedish cavalry was too much for the Imperialists, who tried to turn them back with pistol fire. In the center, Wallenstein's musketeers were hiding in the sunken road. They blasted the Swedish cavalry. Then, instead of fleeing, the usual reaction of musketeers about to be overrun by cavalry, they ducked under the broadswords as the horsemen rode through them, reloaded and blasted the Swedish infantry. Finally overwhelmed, they withdrew behind their pikemen.

In spite of his gout, Wallenstein climbed on his horse and led the counterattack. All his attendants were shot down, a canister shot took off one of his spurs, and several musket balls passed through his coat. Wallenstein's pikemen charged the Swedes ferociously, and the Swedish pikemen were forced back across the road.

On the Imperialist right, where the cavalry was reinforced by infantry, Bernard of Saxe-Weimar, leading the Swedish left, ran into trouble. Gustavus, who had been leading the Swedish right, took a cavalry regiment out of line to reinforce Bernard. The king had just arrived when an Imperialist pistol ball hit him in the chest. Weak and in shock, he had turned his horse to the rear. For some time, his absence was not noticed. When it was, Bernard told his men the king was in another sector.

Meanwhile, the action on the Swedish right was turning from a victory to a disaster for Gustavus's men. Pappenheim and his Black Cuirassiers had arrived. Basically a cavalryman, Pappenheim had returned at full speed, letting his infantry follow as best it could. The Black Cuirassiers hit the Swedes with an old-fashioned hell-for-leather charge with swords instead of pistols. The Swedish cavalry reeled from the impact. But before a rout could begin, an unknown musketeer fired at a big horseman in black armor. Brave, charismatic and hare-brained Gottfried Heinrich von Pappenheim, one of the seventeenth century's *beau sabreurs,* received a fatal wound.

There was no way to hide the death. Too many Imperialists had seen it happen. The Black Cuirassiers, who owed their loyalty to Pappenheim alone, were thrown into confusion. The Swedes rallied and again threw the Imperialists back.

On the other flank, Bernard of Saxe-Weimar realized what had happened to Gustavus, and he didn't want the Swedes to react like the Black Cuirassiers. But something had to be done. Wallenstein was leading his pikemen into the center of the Swedish line, and the Swedish cavalry under

Bernard was being defeated by the Imperialist cavalry-infantry combination. And the Imperialist left was again advancing.

Bernard decided on the bold course. "Swedes!" he shouted, "They have killed the king! Avenge the king!" Bernard waved his sword and, along with his personal bodyguard, charged the Imperialists. All along the Swedish line, men took up the shout: "Avenge the king!" Saxe-Weimar's charge, after two hours of hard fighting, took him past the Imperialist guns on Windmill Hill. The Swedish center rallied, cleared the sunken road and captured the seven guns in their sector. The situation was almost a replay of the Visigothic counterattack at Chalons more than a thousand years before, and it had the same result.

Then Pappenheim's infantry arrived to rescue the Imperialists—outnumbered, out-gunned and now out of artillery. At nightfall, Wallenstein, half-dead from the pain of his gout, ordered a retreat. He had lost 10,000 men and all his guns and baggage. The Swedes had lost 7,000 and were too tired to pursue their foe.

9

The Swedes had defeated the greatest of the Catholic leaders, but they paid a heavy price. It wasn't for a while after they had found the body of the king that they realized how heavy a price.

Gustavus had created an army that was a century ahead of its time—a fighting machine that was quick, flexible and immensely powerful. But it was an intricate machine, so intricate only Gustavus knew how to operate it.

Wallenstein's army wasn't nearly so advanced, but it was still intact, and he was still able to lead it. Both Wallenstein and the Swedes went into winter quarters after Lützen. Men still wanted to enlist in the Friedlander's army. He had defeated the northern devils once, and he could do it again.

And he did. In what the British military commentator Basil H. Liddell Hart called his "military masterpiece," Wallenstein went after a Swedish-Saxon army near Steinau in the spring of 1633, separated the two with a feint and lay in ambush. He let the Saxons go, then surrounded the Swedes, now led by the Bohemian, Count Thurn, leader of the mob at the Defenestration of Prague. Thurn surrendered his army and a number of fortresses in return for his own parole. Wallenstein later remarked that Thurn was so incompetent there was no danger in freeing him.

Ferdinand's courtiers, though, saw the release of Thurn as an act of treason. They also objected to Wallenstein's continued negotiations with Protestant leaders, although the emperor himself had agreed to let the

Czech make treaties. The courtiers told Ferdinand it was his duty to get rid of Wallenstein.

The emperor didn't need much urging. He already owed the Czech adventurer everything but the crown jewels. And Wallenstein was clearly setting up an empire based on religious liberty, a concept Ferdinand loathed. But he was afraid to again demand his general's resignation.

Instead, he ordered that Wallenstein be killed. Wallenstein learned that he had been outlawed and tried to flee with a few troops. At midnight, February 24, 1634, eight men—mercenaries led by a Colonel Walter Butler, an Irishman, and an English captain named Walter Devereaux, with the aid of two Scottish officers named Gordon and Leslie—broke into the general's chamber and murdered the Czech-born German patriot.

They killed not only the greatest Imperialist leader, but the only chance of quickly ending the war. If Gustavus had lived, he might have ended the war, although the result would have been a Germany under Swedish tutelage. The price of the Swedish victory at Lützen eliminated that possibility. Wallenstein, too, might have created a united Germany for all Germans, Catholic and Protestant. His victory over Thurn was his undoing.

The Thirty Years War continued for 16 more years, the destruction and killing growing worse each year. For a while, it looked as if Bernard of Saxe-Weimar, with what was left of Gustavus's army, might reestablish Swedish primacy. Then Bernard met an Imperial army under the emperor's son, Ferdinand, and the crown prince of Spain. The numbers were about equal, and Bernard of Saxe-Weimar had considerably more experience than the two young princes who shared command of the Imperialists. The battle demonstrated that Gustavus had built a machine too sophisticated for anyone but him to command. When the fighting ended, 17,000 of Bernard's men were dead, 4,000 injured, and the rest scattered to the wind.

Still the fighting went on. More villages were burned; more civilians were slain; more diseases were spread; more burghers starved to death. Some estimate that Germany lost three-quarters of its population during the Thirty Years War.

The war ended with the center of Europe burned out. The Holy Roman Empire, the last incarnation of the empire founded by Augustus Caesar, was for all practical purposes dead. (Napoleon would later write the obituary.) Sweden was almost exhausted, Spain totally exhausted, Holland growing in power, England just finishing a religious war of its own, and France trying to recover from a multitude of wars, internal and external. Europe, a cluster of peninsulas and islands on the western edge of Eurasia, filled with contentious and quarreling people, was totally unstable. The stage was set for another series of wars—wars which would set world history on a new course.

POWER

TO THE

PEOPLE

6

1709, MALPLAQUET
(WAR OF THE SPANISH SUCCESSION)

"My Enemies, Not My Children"

"MY DOMINANT PASSION IS CERTAINLY LOVE OF GLORY," LOUIS XIV WROTE in 1666. That was why, six years later, the Sun King was riding at the head of an army, his normal finery hidden by a thick leather buff coat and heavy jack boots. The army was approaching the Rhine, en route to Amsterdam, the capital of Louis' enemies, the burghers of the United Provinces of the Netherlands.

This was not Louis' first foray into the Low Countries. Six years before, he had annexed part of the Spanish Netherlands (roughly where Belgium is now) to compensate for his wife's unpaid dowry. The dowry was the official explanation for the expedition. As he wrote at the time, his real reason was his quest for *gloire*. There was little glory, though, in beating Spain, the bankrupt shell of a great empire. England, Sweden and Holland had come to Spain's aid. Louis ended the war by giving back the province of Franche Compté, which he really didn't want, while he kept the land he had seized in the Netherlands.

Holland was another matter. Beating the Dutch would surely add to his glory. They had organized the alliance that opposed Louis on Spain's behalf. They still controlled much of Europe's trade with the rest of the world, having taken over Portugal's monopoly of the Far Eastern trade.

They were also republicans, while Louis was an absolute monarch. Their leaders were Protestants who had outlawed Catholicism, while Louis was a Catholic who would soon outlaw Protestantism.

Louis' main reason for fighting them, though, was that they would be worthy opponents.

Religious bigotry was far from dead, but it was no longer the sole cause of most major wars. A new factor had become apparent during the Thirty

81

Years War—the divine right of kings to do whatever they pleased. The German princes had no qualms at all about deciding their subjects' religion. Religion was hardly one of Louis' main concerns at this time. In fact, religion mattered not at all to the King of France when weighed against a chance to hurt his dynastic rivals, the Hapsburgs.

With this change in attitude went a change in the way of making war. Armies no longer consisted of masses of peasants impressed into the service of mercenary generals, and they no longer swarmed over the countryside killing, burning and looting. Now they were composed of professional soldiers, better trained than even the armies of Wallenstein and Gustavus. More important, they had given up "living on the country," the practice of every European army since the Romans. These armies were supplied from fortified magazines at strategic locations. They seldom attacked peasants or townspeople. This change was not prompted by consideration for the common people. During the Thirty Years War, generals learned that their armies couldn't live off the land after they had killed all the peasants.

Now, the generals depended on magazines. Protecting their communications with the magazines, and cutting their opponents' communications, were of the utmost importance. That put a premium on rapid maneuver. And that made a small, highly trained force infinitely more formidable than the armies of the previous era. Troops of the late seventeenth and eighteenth centuries were, in many ways, more like those of the Romans than those of any previous era. Trained troops were especially important at sieges. Sieges of the heavily fortified cities containing magazines were the most important feature of late seventeenth and eighteenth century warfare in Europe. Wars became less like extended sessions of mass murder and more like games.

All of these changes occurred during Louis' lifetime. Although he never said "L'Etat c'est moi," he very well could have. He was France; Charles II was England; William of Orange was the United Provinces, etc. All were engaged in a great game with glory the reward for the winner.

A small force of Dutch infantry tried to oppose the French as they crossed the Rhine. The Prince of Condé, France's greatest hero during the Thirty Years War, ordered a wild charge which drove back the Dutch but resulted in the deaths of a number of French cavaliers. Louis, who had quite competently positioned the French artillery to prepare the crossing, was shocked to see a marshal of France behaving like a corporal.

"With a little patience, we would not have lost one of those men," he wrote to his wife that evening. "The Comte de Guiche could have enveloped [the Dutch] from one side, and from the other we could have pushed them with the other squadrons and with the infantry . . . in place of this wild-eyed action that cost us so dearly."

The French losses were not the sort that would have disturbed many field officers, to say nothing of supreme commanders. Louis, though, was hardly the normal supreme commander. His notion of *gloire* definitely excluded both mud and blood. In the last war, he went campaigning with a multi-room silk tent staffed by a corps of beautiful young noblewomen. This time, he left the ladies at home, but he still had the silk tent. It was harder to avoid blood than mud, but the king tried hard. He brought along a Flemish artist to record scenes of the invasion, but the painter was forbidden to show any violence. Eventually, Louis went back to Versailles, where there were no unpleasant sights.

He had seen more than enough violent death in his childhood. Although now, at the start of the Dutch War, Louis was 35, he had been king for 29 years. During the regency of his mother, the strange War of the Fronde broke out. Begun by the Paris mob and spread by the nobility, it ended with an English Royalist force aiding the Frondeurs while the army of Cromwell's Commonwealth helped the French Royalists. During the fighting, the young king had to flee from his enemies twice. Now king in fact as well as name, Louis felt that conquest was glorious, but the cost of conquest was something he preferred not to think about.

When Louis was only two days march from Amsterdam, the Dutch opened their dikes, and the French suddenly found themselves standing in four feet of water. All progress ceased until winter, when the invaders were able to advance over the ice until a thaw again halted them.

The French were deep in Holland, though, and the Dutch government sued for peace. But Louis offered such humiliating terms that a mob tore the leaders of the peace party to pieces—literally. The Dutch then rallied around William of Orange, who, though a republican leader, was also a prince of the blood. William became stadtholder, captain and admiral-general.

William quickly proved himself an incompetent general but an implacable foe. He loved battle with an unholy fervor, and he was almost always defeated. But he hated Louis with a superhuman hatred, and he could always persuade other governments to join in an alliance against the French king.

Blocked by floods, Louis changed direction and besieged the powerful fortress of Maastricht. The king personally led one of the assaulting parties and his brother, Philippe, the other. Taking part in the action was a captain of musketeers named D'Artagnan, who was killed under the walls and became famous almost two centuries later as the friend of the "Three

Musketeers." There was also a young cavalryman named Claude-Louis-Hector Villars, who volunteered for the assault because he wanted to see what it was like to fight as an infantryman. Another volunteer was an Englishman named John Churchill, who wanted to learn war from the greatest general of the day, France's Marshal Turenne. Both Villars and Churchill would achieve fame before Louis' reign was over.

The most important soldier at the siege, though, was Sebastien le Prestre, a commoner's son who had enlisted as a sapper. Now known as the Sieur de Vauban, he was perhaps the greatest military engineer in history. He was one of a number of men whose lack of noble birth had not prevented them from rising to power under the autocracy of Louis XIV. There was also Colbert, the minister of finance and founder of French naval power, who rose from clerk, and Louvois, who had reorganized the French army as drastically as Gustavus Adolphus had reorganized the Swedish.

The *metier* of Colbert and Louvois was the French bureaucracy; the *metier* of Vauban was the siege. At Maastricht he first had a chance to show what he could do. It may have been the first siege in history directed entirely by an engineer instead of by a commanding general. It was not the last. After Maastricht, Vauban directed every important siege while he was on active duty.

Before Vauban's time, a besieger would dig a trench around the enemy stronghold. The concentric circle would be far from the enemy's guns, but from it, the attackers would dig another trench, or sap, close to the walls. The attackers would then mass troops at the end of the sap. Under the cover of a heavy barrage, these troops would attempt to rush the walls. There were two drawbacks to the system. First, the attacker's guns were usually too far back to do much damage. Second, the attacker often couldn't concentrate enough men in the narrow sap. Instead of one big assault that carried the walls, the attack would become a series of rushes, each bloodily repulsed before either the fortress capitulated or the attackers gave up.

Vauban's siege began in the usual way, with a concentric trench. The attackers then dug a wide trench toward the city, but it went only about 250 yards. When they reached that distance, the attackers dug another concentric trench, 12 to 15 feet wide and about three feet deep. They threw the dirt up on the side facing the city and made a high parapet. This "parallel" held far more men than the old narrow type of trench, and they could move quickly from one sector to another. Having completed their second parallel, the besiegers dug another short approach trench, then another parallel. And so they continued, until the last parallel was only about 30 yards from the enemy walls. Under the old system, with its single approach sap, the direction the attack would take was obvious. With Vauban's system the attack could hit any point, or several points, on the fortifications.

The besiegers placed their guns at convenient points in the nearest parallel and began digging mines under the enemy fortifications. The final assault on Maastricht, led by Louis and his brother, was almost unnecessary. Vauban's works were so cleverly constructed that, in spite of the assault, the French casualties were lower than the Dutch. After Maastricht, when a besieger reached the position achieved by Vauban before the assault, capture of a fortress was considered inevitable. The besieged commander usually surrendered at that point and retained his honor.

Vauban's siege technique suited Louis' taste. It was neat, clean and relatively bloodless. Scores of other strongholds would fall to the formula. The most notable modern application of Vauban's method was at Dien Bien Phu in 1954. And a pseudo Vauban-type siege distracted the American high command at Khe Sanh in 1968.

Directed by Vauban, Louis' armies took magazine after magazine when they could not, following Turenne, simply maneuver their enemies out of their fortresses. But Turenne was killed in 1675 at the battle of Sasbach. And William of Orange built one alliance after another to oppose the French.

Louis countered William's activities by fomenting revolts among William's subjects and allies. French secret agents tried to undermine the authority of the Prince of Orange at home. The French wife of the King of Poland and the French mistress of the King of England weakened the ties between William and his allies. Louis bribed leaders of the British parliament wholesale, and he even got Charles II on his payroll. At one point, Louis had a Frenchman representing himself to the courts of Europe as a special ambassador from the King of Sweden.

Though outnumbered and surrounded by enemies, Louis defeated them all psychologically. At the peace conference at Nijmegen in 1677, the Dutch and their allies were glad to leave France with a lot of new territory, including, this time, Franche Compté. Louis had much of the "dueling field" beyond the frontiers of France proper that Vauban had told him their country needed for defense.

2

So Louis gained his glory. The boy who fled from his rebellious subjects now ruled over a united and greatly expanded kingdom. The power of the French nobles was broken forever, and his foreign enemies had been humbled. He had become the arbiter of Europe—the "Sun King" around whom all the other powers revolved. French replaced Latin as the language of diplomacy.

Louis did not merely bask in all this *gloire*. Like Gustavus Adolphus, he was "hard to content." The Sun King's secret agents were everywhere. So were his armies. He had developed the knack of finding obscure claims to frontier towns he coveted, then invading and capturing them without warning—often overnight. It wasn't hard, as long as his enemies were fragmented and their attention was diverted away from France. To help divert them, the "Most Christian King" helped the Moslem Turks in their last attack on Austria. That gambit had a result Louis hadn't wanted. The German states, Protestant and Catholic, united to push the Moslems out of Austria. The prestige of his ancient rivals, the Hapsburgs, grew. Many German and Italian states allied themselves with the empire and the empire's allies, Holland and Spain. When Louis revoked the Edict of Nantes, which had granted religious freedom to the French Protestants, Sweden, France's ally in the Thirty Years War, joined what came to be called the League of Augsburg. According to the Marquis de Dangeau, one of Louis' courtiers, the League, ostensibly an alliance against the Turks, was basically anti-French.

> . . . the ninth of this month a league was signed at Augsburg that seems to be directed uniquely against France. It is composed of the Emperor, the Kings of Spain and Sweden for their estates in the Empire, the Elector of Bavaria, Franconia and the Upper Rhine. They say in the treaty it is for the protection of Germany and the execution of the treaties of Westphalia, Nymwegen and the Truce of 1684, but there are clauses by which the Emperor, if he wishes, can call upon them to declare war on France . . .

Louis had the recurrence of an old nightmare—a united Germany that could halt his nibbling toward the east.

The Sun King feared that his years as the unquestioned leader of Europe were threatened. To aid his crumbling Turkish allies and regain his old prestige, Louis launched a new invasion on the Rhine in 1688. Years of profligate spending had diminished French resources. Louis hoped for a short war in the Rhineland, one that would take the pressure off the Turks and result in a favorable peace. He had reasons for his optimism: the German states were busy fighting the Turks, and William of Orange was planning to invade England at the invitation of an English faction opposed to their current king, James II. That would not only get William out of Dutch affairs, it would, he hoped, create a civil war in England, another potential major enemy. And, of course, he had the matchless army created by Louvois, a corps of competent generals and the great Vauban.

Instead of a blitzkrieg, though, Louis touched off the first world war of modern times—a war fought not only in Europe but in the Americas, Asia and Africa. The war would last for nine years.

Even Louis' army could not conquer all of Europe. His only European ally was Turkey, by now well on its way to becoming "the Sick Man of Europe." To add to the Sun King's troubles, there was no civil war of consequence in Britain and only an easily suppressed revolt by poorly armed rebels in Ireland; Louvois died in office, and the treasury began to run dry. The Duke of Luxembourg, however, turned out to be a master tactician, and Vauban continued to work his magic. The French managed to hold on.

In 1697, nine years after the War of the Grand Alliance (or the War of the League of Augsburg) began, Louis agreed to make peace. His armies had won victories everywhere, but his resources were strained to the breaking point. And the Sun King himself had grown old and tired. He had even stopped collecting young mistresses. After his wife died, he contracted a second, morganatic, marriage with the middle-aged royal governess.

Still, Louis held on to most of his conquests.

3

As the new century dawned, the old king settled down. He found joy in watching his grandchildren grow up and consolation in religion and in Madame de Maintenon, his commoner wife.

While Louis concentrated on his family, international politics continued. Across the Pyrenees, King Carlos II of Spain lay on his deathbed. He had no direct heirs, and all of Europe was waiting to see who would succeed him. The leading claimants were Archduke Charles of Austria and Louis' son. Just before he died, Carlos dictated a will, leaving the kingdom to Louis' second grandson, the Duke of Anjou, who was not in line for the French throne. Carlos knew that his people would never accept union with France.

Louis had already proposed to the powers of Europe that part of Spain's domain—the kingdom itself, the Spanish Netherlands and the Spanish possessions in the Americas—go to Archduke Charles, the emperor's son, and that the Spanish territories in Italy go to the French Dauphin. England and Holland agreed, but the emperor wanted everything for his son. Then the messenger from Spain arrived and announced Carlos's will.

The rest of Europe might become nervous at the prospect of the Spanish and French crowns in the same family, opening the possibility of Louis financing further aggression with the gold and silver of the Americas. On the other hand, under the terms of the will, if the Duke of Anjou should decline the inheritance, it would be offered to Archduke Charles, a prospect that might make every non-Austrian shudder.

Word of Carlos's will arrived at Louis' court in Paris November 9, 1700. The king told only his wife and his closest advisors. He moved the court from Paris to Versailles, and on November 16, he invited all the courtiers to his study. Standing next to Louis was the young Duke of Anjou. The Sun King gestured toward his grandson.

"Gentlemen," he said, "here is the King of Spain. Birth called him to the crown, the late king also, by his will; the whole nation wants him and asks for him urgently: it was an order from heaven. I have granted it with pleasure."

To the new king, he said, "Be a good Spaniard, that is your first duty now; but remember that you were born a Frenchman, so maintain union between the two nations; that is the way to make them both happy and keep the peace in Europe."

Because the Duke of Anjou had not been in line for the French crown, most of the European powers recognized him as King Philip V of Spain. Britain recognized Philip but wasn't happy about it. Holland refused to recognize him. Austria, as expected, declared war. Louis, for once, didn't want war, but he knew it was inevitable. The fighting, confined to northern Italy, looked as if it could be ended by some sort of compromise, as long as England and Holland kept out. It was a time for tact and diplomacy.

But so many years of absolute power at home and overwhelming prestige abroad seem to have affected Louis' diplomatic sense. First, he shocked the Dutch by occupying some frontier fortresses in the Spanish Netherlands—territory evacuated by the Dutch after the peace—to hold them in trust for Spain, he said. Then, as his 19-year-old grandson was having trouble learning to be a ruler, he sent French ministers across the Pyrenees to help him. French warships began convoying Spanish treasure ships across the Atlantic, and the English began to feel as if their American colonies were caught between a French hammer in Canada and a Spanish anvil in Florida and the lands to the south.

At first there was some hope in England that Spain and its possessions might be secured for the Archduke without British armed forces becoming involved. As tensions increased, Britain declared war, but it sent no troops. Then the exiled James II died, and Louis recognized James's son as King of England. Parliament, which had just decreed that on William's death the crown should go to the House of Hanover, was outraged. "No peace without Spain" became a British battlecry. Holland took an active part in the war, and was followed by Denmark and all the German states but Bavaria.

France now faced as many enemies as she had in the War of the Grand

Alliance. But this time, the odds were weighted more heavily against Louis.
All of the great Frenchmen of the past, except Louis, were out of the
picture. Louvois was dead; so was Colbert, who had manipulated the budget
to finance Louis' wars. Luxembourg had joined Turenne and Condé on the
rolls of France's dead heroes. Vauban had asked Louis to restore full liberty
to the Protestants. Louis refused. The two old men had quarreled, and
Louis retired the great engineer. That was one more loss of talent added
to the losses France sustained when Louis revoked the Edit of Nantes.
France was poorer in wealth, too. The high-living court had become more
sober in Louis' old age, but the War of the Grand Alliance had drained the
treasury, and Louis couldn't find another Colbert.

If France lacked leadership, the Allies had finally found some. Austria
had found a Frenchman, Prince Eugene of Savoy, who had left his native
country vowing never to return except as an armed enemy. In England,
that hate-driven incompetent, William of Orange, had died. In his place, the
British had John Churchill, the youth who had fought under Turenne at
Maastricht. Now the Duke of Marlborough, he was probably one of the two
or three best soldiers his warlike nation ever produced.

Marlborough commanded, besides the British expeditionary forces in
the Low Countries, the Dutch and German troops in that area. The emperor
had made him governor-general of the Spanish Netherlands, territory he
now claimed. The Dutch, who supplied the bulk of his troops, followed a
policy of bluster at the conference table and caution on the battlefield. They
demanded a campaign of sieges, while Marlborough yearned to deliver a
decisive stroke.

While Marlborough chafed under restrictions in Flanders, the French
began to turn the tide farther south. In 1703, another veteran of Maastricht,
Claude-Louis-Hector Villars, trounced the Imperialists at Hochstett, losing
1,000 men to their 11,000. Then Villars joined Louis' only continental ally,
the Elector of Bavaria, in a drive for Vienna. Villars quarreled with the
Elector, a jolly drinking companion but a haughty prince who never let
cooperation with an ally stand in the way of his personal convenience.
Elector Max's dawdling wrecked Villars' plan for closing a giant pincers on
Vienna. The Frenchman resigned his command in disgust. Louis replaced
him with Marshals François de Villeroi and Camille d'Hastun, Compte de
Tallard, two well-connected gentlemen not known for their talent.

The French and Bavarians remained a threat to the Allies, however.
Marlborough took advantage of his office as an imperial governor-general to
come to the aid of the empire. In 1704, he left his base in Flanders and
marched southeast. His course was such that the French couldn't discover
where he would strike and so were unable to concentrate the forces

necessary to stop him. Finally, he attacked the French and Bavarians at Donauworth and defeated them heavily.

In an age that had replaced wholesale slaughter with maneuver and had developed relatively bloodless sieges, Marlborough was an atavism. At sieges, he introduced new storming tactics based on the recently reintroduced hand grenade. His troops overran fortresses in gory charges before the garrison commander could surrender and march out with the honors of war. Moreover, Marlborough refused to parole prisoners, as had been customary.

After Donauworth, Marlborough joined the Imperial army of Prince Eugene, establishing what was to become one of the most successful international partnerships in military history. The two Allied generals then moved against a slightly more numerous Franco-Bavarian army under Tallard.

Tallard had drawn up his troops with one flank on the Danube, near the village of Blenheim, and the other on a range of hills. The English general decided that the weak point of Tallard's army was in the center, where the French joined the Bavarians and there were likely to be problems of coordination. Marlborough had Eugene attack the Bavarians on Tallard's left flank, while his subordinate, Lord Cutts, did the same to the French on Tallard's right. When the center seemed sufficiently weak, Marlborough threw the rest of his weight against it. Coordinating his infantry, artillery and cavalry, Marlborough broke through the center over the bodies of the French infantry, which refused to flee. The Allied cavalry poured through the gap, Tallard was captured, and the Franco-Bavarian force ceased to exist as an army.

With Bavaria out of the war, Marlborough returned to the Low Countries. In the Allied camp, the first rejoicing over Blenheim was followed by grim muttering over Marlborough's "butcher bill." Louis took advantage of the reaction by dictating a broadside giving the names and stations of hundreds of British, Dutch and Imperial officers killed in the battle. It took three pages to list all the names on the broadside, which Louis' agents distributed in the enemy countries. The Allies kept Marlborough on a tight leash for the next year.

On other fronts, the British had taken Gibraltar and could not be dislodged, and French efforts had bogged down in Italy. Louis, under the influence of his pious new wife, began to think God was punishing him for the sins of his youth, particularly the quest for glory that led to the Dutch War.

In 1706, Louis' old friend, Marshal Villeroi, moved out of his fortification at Namur and gave Marlborough a chance to attack him near the town of

Ramillies. The Englishman ran into trouble on one flank, so he withdrew almost all his cavalry on that flank, marched them behind his front to the other flank and delivered a devastating attack on the French left while Villeroi still thought his right was the threatened flank.

Villars had some success in the Rhineland, but the defeat at Ramillies canceled out any good effects that might have had. The French were driven out of the Spanish Netherlands. Then Eugene routed the French around Turin. In Spain, an Imperial army reached Madrid.

Things improved slightly for Louis the next year. The Dutch politicians again "chained" Marlborough, permitting the French under Vendome to retake a number of towns in the Spanish Netherlands. The conduct of the British and Imperial armies in Spain outraged the inhabitants. Money and volunteers came to Louis' grandson, Philip V, a monarch for whom the Spanish public had previously shown little affection. A guerrilla movement began. Then the Duke of Berwick, a Catholic Englishman fighting for the French in Spain, defeated the Earl of Galway, a Protestant Frenchman with an Irish title leading an English army in support of the Austrians in Spain. Villars pushed farther into Germany. Prince Eugene and the Duke of Savoy, supported by an Anglo-Dutch naval force, tried to take Toulon, but the fury of French soldiers fighting on French soil was too much for them.

Then Eugene took his army up the Rhine, and the firm of Marlborough and Eugene was again in business. At Oudenarde, on July 10, 1708, they caught the main French army in Flanders, commanded by Vendome and the Duke of Burgundy, another of Louis' grandsons. The French were routed. The Allies then besieged Lille and fanned out through northern France, levying contributions on the people. Meanwhile, Anglo-Dutch naval power had driven French ships out of both the Atlantic and the Mediterranean. Everything that had to be imported was in short supply; prices climbed out of reach. Then came the freeze.

The winter of 1709 was the coldest in a century. Even the canals of Venice and the mouth of the Tagus in Portugal froze. In France, it was a disaster. Wheat seed died in the ground. Half the livestock in the country froze to death. Famine was following defeat in war. Louis, the crushed vestige of the world's proudest monarch, was convinced that God was punishing him for beginning the Dutch War. He sued for peace.

4

Louis' foreign minister, the Marquis de Torcy, went to Holland to seek terms. They were harsh, and each day of the negotiations, they became harsher. Louis would have to give up all his conquests. He would have to cease all aid to his grandson in Spain. Torcy tried to argue, but the Allies, especially the Dutch, were intransigent. France was in no position to resist.

The last of the forty Allied demands shocked Torcy profoundly: Louis would have to drive his grandson from the Spanish throne. Torcy took the demands to the king, stopping to confer with Marshall Villars. Villars counseled resistance.

When Louis saw the demands, he went into deep depression. Finally, he said, "If I have to have war, then I would rather fight my enemies than my children."

Louis then did something unprecedented for any monarch of that time, something nobody could have expected of the Sun King. He turned to his people.

The king wrote an open letter to the Cardinal Archbishop of Paris, which was printed and distributed nationwide. It declared that Louis had regarded securing peace for his people his most important duty and that his enemies, confident in their strength, had opposed his best efforts. Consequently, the outcome of the conflict was now in the hands of God.

The same day, he wrote to the governors of the provinces detailing the unreasonableness of the Allies and their impossible demands. And he wrote a propaganda broadside aimed directly at the people of France:

> I can say that I have done violence to my character . . . to procure promptly a peace for my subjects even at the expense of my personal satisfaction and perhaps even my honor. . . . I can no longer see any alternative to take, other than to prepare to defend ourselves. To make them see that a united France is greater than all the powers assembled by force and artifice to overwhelm it, and I have put into effect the extraordinary measure we have used on similar occasions to procure the money indispensable for the glory and security of the state. . . . I have come to ask . . . your aid in this encounter that involves your safety. By the efforts that we shall make together, our foes will understand that we are not to be put upon.

The people responded. Money poured into the treasury and volunteers swarmed into the army. Villars put the soldiers to work constructing field fortifications which, with fortresses and watercourses, would make defensive "lines," protecting territory and communications. Most of the troops were raw, most of them were ill-equipped, and all of them were close to starvation. But they were driven by patriotism.

"I am humble," Villars wrote, "when I see the backbreaking labor men perform without food." Villars labored, too, trying to train his troops, to form them into an army that could meet Marlborough's veterans.

The English general had drilled his men in musketry. They could fire faster than any other infantry in history. They fired by platoons, instead of by lines, giving their commander new flexibility in directing fire. Cavalry was Marlborough's favorite arm, as it was Villars', and the British cavalry was considered the best in Europe. Marlborough had Eugene, while Villars had only Boufflers. Boufflers was both brave and intelligent, but he was also old, cautious and sick. In addition to everything else, Marlborough had more men.

Marlborough set out to besiege Mons. He began with his usual deceptive preliminaries, threatening several places at once to prevent the enemy from knowing his true objective. Villars, though, had no intention of preparing for a siege, the normal reaction of an outnumbered general at this time. He brought his army out to give battle. The Allies could have moved on to Mons and set up a siege without any sort of battle, but the chance of a good fight was too much for Marlborough. The only Dutch politician with Marlborough's army when he began his march was Sicco van Goslinga, an uncharacteristically pugnacious Hollander. Marlborough and Eugene saw a chance to end the war with one stroke. They moved against Villars' fortified position, near the town of Malplaquet.

5

The position Villars had chosen was strong. The flanks were protected by woods, which did terrible things to infantry attempting eighteenth century linear tactics. Marlborough decided the situation called for a replay of Blenheim. He would assault Villars' flanks until the Frenchman weakened his center. Then Marlborough's troops would burst through the center and attack both French wings from the rear. (More than 200 years later, in 1940, Erich von Manstein did almost the same thing in almost the same area.)

On the French left, a line running through the Wood of Taisniers curved out toward the Allied front. Marlborough ordered Schulenburg, leading 20,000 Germans in forty battalions, to advance towards the French center, then suddenly wheel to his right and hit the defenders of the Taisniers woods from the side. Altogether, the Allies in this sector would outnumber the French at least four to one. A half-hour later, the Dutch were to attack the other flank, aided by other German forces and a Scottish brigade.

The attack opened as planned. A battery of 40 guns—an enormous number in that age—opened up on the Taisniers woods. Schulenburg's troops set out, bayoneted muskets on their shoulders, marching at the stately pace of eighty steps a minute to the beating of drums. They came in three waves, 200 yards apart, their colonels' colors fluttering before them.

They were marching across 800 yards of rolling land to meet an unseen enemy.

Before the first line could reach the woods, the French artillery opened fire. Round shot, four-pound iron balls about three inches in diameter, blasted out whole files with a single discharge. The Germans kept coming. The French changed to grape shot, one-inch iron balls bagged around a wooden spindle, which knocked down the Germans in bunches. The attackers closed their ranks and kept marching. When they were only a few yards from the French trenches, the defenders greeted them with a tremendous volley of musketry and charged with their bayonets before the Germans could repair the gaps in their line. Eighteenth century bayonet tactics placed a premium on mutual support. Any Frenchmen who got through the gaps, though, were immediately met by the rank behind the front line. The struggle became a bloody mêlée. The first wave of Germans had suffered heavily—two of its three major generals and all of its colonels had been killed, along with thousands of privates. After a few minutes, the French overwhelmed Schulenburg's first wave and sent it crashing back against the second.

Meanwhile, Lottum's battalions, part of the attacking force, had turned as Marlborough ordered to hit the projecting French flank from the side. The change of direction was supposed to be deceptive, but it was disastrous. The French had pushed their artillery to the front of their position as soon as Lottum's men appeared. Before they turned, they were enfiladed by the French cannons. Cannon balls wiped out dozens of men in a rank with a single shot. The Germans turned and made for the French line. As the attackers struggled through an abattis made of trees felled with their branches pointing outward and sharpened, the cannoneers switched to grape shot and the musketeers began firing. Lottum's first line, like the rest of Schulenburg's leading edge, fell back.

The German first lines, though, came back with the second lines. As the second wave was engaged, the third wave arrived to join the fight. The French brought up their reserves, and the fight continued.

On the other flank, the Dutch began their attack under the young Prince of Orange. As they marched toward the main French line, the plumb-straight ranks of Dutch and Scots passed a hidden battery, which took them in the flank. In the incredible way of eighteenth century troops, they continued marching toward their designated objective, ignoring the guns which were carpeting the ground with blue Dutch uniforms and plaid Highland kilts. The Dutch and Scots waded into the musketry and grape shot which was hitting them from the front, tore away the abattis and actually crossed the French parapet. Then a counterattack by the French reserves drove them back. Covered for a few moments by a charge of the Hessian cavalry, the Dutch and Scots reformed and again attacked. Once again they were driven back, and once again, the Hessians saved them from destruction. Some British were sent from the center to keep the Dutch in the fight.

On the French side, Villars had also withdrawn troops from his center. He was forming them up for a counterattack against Eugene's Germans when a musket ball hit him in the knee. He fell from his horse, but refused to be taken to the rear. His aides found a chair for him in a nearby farm house, and Villars sat on the chair directing the battle until he fainted and was carried off the field.

Meanwhile, Marlborough had ridden up to the French positions in the center and seen that they were not occupied. He ordered his infantry to advance into the gap. Then the English cavalry rode through and appeared in the French rear. But they appeared on trembling horses, worn out from a day of rushing from crisis to crisis. Their fight with the French cavalry was indecisive, and Marshal Boufflers, commanding in Villars' absence, was able to retire in good order.

And so ended the bloodiest battle since the invention of gunpowder.

6

The French had lost some 10,000 men. But the Allies losses were almost three times that. Of the eighty Dutch battalions that fought, there were not enough men left to make eighteen.

"If it please God to give Your Majesty's enemies another such victory," Villars wrote to Louis, "they are ruined."

Villars sounds as if he were paraphrasing Pyrrhus of Epirus, but Malplaquet wasn't exactly a pyrrhic victory for the Allies. Marborough was still in the field, so were Eugene and the Dutch. And Louis was still depressed.

The king had seen other attempts by generals to put a good face on a disaster. The facts he knew were not encouraging. Ten thousand of his soldiers were dead. His best general was severely, perhaps mortally, wounded. And Mons had fallen. The Dutch were breathing fire; food was still scarce; and the treasury was almost depleted.

As winter approached, the military on both sides appeared stunned by Malplaquet, but Louis saw no reason for hope.

"I am infinitely miserable," he told his personal surgeon.

Then the king's oldest son, the dauphin, caught the smallpox and died in a few days. Louis was still in mourning when the wife of his grandson, the new dauphin, died of the measles. Five days later, the new dauphin himself became sick. In four more days, he, too, was dead. The king was now utterly convinced that God was punishing him as He had punished David. "You are a man of war and have shed blood," a prophet told the Hebrew king. The French king could not say that he was different.

Things were happening, however, that the grief-stricken Louis could not see. More volunteers had joined the army, and more money had been donated to the treasury, in response to another appeal to the people Louis had issued after Malplaquet. In Spain, Philip V now had the whole-hearted support of his people and was driving the invaders out. Then Villars recovered and got back into the field. Now it was Marlborough and Eugene who avoided pitched battle. The Dutch deputies, no matter how fiercely they talked, were positively terrified of a fight in the field.

Best of all, from Louis' point of view, was what happened in England. Jack Churchill was, by all accounts, a charming man. But no one so ruthless and venal—he had once requested payment from the French for his services in attempting to bring about peace—survives without making enemies. The ghastly price of victory at Malplaquet was all those enemies could have asked for. Marlborough was removed from his post, and the British let it be known that they would make a separate peace.

The Allies still had Eugene, and even with the British troops at home, he still had more men than Villars. No matter how miserable he was, though, Louis was not going to wait passively for Eugene and the Dutch to devour his country. He ordered Villars to "march against the enemy and launch an attack in order to save Landrecies."

In those day, rivers and canals were supply lines as necessary as railroads became in the nineteenth century. Landrecies blocked the Allied advance up the River Sambre, and Valenciennes blocked the Escaut (or Scheldt). Prince Eugene had his headquarters between the two towns. He had established a base at Denain, behind Valenciennes on the Escaut, which cut off the French fortress from river-borne supplies.

Villars marched on Landrecies, under siege by the Allies, but he found Eugene's troops well entrenched. At dusk, the French formed up in view of the besiegers and marched east. As soon as it became dark, they turned around and marched west. They marched all night and crossed the Escaut on pontoon bridges the next day.

That morning, on his regular reconnaissance, Eugene saw masses of French troops in the distance. It never occurred to him, though, that Villars would attempt to attack a fortress like Denain with his back to a river. He decided that he was looking at a retreating French force.

"Gentlemen," he told his staff, "let us go back for lunch."

As Villars approached Denain from the south, the garrison of Valenciennes marched on it from the north. The commander of the Denain garrison, the Dutch-born Duke of Albermarle, sent a courier to Eugene. Villars expected that he would, so he launched the sort of rapid storm Marlborough had used so often. It cost him 1,200 men, but the Dutch garrison panicked. So many crowded on the one remaining bridge that it collapsed, and hundreds of the garrison drowned. By the time Eugene got his troops to Denain, the French controlled the river and frustrated his attempts to cross. Villars then snapped up the isolated garrison at Douai and reversed his direction to take Bouchain, another town commanding the Escaut. In six weeks, Eugene lost fifty-three battalions and strongholds that took years of campaigning to capture. He fell back to Brussels. For all practical purposes, the war was over.

Villars' last campaign was undeniably brilliant, but it was really a mopping-up operation. With Britain looking for an out, the Alliance was already crumbling. Without Marlborough, the Allies had no leader who could meet Villars on anything like even terms. After that shockingly bloody victory at Malplaquet, everything had fallen apart for the Allies.

Louis gained an honorable peace. France kept all the Sun King's ill-gotten gains in Europe although it lost some territory in the New World. Spain lost Gibraltar to Britain and Naples and the Spanish Netherlands to Austria. But Philip V remained king, and under the same conditions Louis had laid down to him when he accepted the crown: "Be a good Spaniard . . ."

Europe remained as unsettled as it had been after the Thirty Years War. There were fewer contenders for hegemony, however. Holland was pretty much out of contention, and Sweden, after the Great Northern War that ran concurrently with the War of the Spanish Succession, was also out, although it didn't understand that for a few more decades. Britain and France were left. They watched each other intently in Europe, but they were already dueling for supremacy in America.

Louis himself had two years to enjoy the peace. On August 13, 1715, the king felt a stabbing pain in his left leg. Four days later, his surgeon noticed a small black spot on his foot. In spite of such treatments as bleeding and draughts of ass milk, the entire leg became gangrenous. On August 31, Louis XIV died at the age of 77 after a reign of almost 62 years, the longest in European history.

A few days before he died, the King called for his great-grandson, the five-year-old dauphin.

"Soon you will be king of a great kingdom," Louis told the wide-eyed boy. "Try to remember your obligation to God; remember you owe Him everything. Try to remain at peace with your neighbors. I have loved war too much."

Louis spoke to the child as his successor to an absolute monarchy. The king himself, though, had already planted the seeds of an idea that would destroy absolutism when, in his darkest hours, he appealed directly to his people. The idea would, in a couple of generations, change France forever.

First, though, it would take root in North America.

7

1755, NEAR FORT DUQUESNE
(FRENCH AND INDIAN/SEVEN YEARS WAR)

A Different
Kind of War

ATHANASE MIGHT HAVE GASPED IN SURPRISE IF HIS ENTIRE UPBRINGING HAD
not prevented his ever displaying such a sign of weakness. He and the party
of Lorette Hurons he led had never seen such a sight. Neither had Pontiac,
that mighty warrior who had seen so much.

The enemy soldiers were marching four abreast on a narrow road.
They were packed tightly together, but they covered the trail for a mile and
a half. From where the Indians lay on the mountain, the army looked like an
enormous banded snake—red and blue with a white belly—swaying in time
with beating drums as it crept up and down the hills and across the shallow
streams. That half-white Ottawa, Langlade, had told them there would be
no problem. All they would have to do would be to surprise a small party of
English. Just that, and it would save France, save their holy religion and
drive away the English, who were trying to steal the land of the peoples of
the Ohio Country. The French would express their gratitude most gener-
ously, said Langlade, who was a minor chief of the French. There would be
plenty of booty—muskets, ammunition, scalps and captives—from the
defeated army and the English settlements.

At times, Athanase felt almost as French as Langlade. The French,
after all, had let him know the true God. As a good Christian, though, he
knew that suicide was a sin. Trying to attack this army would surely be
suicide. They could not be surprised. A thin, scattered line of redcoats
continually crunched through the brush at either side of the army, and an
advance party took up firing positions at every river crossing. And there
were so many of them. There were fifteen hundreds of English. The English
were of the same race as the French, from those mysterious lands beyond
the sea. They were clumsy, boorish, stupid men, but men who possessed

an enormous number of muskets, and big guns, too. You could hear them coming before you saw them, and they couldn't follow a trail. They could, though, build strong houses that resisted bullets and cannon balls, and they could use their guns with a skill that was truly terrifying. In short, these pale, light-eyed warriors were an enemy you did not fight without a clear advantage.

Athanase knew his side had no advantage. He looked at his brothers. They knew it, too. The French chief, Contrecoeur, knew it. Hiding in his strong house at the forks of the river, he became visibly more terrified each day the English approached. The English moved so very slowly, the Frenchman might die of fright before they arrived. Langlade gave no sign of recognizing the danger, but Langlade was mad, as he had demonstrated at Pickawillany. Athanase gave an almost imperceptible gesture, and the Hurons got up and trotted silently through the woods.

In the big red-and-blue snake creeping along the road, a tall young redhead looked over his shoulder at the troops behind him and was sure that never in his twenty-three years had he seen such a magnificent sight. The sun was high, and the air was so clear he imagined he could have seen all the way back to his plantation if the mountains didn't block the view. The bright uniforms of the soldiers contrasted vividly with the deep green of the summer foliage and the blue of the river. Even better than the beauty of the scene was the sense of power it gave him. For Colonel George Washington, it had been very different a year ago.

2

In 1754, the British and French had been fighting over North America almost continuously since the War of the Grand Alliance began in 1689. They had theoretically been at peace since the Treaty of Aix-la-Chapelle in 1748, but there were Indian raids incited by both sides and a kind of muted guerrilla war, acknowledged by no one. The problem was that none of the treaties signed in Europe had set any definite boundaries for the rival colonies in America.

The colonial authorities were mostly men who enjoyed fishing in troubled waters. They were out to make their marks by taking advantage of their semi-autonomous positions in the unstable lands across the sea. It was dangerous work. With the constant friction and frequent fighting in America, a great European war could more easily start in the forests of the New World than in the councils of the Old.

The Ohio Country, the vast area of woodland drained by the Ohio River, was the greatest source of trouble between the two nations. Both

British and French fur traders were active there, and each group had its Indian allies.

In 1749, a French officer, Captain Pierre Joseph Celeron de Bienville, set out with 200 soldiers, thirty Indians and a pile of lead plates. He buried the lead plates at strategic places to establish France's claims to the disputed territory. Where he found English traders, he told them they were trespassing on the property of His Most Christian Majesty and warned them to leave. At Pickawillany, a town that was a kind of meeting place of the tribes, he was coldly received by the ruler, Unemakemi, paramount chief of the Miamis. Because of his hospitality to them, the English called Unemakemi "Old Briton." The French, for reasons in no way apparent, called him "La Demoiselle."

Celeron's expedition convinced the French that they must take further steps to secure the Ohio Country. It convinced the English, particularly those belonging to the Ohio Company, headquartered in the colony of Virginia, of the same thing. The Virginians had been stepping up their trade with the Ohio Country Indians and trying to establish settlements in the area.

The new French governor, the Marquis Duquesne, sent Captain Claude Pecaudy de Contrecoeur to improve the portage road near Fort Niagara and ordered the Sieur de Marin to build three forts protecting the approaches to the Ohio.

Lieutenant Governor Robert Dinwiddie of Virginia, who was a major stockholder in the Ohio Company, got permission from the crown to build a fort where the Ohio, Allegheny and Monongahela rivers converge. To get the project under way, he sent a young militia officer named George Washington to warn the French in the area to leave. The French politely refused.

The Virginians, however, got the benefit of Washington's acute observations of the situation. As a wilderness surveyor, he missed few details. The Virginia government sent Washington back with 200 militia and the rank of major to protect a detachment of fort-builders already at work where the Allegheny and Monongahela rivers merge to become the Ohio. Before Washington and his troops could reach the builders, though, Contrecoeur arrived with 1,000 soldiers and took possession of the fort site. They started a much bigger fort and named it Fort Duquesne. Washington heard about the capture en route. He decided to push on to the Ohio Company's storehouse on the Monongahela and wait for reinforcements. To make it easier to bring up reinforcements, he had his troops widen the trail into a wagon road. Along the way, he met a party of French troops—28 enlisted men, two officers, some cadets and an interpreter. There was a fight and ten of the Frenchmen, including their leader, Ensign Joseph Coulon de Jumonville, were killed.

Fearing a French reprisal, Washington fortified his camp with a crude stockade and called it Fort Necessity. At Fort Necessity, reinforcements arrived—an independent company of regulars from South Carolina and three new companies of Virginia militia. The militiamen told Washington that he was now a colonel. With the new troops, he had 450 men. Some Indian allies arrived, too. But they heard that there was a French expedition on the way, and they examined Fort Necessity. The Indians put two and two together and melted into the woods.

The French came, 750 of them, along with 350 Indians. They were led by Captain Coulon de Villiers, the brother of Jumonville.

Fort Necessity was no masterpiece of military engineering. Built on a poorly drained meadow, it was a simple stockade surrounded by a knee-deep trench. The woods around it were within musket range—100 yards away on one side and only 60 yards on the other. It was overlooked by hills from which attackers could fire into the enclosure.

It began to rain when the French and Indians arrived, and it rained all night and most of the next day. The trench filled with water, and the inside of the stockade became a morass.

By the end of the day, 13 of Washington's men had been killed and 54 wounded. Besides those, another 100 were sick. The Virginians' food could stretch no longer than three days. They were short of powder, and most of that was wet.

Villiers didn't know things were so bad for the English. He did know that two Delawares told him they were scouting to the east and heard drums. He sent a man under a flag of truce to request Washington's surrender.

The young colonel was a better psychologist than an engineer. He would not let the Frenchman into the fort, and he curtly refused to surrender. The messenger went back to Villiers, then returned with the word that the French commander requested Washington to send an officer with whom terms could be discussed. By the terms agreed to, the English would go back to Virginia, and the captives from Jumonville's force would be released. Washington had to sign an agreement in French, which he could not understand. In so doing, he unknowingly took responsibility for "the *murder* of Sieur de Jumonville."

The next world war had begun. Britain wisely decided to send regulars to America. Two Irish regiments, the Forty-fourth and the Forty-eighth, were sent across the Atlantic, where they would recruit colonists to raise them to full regimental strength. Two more regiments would be raised in

America, joining the seven independent companies already in New York and South Carolina and the three regiments in Nova Scotia. The colonists would supply all of these troops, plus their own militia, with food, transportation, bullets, powder and other necessities.

Commanding the whole force was Major General Edward Braddock, a short, stout, hot-tempered man of 60 who knew everything about the parade ground tactics of Europe and nothing at all about the American wilderness. He was not disposed to learn, being convinced that all colonists were shiftless and crooked and that all Indians were witless savages. He needed colonial troops to fill out his army, but he dispensed with aid from the Indians.

Braddock liked Washington, though, and offered the young colonel a position as his aide de camp. He also liked a colonial official named Benjamin Franklin. Franklin secured the wagons Braddock used for his supply train, and also arranged for gifts of special food for the army's officers.

Braddock told Franklin of his plans. Franklin later recalled that he replied:

> "To be sure, sir, if you arrive well before Duquesne with these fine troops, so well provided with Artillery, that Place, not yet compleatly fortified, and as we hear with no very strong Garrison, can probably make but a short Resistance. The only danger I apprehend of Obstruction to your March is from Ambuscades of Indians, who, by constant Practice, are dexterous in laying & executing them. And the slender Line, near four Miles long, which your Army must make, may expose it to be attack'd by surprize in its Flanks and be cut like a Thread into several Pieces, which from their Distance, can not come up in time to support each other." He smil'd at my ignorance and reply'd, "These savages may indeed be a formidable Enemy to your raw American Militia but upon the King's regular and disciplin'd Troops, Sir, it is impossible they should make any Impression."

Under the British plan, Sir William Johnson, an Irishman who after adoption into an Indian tribe was also the Mohawk warrior Warraghiyagey, would lead the northern militia and the Iroquois to take Crown Point on the Hudson. Governor William Shirley of Massachusetts would attack Fort Niagara. But the main thrust would be delivered by Braddock, who would take Fort Duquesne, then sweep north, along the Allegheny and Lake Erie to join Shirley at Fort Niagara.

The British leaders in London had carefully studied maps of North America before drawing up the plan. Never having been to America, though, they could not imagine how the mountains, virgin forests and unbridged rivers of the New World differed from the topography of England.

In his bastioned fort at the forks of the Ohio, Contrecoeur felt terribly exposed. He was holding the last outpost of New France a traveler would see before arriving in the English lands. There were a million and a quarter English in those colonies, while there were only about eighty thousand French in all North America. Six thousand regular soldiers from France had arrived at Montreal under Baron Ludwig Dieskau, but they were still learning to adapt themselves to the wilderness. Here at Fort Duquesne, Contrecoeur commanded only a few companies of regulars and some untrained Canadian militia. He heard the English were planning to send some 2,000 soldiers against him. Contrecoeur did not enjoy the prospect of martyrdom.

Then Langlade arrived. Lieutenant Charles Michel de Langlade, leading a horde of Ottawas, Chippewas and Potawatomies, with a fringe of Hurons, Delawares, Shawnees and Mingoes—there were perhaps 800 in all. Contrecoeur would have greatly preferred half that number of soldiers, even militia soldiers. He considered the Indians untrustworthy, cowardly brutes, notable for nothing but their fiendish cruelty. The governor, though, had decided that they would strengthen his force. Perhaps they might be of some help if they would take orders from anybody but Langlade. Langlade, in spite of his title, was not a soldier.

3

Langlade had achieved that title in a unique way. He did not even want a commission. All he wanted to do was trade with the Indians.

But a couple of years before this, while he was staying at Pickawillany, some English traders had stolen all his property. He complained to the chief, Unemakemi. But "Old Briton" told Langlade he wasn't wanted in Pickawillany. He added that if the trader didn't leave, he would cut Langlade's heart out and throw it to the dogs.

Langlade left, but on the way back to his home at Green Bay, he stopped off at Detroit, where Celeron was in command. He told the captain how Unemakemi had insulted him. Celeron told Langlade that he knew Pickawillany was a center of subversion and would have destroyed it long ago if he were strong enough.

"Captain," Langlade said, "you wish Pickawillany destroyed. I will destroy it." He told the officer he would welcome any help, but with or without help, he'd destroy the town and kill Unemakemi for his insult.

Celeron thought for a moment. Ordinarily, he would not even have listened to the wild ravings of a 22-year-old fur trader, but Langlade was different. He already had immense influence with the western Indians—not only with the Ottawas, his relatives by blood and marriage, but with the Chippewas and Potawatomies as well.

He gave the young man two wampum belts, signifying that the governor of Canada was commissioning the Indians to destroy Pickawillany. If Langlade could raise the Indians, Celeron said he could also have supplies, powder, bullets and perhaps eight or ten French soldiers.

About a month later, Langlade returned with more than 200 Ottawas and Chippewas in a flotilla of 22 canoes. Pontiac, the Ottawa war chief, was at Detroit. He had opposed the expedition to Pickawillany, but after conferring with Langlade, he agreed to join it. Celeron gave the Indians the supplies he had promised and threw in a dozen soldiers.

Pickawillany was a town of 8,000 people, the creation of Unemakemi. The Miami chief had established a reputation for wisdom and friendliness which attracted individuals and groups from other tribes—Delawares, Shawnees, Piankeshaws and Hurons. Tribal society was starting to break up under the impact of the alien European culture. Warriors gravitated toward strong chiefs like Unemakemi. Pickawillany's size attracted English traders, and the traders, in turn, attracted more Indians. As Pickawillany grew strong, Unemakemi grew arrogant. His bias toward the English increased to where he secretly allowed his people to attack and kill French traders. He could call up some 2,000 warriors of many nations, and he didn't care what the governor of New France thought.

When Langlade and his 250 warriors attacked, though, most of the able-bodied men of Pickawillany were away, hunting, fishing or trading. When Langlade's men appeared out of a cornfield and started firing, there were about 200 surprised and unprepared men in Pickawillany. Unemakemi was hit before he could reach the fort the English had built. Langlade was on the chief before he could reach his musket. The trader cut Unemakemi's heart out while he was still alive and ate it before his eyes.

The fort, sheltering five Englishmen and a number of warriors, held out for a while. Pontiac said he would let the defenders leave in peace to go back to their home villages. Two of the Englishmen slipped out unnoticed and got away through the woods. Three others were captured, but one was mortally wounded. Pontiac killed the wounded man, but before he could do the same to the others, Langlade claimed them as prisoners to be taken to Celeron.

Pontiac and his men cut up the body of the dead trader, the body of Unemakemi and the bodies of two other Pickawillany warriors and put the pieces in a huge iron kettle. Then he, the attacking Indians and Langlade cooked and ate them.

The English fur traders who escaped arrived at the lodge of another

Miami chief, Michikiniqua, and told him what happened. Michikiniqua asked them to write a letter he wanted to send to Governor Dinwiddie. It was not the sort of diplomatic message familiar to Europeans.

Elder Brother:

This string of wampum assures you that the French King's servants have spilled our blood and eaten the flesh of three of our men and one of yours. Look upon us, and pity us for we are in great distress. Our chiefs have taken up the hatchet of war. We have killed and eaten ten of the French and two of their Negroes. We are your brothers.

That was two years before Washington met Jumonville and four years before the formal opening of what Europeans came to call the Seven Years War.

For the part he had played in taking Pickawillany, Charles de Langlade was commissioned a lieutenant and given new clothing and equipment. Governor Duquesne promised to call on him soon.

4

Langlade heard from the Governor while he was among the Chippewas near Michilimacinac, on the straits between Lakes Michigan and Huron. He recruited some 800 of the best warriors of the western nations, including Pontiac, and came to Fort Duquesne. Captain Contrecoeur, who preferred allies who had demonstrated more conventional military skills than massacre and cannibalism, greeted them with greatly restrained enthusiasm. Contrecoeur's scouts were giving him daily reports on the English progress, and he became more depressed with each report.

The Indian scouts themselves found the sight of the English army depressing. They did not want to fight so many soldiers. But, they reasoned, with all those soldiers here, there would not be many defending the frontier settlements. The Indians began drifting away from Fort Duquesne to take advantage of the easy pickings in the scattered English settlements.

With Braddock only days away, Contrecoeur called a council of war with his three subordinate captains, Daniel de Beaujeu, Jean Dumas and François de Ligneris. (It must have seemed to Contrecoeur that the only things Fort Duquesne had in excess were Indians and captains.)

The senior captain pointed out that the English not only had overwhelming numbers, they had cannons. They had large cannons—ten six-pounder and twelve-pounder guns and four eight-inch howitzers—that could smash

Fort Duquesne. They also had 14 small Coehoorn mortars that could drop shells inside the walls. Contrecoeur suggested that their best move might be to ask the English for terms.

Daniel Hyacinth de Beaujeu protested. He was the scion of a French military family that went back to the eleventh century. His ancestors included a constable of France and a grand master of the Templars. He did not want to surrender without a fight. He begged Contrecoeur to let him take the troops and Indians out and attempt to ambush the English. Contrecoeur reluctantly gave his consent.

Beaujeu called a council of war with the chiefs. He told them that the time had come, the event for which they had traveled so many days from the far northwest. Tomorrow they would attack and wipe out the English.

"I have seen the English," said Athanase. "I do not like what I have seen." He pointed out that there were more than twice as many English soldiers as there are of all of them—Indians, soldiers and Canadians. And they had artillery, the big guns that could knock down a wall or kill a crowd of men with one shot. He concluded that none of the Indians wanted to die on a fool's errand.

There was a murmur of agreement. Beaujeu looked from face to face.

"Do you all feel this way?" He turned to Langlade. "I have been misinformed. I was told that all the men of the western nations were great warriors." He looked at the chiefs again. "Well, if you all wish to stay by the fires like women, that is your choice. But hear me! Frenchmen are men, and we go to fight. Counsel among yourselves and give me your answer in the morning." He stalked away.

Langlade pointed out the booty the warriors could take from the enemy army — an army of clumsy Englishmen from across the sea and English farmers who knew nothing of the woods. This was the best opportunity they'd ever have to save their own lands, and after wiping out this enemy army, the enemy settlements could be sacked and destroyed with ease. If they turned away from this chance, all the other nations would hold them in contempt.

The chiefs, already shaken by Beaujeu's scorn, told Langlade that in the fight tomorrow, he could count on them.

The next morning, after receiving communion from the fort chaplain, Beaujeu took off all his clothing but his breeches, his hat and his gorget, a small metal plate hung from his neck that had once been armor and now was a symbol of rank. Then he smeared paint on his face and chest in grotesque designs. Langlade and all the French did the same. When everyone was ready, Beaujeu and his force trotted off into the woods—36

French officers and cadets, 72 French regulars, 146 Canadian militiamen and 637 Indians.

5

George Washington had been confined to a wagon for the last three weeks of Braddock's painfully slow march. He had dysentery, but the worst of the sickness was over. He was still almost too weak to stay on his horse, but, as he wrote to his brother, he would not miss the fall of Fort Duquesne for 500 pounds.

There were better roads to the west than the one the British army was taking. It was not really a road at all. It was a trail. One of the reasons the march was so slow was that Braddock had 300 axe men widening the trail so wagons could use it. Although there were better roads, Braddock had been ordered to take this one. It was an Ohio Company trail. Some of the company's stockholders who had influence in London thought it would be most convenient if the army, on its march west, could take this route, thus turning the footpath that led to company territory into a wagon road.

If Braddock moved slowly, he moved strongly. He took no unnecessary risks. At the head of the Potomac, his jumping off place, he established a fortified base and named it Fort Cumberland, after the commander-in-chief of the British Army. His supply train included a herd of cattle—beef on the hoof—and scores of supply wagons. But the supply train bogged down so much he left it at Great Meadows, near Washington's Fort Necessity, and proceeded on with his artillery, a troop of cavalry and 1,400 infantry.

Lieutenant Colonel Thomas Gage led the advance guard. He sent flankers out into the woods at every river or stream crossing, and he sent a platoon to occupy the top of any hill the army would pass close to.

Along Turtle Creek, Braddock's scouts reported that a steep defile made a likely spot for an ambush. Braddock had his troops cross the Monongahela twice to avoid it.

As the army drew closer to Fort Duquesne, an ambush seemed less and less likely. It looked as if the French were going to stay in the fort and sit out a siege. A kind of fever gripped the army. Everyone was hurrying as fast as he could to get to the fort and end the campaign. Gage neglected to order any flankers to cover a hill that stood near the trail.

Suddenly, only two miles from Fort Duquesne, a painted man wearing a hat, a gorget and European breeches appeared on the trail, running toward them. He stopped short, shrieked and waved his hat to the left and the right. Puffs of white smoke burst from the woods. The troops in Gage's column saw movement in the forest and saw shapes darting from tree to tree on either side of them, apparently trying to encircle them.

Gage's men formed a line facing the painted man and the woods from which the first shots had come. They fired a volley, shouted "God save the king!" swiftly reloaded and fired again.

The painted man was still standing in the trail. "Attaquez!" he shouted. But the raw Canadians panicked. At the second British volley, they ran to the rear screaming, "Back to the fort!" Other troops heard them and thought it was a command. They, too, began to run.

"Attaquez! Attaquez!" the painted man was yelling. The retreating Canadians paused. One of Gage's officers told the troops to direct their next volley at the painted man.

Six one-ounce balls struck Daniel Hyacinth de Beaujeu, killing him instantly.

Captain Jean Dumas, now in command, was sure that the end had come for him and his tiny army. But if he were going to die, he'd die like a soldier, as Beaujeu had already done. He ran out in front of his men shouting like a berserker, "Follow me! Fire! Kill them!"

Dumas' boldness had an effect. The troops turned their attention to the enemy. The French, and the Canadians still in action, fired volley after volley from cover into the exposed, red- and blue-coated mass.

The Indians recovered from their panic to hear Langlade, Pontiac and the other chiefs shouting at them. The English were still standing in the road, exposed to fire from all sides. The Indians knew all white men were stupid, but the stupidity of the English was beyond belief. They were like cattle waiting to be slaughtered. All the Indians had to do was crouch in the thick cover and keep shooting. Occasionally, one brave, consumed with a thirst for glory, would sneak to the edge of the road to dart out and tomahawk a soldier who was reloading.

Dumas had succeeded in one of the most difficult feats of leadership—turning an incipient rout into an attack.

As soon as the firing started, Braddock left the baggage with a 400-man detail and brought up the rest of the army to join Gage. At the same time, the French and Indians were moving through the woods so they could attack the entire column. By the time the main force reached Gage's party, the advance guard was in retreat, having abandoned its cannons. As the two forces met, a large party of Hurons and other mission Indians led by Athanase opened fire from a steep hill above the trail—fire from which no cover was possible.

Braddock was all over the battlefield, bellowing at soldiers to stand up and keep firing.

"But we can't see anything to fire at," one of them complained.

Another group of redcoats did see something—dim figures in the brush crouched behind a log. The troops fired their next volley at the dim figures. And killed a number of Virginia militiamen.

Five horses were shot from under Braddock, but the general still exhorted his men to stand fast, stand up and fire.

Colonel Gage was hit in the shoulder; Captain Horatio Gates, another regular, took a ball in the thigh. Today, the .45 pistol is considered by many to be an almost infallible manstopper. The standard French musket in 1755 was .69 caliber, and a ball from it had far more weight and velocity than anything that ever came out of a .45 pistol. But Gage, Gates and scores of others hit solidly by musket balls went on fighting. Lieutenant Henry Gladwin of the Forty-eighth Regiment took a ball in his upper arm. The impact staggered him; he stumbled and almost fell. His men looked at him with terror on their faces. Gladwin pulled himself erect. Holding the wound with his good hand, he grinned at the troops. "Well, dammit," he said. "I'm the one who's shot, not you. Keep firing."

The fever-ridden George Washington, like Braddock, dashed from one part of the firing line to another (along the trail, there was no part that was not the firing line) encouraging troops who looked about to bolt, helping to move the wounded out of the way, making sure ammunition was distributed evenly. Four bullets passed through his clothing; two horses were shot from under him, but, miraculously, he was untouched.

At the rear of the column, where Braddock had left the wagons for safety, word reached Major Peter Halket, commander of the rear guard, of the main army's troubles. He ordered William Shirley, Braddock's secretary and the son of the governor of Massachusetts, to take a detachment forward and help the general. Shirley had just saluted when Halket fell off his horse, a musket ball through his heart. Halket's son, a lieutenant, ran to his father's side, and another musket ball took the top of his head off. A third shot hit Shirley in the head. With the soldiers falling all around them, the wagoners and packhorsemen fled screaming down the road, on foot or mounted on the wagons or pack horses. Few of them reached safety.

For three hours, the slaughter of the British army went on. Braddock stood in the stirrups on his exhausted sixth horse and bellowed, "Retreat! Back to the river and cross it!" Then a bullet struck him in the chest. In spite of his demands to be left, a group of Virginians picked up Braddock and carried him to the rear. Washington, Gage, Gates and some other officers tried to prevent the retreat from becoming a stampede.

Somehow, they all got across the river. Only about 50 Frenchmen under Dumas and Ligneris bothered to pursue them. The Indians were too busy scalping the dead and wounded and looting the battlefield. With the enemy across the river, Dumas knew he and his 50 men could do nothing.

The Indians took only a handful of captives. Some, they killed by tying them to posts between two huge fires so that they roasted for eight or ten hours before dying. The rest, they ate.

At Fort Cumberland, a panicked wagoner brought word of Braddock's defeat. Colonel James Innes, commander of the fort, sent messages to the Virginia authorities and to Colonel Thomas Dunbar, commanding the advance base. Dunbar sent reinforcements to join Braddock's army. On the way, they met Washington and seven other men who had been sent by the dying Braddock to go to Dunbar for reinforcements. Washington told the reinforcements to hurry, then he continued on to tell Dunbar what had happened.

The reinforcements reached Braddock and told him Dunbar's camp was only six miles away. The general ordered a march back to the camp after detailing a party to collect as many stragglers as possible. At the camp, they found a disorganized crowd of soldiers who had fled, but had been stopped by Dunbar.

Braddock ordered the surplus supplies, cannons and powder destroyed and a general retreat begun. The second day of the retreat, the army camped near Fort Necessity. Braddock looked at the officers gathered around him and said, "We shall better know how to deal with them another time." Then he died. His troops buried him and erased all signs of the grave so the Indians could not defile the body. The retreat continued under Dunbar.

6

The battle was the worst defeat the British had ever suffered in America. Of the 1,459 men engaged, 456 were killed and 421 wounded. British casualties came to *more than eight times* the number of French troops even engaged, more than seven and a half times all the French and Canadians who went out to meet Braddock. Three French officers and five enlisted men were killed; two officers, two cadets and four enlisted men were wounded. Only 27 Indians were killed or wounded. The French and Indian victory exposed the western frontier of the middle British colonies to French attack. The long-range consequences of the victory, though, utterly destroyed French chances to win control of North America.

The consequences were a series of misconceptions.

First, the performance of their own colonial militia at the beginning of the battle convinced the French authorities that colonial troops were useless. They also knew that a large proportion of the British forces were colonials. Therefore, the huge disparity in population between the British and French colonies was militarily irrelevant.

Second, although the French knew that the British regulars were anything but a despicable foe in Europe, the battle strengthened their belief that the British could never understand wilderness warfare as the French did.

Third, the performance of Langlade's Indians convinced them completely that native warriors, directed by French officers, were the best kind of wilderness troops.

As a result, the nation with the largest army in Europe sent few regulars to America after Braddock's defeat. Dieskau and his 6,000 soldiers had arrived before the battle on the Monongahela. New France would wait a long time before it saw another such reinforcement.

The British, on the other hand, poured regulars into America, raised a new regiment in the New World and activated the colonial militia on a vast scale. The French were doomed to fight a war in which they were always and everywhere outnumbered, sometimes grossly outnumbered.

The Indians did not make up the difference. After the battle, the French authorities remembered only the victory, not how Beaujeu had to shame his allies into participation. And even Beaujeu's performance might not have been sufficient if Langlade had not added his influence and his persuasive tongue to the effort. For most of the war, the Indians refused to move against enemy forces unless they were accompanied by one, or more usually, two, soldiers or militiaman for every warrior. Attacking civilian settlements proved to be the Indians' *forte*. The fight before Fort Duquesne was the exception that proves the rule.

In most cases, the Indians were anything but reliable. Later in the war, when the British were besieging Fort Niagara, the French called on western Indians, some coming from the upper reaches of Lake Superior, to help them lift the siege. The western tribesmen paddled their birch bark canoes hundreds of miles through the lakes. When they arrived at the fort, they saw Iroquois canoes pulled up on the shore. They had no wish to tangle with the dreaded Six Nations. They immediately began paddling back to Minnesota. But in 1660, a French Jesuit missionary had said of the Iroquois themselves, "None are more courageous when no resistance is offered them, and none are more cowardly when they encounter opposition."

The Iroquois had once been overlords of all the nations from Massachusetts to Indiana and from the Adirondacks to Virginia. Their power had declined somewhat, but they were still the strongest of any Indian group. Irish-born William McShane, who became William Johnson, who became

Chief Warraghiyagey of the Mohawks, kept the Iroquois firmly on the British side. But these mightiest of warriors were never a decisive factor in the war.

In contrast, the despised colonists proved that they could fight as well as Europeans. The Sixtieth Regiment, the Royal Americans, was raised in the colonies at this time and became one of the crack units of the British Army. In August of 1758, a force of New Englanders took Fort Frontenac, a major supply depot at the mouth of Lake Ontario. That cut off supplies to Fort Duquesne. And in November of that year, Brigadier General John Forbes led an army against Fort Duquesne itself. Forbes' column was composed of Virginia militia (under George Washington), Pennsylvania militia, the Royal Americans, assorted colonial troops and some companies of the Seventy-seventh Highlanders. The French burned the fort and fled. Through the efforts of the British colonial troops, France had been pretty well pushed out of the Ohio Country before Wolfe met Montcalm on the Plains of Abraham.

At the end of the war, the French realized the mistake they had made about the British colonists. After the peace was signed, Charles Gravier, Count of Vergennes, told the British:

> Delivered from a neighbor they have always feared, your other colonies will soon discover that they stand no longer in need of your protection. You will call on them to contribute toward supporting the burden which they have helped to bring on you, they will answer you by shaking off all dependence.

That was a lesson the British had yet to learn. It would cost them their American colonies and defeat in still another world war. It would also result, eventually, in a new world power—a democratic republic, whose birth would usher in a new age.

8

1775, BUNKER HILL (AMERICAN REVOLUTION)

Regulars
and Rabble

TO BE A MEMBER OF ONE OF THE FLANK COMPANIES OF A BRITISH REGI-
ment—a grenadier or a light infantryman—was to be someone special.
Flank companies, named from the positions they took when the regiment
was in combat, were composed of men who had received special training.

The grenadiers had once been specialists in throwing hand grenades.
But the grenade, which promised to be such a devastating weapon in
Marlborough's time, had turned out to be too dangerous for general service.
The army had dropped the grenade, but not the grenadiers. The big, strong
men selected to throw grenades were just too impressive on the parade
ground. So the military authorities made them shock troops. But they kept
their tall, brimless hats, which made it easier to throw the non-existent
grenades.

Physically, the light infantry were the exact opposite of the huge
grenadiers. They were wiry men who wore small leather caps and carried
light muskets called fusils. While the grenadiers had almost a century of
tradition behind them, the light infantry was born less than 20 years before
this, here in America during what the Americans called the French and
Indian War. The world's first light infantry regiment had been raised by the
present commanding general, Thomas Gage. While other troops advanced
at 80 steps a minute to meet the enemy in long, neatly dressed lines, light
infantry charged at the run in small groups. They could negotiate woods
and broken country that would disorganize ordinary troops. When they
closed with an enemy, though, their bayonets were as deadly as those of
the grenadiers. If Braddock had had light infantry, any light infantryman
would tell you, his fight on the Monongahela would have ended differently.

114

Right now, though, neither the grenadiers nor the light infantry were enthusiastic about the honor of being in the flank companies.

First, General Gage had detailed the flank companies of each of his regiments for what he called special training. That was to confuse the rebels. Then he had the flank companies wakened in the middle of the night and rowed across the Charles to Cambridge. They waded up to their knees getting ashore. Then Fat Francis Smith, their colonel in this Godforsaken enterprise, they grumbled, moved them to another point on the shore, and that involved wading chest-deep. And in America, this country of extremes—climatic and political—early spring was colder than the depths of winter in England and Ireland.

Now they were on the road to Concord, where the officers—not their regular officers, but volunteers from other units—said the rebels had stored munitions. They were wet and cold, carrying 60 pounds of equipment, and Concord was 20 miles away.

In his Boston headquarters, General Thomas Gage hoped that seizing the munitions would take the starch out of the militant element in Massachusetts. Gage did not dislike Americans. His wife was an American from New Jersey, and he had spent most of his adult life on the continent. He owned property in New York and hoped to live there after his retirement.

2

Most of Gage's fighting had been in North America. After recovering from the wound he received leading the vanguard of Braddock's army, he had fought with Abercrombie at Ticonderoga. He had demonstrated commendable bravery at those bloody disasters but no particular tactical ability. His *forte* was organization and administration. When the French and Indian War ended, Gage became governor of Canada. He managed to make himself popular with the Canadians while giving the colony the most efficient government it had enjoyed in generations. As a dedicated administrator, Gage viewed defiance of the law with horror. He pulled strings in his next post, commander of all army units in North America, to have troops moved into the English-speaking colonies when unrest developed there over Parliament-imposed taxes.

A week after the Boston Tea Party, the general had an interview with George III. The king described the meeting in a letter to Lord North.

Since you left me this day, I have seen Lieutenant General Gage . . . his language was very consonant to his Character of an honest and determined Man; he says they (the colonists) will be Lyons, whilst we are Lambs but if we take the resolute part they will undoubtedly prove very meek; he thinks the four Regiments intended to Relieve as many Regiments if sent to Boston are sufficient to prevent any disturbance; I wish You would see him and hear his ideas as to the mode of compelling Boston to submit to whatever may be thought necessary.

"Whatever may be thought necessary" was known in Boston as the Intolerable Acts. The Acts closed Boston to all shipping. The upper chamber of the Massachusetts legislature, the Council, was to be appointed by the king instead of elected. Judges and sheriffs were to be appointed by the governor. No one indicted for a capital offense in connection with either a riot or the revenue laws would be tried in the colony: the trial would either be in England or in another colony.

To enforce these acts, the king appointed a new governor of Massachusetts, Thomas Gage, who remained commander of all British troops in North America. Four regiments of soldiers followed Gage to Boston.

The new governor began enforcing the Coercive Acts, as the British called them, with a vengeance. Then troubles started. The rebels terrorized the newly appointed Council members into resigning. Mobs in outlying towns forced the courts to close.

"Civil government is near its end," Gage wrote. And again: "Conciliating, Moderation, Reasoning is over, Nothing can be done but by forcible means." Until he received reinforcements, he would do his best to avoid "any bloody Crisis." Three weeks later, he proposed withdrawing all troops and blockading the coast until the government could raise an army capable of conquering all New England. To raise this army, he estimated, the government would have to hire German mercenaries.

Troops continued to arrive in Boston, until that town of 20,000 contained 3,000 soldiers. The king and his ministers began to suspect that appointing Gage had been a mistake.

Gage didn't spend all his time complaining. He also developed a remarkably efficient spy network. It included such agents as Dr. Benjamin Church, a member of the Massachusetts Committee of Safety, the highest council of the rebels. Through his spies, Gage came to a truer appreciation of the rebel movement than he had gained from his Tory friends in New York.

For one thing, it had much wider support than he had been led to believe. The colonies, after all, had been settled by people who were dissatisfied with their lives in the "old country." (Even at this early date, there were a number of "old countries" besides England.) The colonists had begun governing themselves, because there was no other government available. That was especially true in New England, now the home of the most virulent rebel movement. When the crown later attempted to abridge their powers, the colonial assemblies resisted with all civil means and were generally successful.

After the French and Indian War, the home government began imposing taxes. British leaders argued that revenues from those taxes would pay only part of the cost of the military establishment that Britain was maintaining in America to protect the colonists. To shirk them would be freeloading—forcing people in Britain to pay for something that mainly benefited Americans.

But the Americans argued that they themselves supplied much of the manpower used in North America during the French and Indian War. The French were no longer a threat, and the regulars had thoroughly proved that they were inept Indian fighters. What was the army supposed to protect them from?

The main purpose of the army was to provide employment for the huge number of colonels—all of whom had to have political influence—that had been created during the war. But that was a reason members of the government would not even admit to themselves. It was easy, on the banks of the Thames, to accept any arguments from military commanders in the wilds of America.

The vehemence of American resistance to the taxes bewildered anyone who did not understand that these descendants of English religious dissenters; debtors and convicts had a built-in bias against any control from London. But they didn't hate Britain. Most of them had friends and relatives in Britain. They considered themselves English.

A moderate American, who was also an honored member of English society, explained the American position in a letter to an English newspaper.

In the past, wrote Benjamin Franklin, whenever the king needed money, resources or men, he asked the colonial assemblies for what he wanted. The assemblies always granted the requests "and, during the last war, beyond their abilities, so that considerable sums were returned to them yearly by Parliament as exceeding their proportion."

Franklin pointed out, "It is well known that the Colonists universally were of the opinion, that no money could be levied from English subjects, but by their own consent, given by themselves or their chosen Representatives. That therefore whatever money was to be raised from the people in the colonies, must first be granted by their Assemblies; as the money raised in Britain is first to be granted by the House of Commons. This right of granting their own money was essential to English liberty; and that if any man or body of men, in which they had no Representative of their chusing, could tax them at pleasure, they could not be said to have any property, any thing they could call their own."

Gage did not think much of the colonists as soldiers. Man for man, he believed, they were no match for regulars in open battle. He had to admit their political sophistication, though. When the Coercive Acts were passed, the Massachusetts rebels had responded by forming a Provincial Congress, a shadow government that immediately took control of the militia and appointed a Committee of Safety to act in its name when the Congress was not in session. Even before that, revolutionary elements in all the colonies had formed Committees of Correspondence, which arranged the first intercolonial assembly, the Continental Congress. Fifty-six delegates from all the colonies but Georgia met in Philadelphia September 5, 1774. Although few of them wanted actual independence from Britain, the majority of colonists were united in resisting any attempt by London to abridge their "rights as Englishmen."

The Massachusetts rebels were now receiving support from other colonies. Although Boston was closed to shipping, food and supplies—including gunpowder, muskets and cannons—were crossing colonial boundaries. Gage's spies told him where a number of rebel military depots had been established.

On February 21, 1775, Gage's secret service had told him that, within five days, 20 wagonloads of flour had passed from Salem and Marblehead towards Worcester. The spies reported that there were 12 brass cannons in Salem, too. On February 26, Gage sent troops to Salem. They were met at a drawbridge by a local militia unit under Colonel Timothy Pickering. Pickering refused to lower the bridge. Finally, a Salem minister intervened and worked out a compromise. Pickering would lower the bridge if the British would promise to march only 30 rods into the town and return. The British did as they promised and returned without finding either flour or cannons.

Gage did not take this as evidence that there were no accumulations of military supplies. Even before the Salem expedition, Gage had, on February 22, sent two disguised officers, Captain William Brown and Ensign Henry de Bernier, with Brown's batman, to Worcester. After several narrow escapes, they returned with word that supplies were indeed being stored in Worcester, due west of Boston. Local Tories, part of Gage's spy network, had pinpointed the locations. On March 20, Gage sent Brown and de Bernier to Concord, a town closer to Boston, lying west-southwest of the capital. They noticed points of military interest in Concord, such as that the houses were arranged in scattered groups. They also learned that a number of field guns and mortars had recently arrived.

A few days later, Gage sent out another pair of spies. One was a corpulent lieutenant colonel named Francis Smith. The other was an enlisted man, probably a sergeant, named John Howe. Not much is known about Howe, who wrote his memoirs in Canada after a long and successful career in espionage in North America. It's certain that he was a trained gunsmith and had a natural talent for secret agentry.

A black barmaid in a Watertown tavern recognized Smith, so he went back to Boston. Howe continued on to Worcester and returned by way of Concord. He convinced the rebels in Concord that he was an American gunsmith who wanted to help the cause, and they showed him all their military stores. Howe told Gage not only about the stores, but about the temper of the people. He told the general he'd need more than 10,000 men to destroy the munitions at Worcester and return. Gage knew that was the sort of overestimate spies tend to make, but it convinced him that the first raid should be on the closer supply center, Concord.

And that was why on April 19, as the sun rose, British light infantry and grenadiers were marching into the town of Lexington, on the way to Concord.

3

The light infantry, commanded by Major John Pitcairn of the Royal Marines, got to Lexington first. Lieutenant Colonel Francis Smith, the would-be spy, who commanded the whole column, followed with the grenadiers. Drawn up to meet them on Lexington Common were about 70 men with muskets. Pitcairn knew they were minutemen, members of militia companies who were picked to respond to alarms immediately. He halted his troops and rode toward the Americans.

"Stand your ground," Captain John Parker told his militia. "Don't fire unless fired upon. But if they want a war, let it begin here."

"Lay down your arms, you damned rebels, and disperse," Pitcairn yelled.

Parker told his men to disperse, but to keep their weapons. Pitcairn again demanded that they lay down their arms. Somebody fired a shot. There was scattered firing on both sides. A light infantryman was hit, and two bullets grazed Pitcairn's horse.

"Fire, by God, fire!" a British officer ordered. A volley blasted the rebels before he could finish his last word.

"Soldiers, soldiers, don't fire!" Pitcairn shouted. "Keep your ranks. Form and surround them."

Pitcairn, a marine, had never commanded light infantry before. Men in the light companies, unlike those of the line companies—"battalion men"— were trained to think for themselves. Wet, cold and miserable, the thoughts these light infantrymen were thinking were not pleasant. When Pitcairn told the light companies to surround the rebels, they cheered and swept around the Common. The minutemen started to run. The light infantry stopped, volleyed by platoons, reloaded and fired again. Then they charged at the double. The Americans ran wildly, except for Jonas Parker, the captain's cousin. Parker reloaded and fired, then the bayonets struck him down.

One British soldier had been wounded. Eight Americans were killed and ten more wounded. The British proceeded to Concord, their wetness and coldness forgotten.

There's no record that any of the British soldiers wondered how the minutemen came to be waiting for them. The reason was that the rebels had an intelligence organization as good as Gage's. The "special training" story had taken no one in. As soon as the flank companies began to move out, rebel agents signaled the message to Colonel William Conant of the Charlestown militia. Then Paul Revere, who headed the intelligence apparatus concerned with troop movements, personally rode toward Concord to warn the rebel leaders and militia. Dr. Joseph Warren, leader of the Committee of Safety, had sent him with William Dawes, another member of the Revere organization. After leaving Lexington, Revere and Dawes fell in with a young physician, Samuel Prescott, who was riding home after a long night of courting. A British patrol intercepted them, capturing Revere and driving off Dawes. Dr. Prescott, though, got to Concord.

By the time Major Pitcairn, Colonel Smith and their troops got there, the supplies had all been moved. And militia were starting to arrive. Some 400 militiamen had already reported to Colonel James Barrett, the local commander. Barrett's house had contained some of the supplies Gage wanted, but the minutemen moved these out as their first order of business. Now, as the light infantry and grenadiers marched into town, the militia stood on a ridge overlooking North Bridge.

Smith and his staff repaired to a tavern to refresh themselves after giving orders to the troops. Four companies of light infantry crossed North Bridge and marched up to Barrett's house. Three more light companies guarded the bridge, their eyes on the long line of armed farmers looking down on them from the ridge. In the town itself, the grenadiers searched houses. They found a hundred barrels of flour and 500 pounds of bullets. They threw the flour barrels and sacks of bullets into a pond without bothering to break them open. The rebels later recovered everything intact. The grenadiers also found some wooden gun carriages. They burned these.

Up on the hill, the militia saw the smoke from the gun carriages.

"Will you let them burn the town down?" Adjutant Joseph Hosmer asked Barrett. The colonel ordered his minutemen to march into the town, but not to fire unless fired upon. They formed a column of twos and started for the bridge.

Captain Walter Laurie, commanding the light infantry at the bridge, sent back to Smith for reinforcements. Then he ordered his men to prepare for street fighting.

The light infantry drill for street fighting was for the troops to form a column of fours. The first rank would fire and peel off. While they were running to the rear, the second rank would fire. They'd immediately run to the rear after firing and the third rank would volley. And so on. It provided for unceasing fire by a firing line about the width of the average street. With the weapons available in the eighteenth century, no better system could have been devised for fighting in a densely populated town.

The only trouble was that Concord, with its scattered houses, was not a densely populated town. And the minutemen, even though they were marching in a column of twos were marching at an angle to the bridge and marching across an open field. In other words, the British firing line was only four soldiers; the minutemen's was about 200.

The first rank of light infantry fired.

"God damn it, they're firing ball!" yelled Captain Timothy Brown as he heard a bullet whistle by.

The light infantry fired again. Captain Isaac Davis and the drummer boy, Abner Hosmer, fell dead.

"Fire, fellow soldiers!" a militia officer screamed.

A ragged volley rippled all along the militia line. Twelve Britishers dropped. Some of them got up again, but three of them were dead and a fourth was unconscious.

It wasn't particularly good shooting on the colonists' part, but it was sufficient. That roaring volley terrified the light infantry. They turned and fled.

The militia followed them into town, then they realized the enormity of what they had done. They had fired on His Majesty's troops. Confused, they withdrew across the bridge. As they watched, a young man with an axe walked up the road as if he intended to join the militia. As he passed the red-coated bodies, the unconscious soldier stirred. Panicked, the townsman struck the wounded man with his axe, then ran as fast as he could in the opposite direction. Later, the British troops would claim that the minutemen scalped fallen soldiers.

The light infantry that had gone to Barrett's house returned after a fruitless search. They stepped along smartly until they caught sight of the bodies of their comrades. Then they, too, dashed into town.

Smith had some 750 men, but, according to survivors of the North Bridge skirmish, the rebels had thousands. Gage had ordered Smith not to fire on the local people unless it was absolutely necessary—an order that apparently was not understood by the light infantry. The colonel hired some carriages for his wounded and led the troops back towards Boston. But the word had spread. Militia seemed to be lining the route home.

At Miriam's Corners, a short distance from Concord, the British fired at some militiamen they thought looked threatening. The militia fired back. All the militia. All the way back. They fired from behind stone walls, through the windows of houses, from patches of dense woods. The grenadiers returned ineffectual volleys. The light infantry charged with bayonets, but the militia simply fled and returned to fire again when the Redcoats were back on the road.

Gage had sent Lord Hugh Percy with 1,000 men and two field guns to reinforce Smith in case of trouble. Percy's force arrived just as Smith's column was about to disintegrate. His cannons awed the militia and helped the British get back across Charlestown Neck and to safety. Of the total of 1,750 men engaged (including Percy's) 73 British were killed and 174 wounded. The losses of the some 4,000 militia who were engaged at one time or another were quite small.

The British army had sustained many more serious defeats. And, as the officers of the expedition were quick to point out, the rebels hadn't fought a proper battle at all. They had engaged in mass sniping at troops on a route march.

4

News of the fighting spread quickly through the colonies. In Connecticut, a young pharmacist named Benedict Arnold led his militia company into a confrontation with the town fathers of New Haven and forced them to give him the keys to the powder house. Then he, his troops and the powder started northeast to help the Massachusetts militia. At the same time, a burly old veteran of the French and Indian War named Israel Putnam heard the news while he was plowing on his Connecticut farm. He left his plow in the field, changed into his uniform and started riding to Massachusetts.

Not every colonist reacted like Arnold and Putnam. Three weeks after the fighting, a second Continental Congress convened. Georgia and New York stayed away. The New Yorkers even apologized for the actions of their delegation at the last congress. The New York delegates, they hinted, had contracted a strange kind of madness in Philadelphia.

That was some comfort to General Gage, or "Blundering Tommy," as they were beginning to call him in London. It wasn't much, though. Rebel forces had captured Fort Ticonderoga on the Hudson. The rebel militia were closing in on the British stronghold in Boston Harbor. They now occupied the land on the other side of Boston Neck and Charlestown Neck. The British position was strong because Boston and Charlestown occupied two peninsulas that looked like a pair of huge polliwogs thrust into the harbor. Each was connected to the mainland only by a tiny, flat neck of land. It would be almost impossible for the rebels to force their way across either neck. On the other hand, they could easily block the only land routes out.

Nevertheless, the government in London was demanding that Gage take bold action to put down the rebellion. London sent him reinforcements, both welcome and unwelcome. The welcome reinforcements were troops. He now had 5,000 men, which, however, he felt was too few to regain control of the countryside.

The unwelcome reinforcements were three new generals, probably the three most ambitious officers in the service. One was Henry Clinton, a native of Newfoundland but a New Yorker by upbringing. Clinton was a cold intellectual who had the greatest difficulty in seeing any merit in anyone else. The second was "Gentleman Johnny" Burgoyne, reputedly the bastard son of a lord. Burgoyne followed three careers simultaneously—he was a general, an active politician and a playwright—and he was good at all of them. The third was William Howe, brother of Lord Augustus Howe, the inventor of light infantry, who had been slain alongside Israel Putnam in the last war. Howe's other brother, "Black Dick" Howe, was an admiral. William Howe himself had been considered by James Wolfe, conqueror of Quebec, to be the most brilliant and daring young officer in the army. He had led Wolfe's climb to the Plains of Abraham and had contributed much to the science of light infantry tactics.

The rebel side had a plethora of generals, too. Nominally, all the militia outside Boston were commanded by Artemas Ward, the ranking officer in the Massachusetts militia. Actually, the Committee of Public Safety really ran the show, with Dr. Joseph Warren running the Committee. To further complicate things, the Provincial Congress had asked the Continental Congress to appoint a commander-in-chief, and thus adopt the army besieging Boston. The new commander-in-chief had not yet arrived. Meanwhile, militia generals and colonels were throwing their weight around, trying to gain power among the citizen-soldiers.

One of the bumptious generals was Israel Putnam. Standing on the mainland side of Charlestown Neck, he looked up at Bunker Hill. The militia should fortify the hill, he said, to forestall a British attempt to break out through Charlestown. It would also discourage other enemy moves. The colonial intelligence service had warned that the British were about to take some action—probably to occupy Dorchester Heights.

Not all the officers were enthusiastic about Putnam's idea. Charlestown

Neck was low ground and only 35 yards wide. The British fleet controlled Boston Harbor. Any troops who went up on Bunker Hill, the dissenting officers argued, would be climbing into a trap.

One who thought fortifying Bunker Hill would be a good idea was a tall, taciturn colonel named William Prescott. The faction of Putnam and Prescott carried the day in revolutionary councils. Prescott was assigned to fortify the hill.

And so, on the night of June 16, Putnam and Prescott led 1,200 farmers into a cul de sac. With them was Colonel Richard Gridley, a man who had studied military engineering until he knew Vauban's principles as well as Vauban. There was a short argument about whether they should fortify Bunker Hill or Breed's Hill, which was lower, but closer to Charlestown. Gridley told them they were wasting time. They agreed to fortify Breed's. An abandoned British fortification on Bunker Hill would cover any retreat. Gridley marked out the works. Putnam gave an order: "Dig!"

The works on Breed's Hill were not a simple trench, but a full-size fort of earth. It was 130 feet square and had earth walls rising 12 feet from a dry moat. Prescott's troops were almost all farmers. At that time, the most sophisticated piece of farm machinery was an ox-drawn plow. They were far from the dead-eye marksmen of legend, but there were no better diggers. When the sun rose on July 17, the officer of the watch on *HMS Lively* trained his telescope on a complete fort crowning Breed's Hill. *Lively* opened fire on the works, but a message from Admiral Samuel Graves, commander of the fleet, stopped the firing. *Lively's* bombardment inhibited work on the fortifications, but when the firing stopped, Prescott got his men working on a breastwork running down the hill toward the Mystic River. On Bunker Hill, in the meantime, Putnam had another detachment improving the existing works.

In Boston, Gage and the other generals held a council of war. They had suggested—no army man could order Sam Graves—that the fleet bombard the rebel fortifications. Now they had to decide what the army should do.

Henry Clinton suggested that they land men on Charlestown Neck and cut the rebels off from the rest of the armed rabble. Howe pointed out that such a landing party would be caught between the rebels on the Charlestown heights—who must number several thousands to have done so much work overnight—and the hordes on the mainland. The British would also be on a narrow strip of semi-swamp while their enemies held the high ground north and south of them. And the tides allowed landing (or evacuation) at only limited periods of the day. It was just too risky, said the master of light infantry tactics. (The master didn't mention that with the guns of the fleet covering them, the men on that low-lying land would have been as secure as if they were in their barracks. He may have cursed Clinton silently for coming up with the obvious plan first.) Why not, said Howe, land men in Charlestown, where they wouldn't be in danger of rebel fire and could form up in good order. The rebel redoubt was open on both flanks. The troops could feint to the left at the redoubt. While the rebels were looking to their own right, the light infantry would run along the beach on the Mystic River side and turn the rebel flank. Then a massive push by the grenadiers and the line companies would smash the Americans.

No one, apparently, thought of the move that worried old Artemas Ward. The militia general was afraid that the British might feint at Charlestown to draw troops away from Boston Neck. Then they could break out of the Boston Peninsula, sweep south, east and north around Boston Harbor and overrun Cambridge, the patriot headquarters and supply center.

Gage approved Howe's plan. So far, everything had favored the rebels. Now, he thought, the tide had turned. On the Concord expedition, there were no pitched battles. But now, the rebels would have to fight like soldiers. When they fled, as he was sure they would, it would show that the ultimate power, military power, belonged to the government. Then the government could offer an olive branch, and he could retire to a country house in New York or New Jersey. Gage ordered Howe, the senior of his three unwelcome subordinates, to lead the attacking force. Clinton, the second-ranking, would command the reserves. Burgoyne would hold himself in readiness for whatever might be required.

Meanwhile, Prescott's men were still digging. The sun was high, and they were wilting from thirst. Asa Pollard took a party of men into Charlestown to get water. Returning, they had almost reached the diggers when Pollard's head disappeared and a geyser of blood spouted from his neck. A cannon ball had decapitated him—the first death caused by the 10,000 rounds the fleet had fired so far. The men in the trenches looked at Pollard's body in horror. Before panic could seize them, Prescott got up on the parapet and walked slowly down the line.

To the rear, on Bunker Hill, Putnam again mounted his horse and galloped across fire-swept Charlestown Neck to get reinforcements. Twice Artemas Ward, fearing for Cambridge, had refused to send them. This time, he allowed Colonel John Stark and the New Hampshire militia to go forward.

5

At one o'clock, Howe's landing force came ashore at Moulton's Point, east of Charlestown village. Howe feared—correctly, as it turned out—that the village might be full of rebel snipers. Checking the American position through his telescope, the British general saw Stark's column approaching Breed's Hill. He sent for reinforcements and halted operations until they came. Prescott continued digging. His breastwork ran down the Mystic River side of the hill and into a clump of woods that bordered a swamp. Beyond the swamp, the land was open. Prescott sent two field pieces and Captain Thomas Knowlton with some Connecticut militia to extend the line. The gunners ran away, but Knowlton's men dug in behind a rail fence with a stone foundation that extended to the bank of the Mystic. The fence was some 200 yards behind the line of the breastwork, but it was the only defensible position in the area. Between it and the breastwork, the militia dug three small entrenchments.

When Stark arrived with two New Hampshire regiments, there was still a gap on the extreme left. The New Hampshiremen plugged it. The took over the end of the fence, then they built a stone wall across the beach. By the time Howe's reinforcements arrived and the British had eaten lunch and smoked a last pipe, Howe's plan to turn the rebels' left flank had been ruined.

On the right, there was little Prescott could do but order some of his men to infiltrate the village of Charlestown. By fighting Concord-style among the houses and stone-walled fields, they could delay a British sweep.

As Prescott was inspecting the line, he saw a foppishly dressed young man approaching. The white satin breeches and silver-laced blue waistcoat caught his eye first. They stood out among the brown homespun, linen hunting shirts and unfashionable broad-brimmed hats of the rest of the troops. As the man came closer, Prescott could make out his face. It was Dr. Joseph Warren, who had just been elected a major general. Prescott immediately offered the doctor his command.

"I shall take no command here," said the chairman of the Committee of Safety and president of the Provincial Congress. "I came as a volunteer with my musket to serve under you."

The British were now ready to move.

Howe's force consisted of all the flank companies of the British regiments in Boston, plus the Fifth, Fifty-second, Thirty-eighth, Forty-third and Forty-seventh regiments and the First Marine Battalion—some 2,200 men in all. He divided his force into two separate wings. Brigadier General Robert Pigot would command the left, consisting of the Thirty-eighth, Forty-third and Forty-seventh regiments, the Marine Battalion and three companies each of light infantry and grenadiers. Howe kept most of the light infantry and grenadiers—11 companies of each—as well as the Fifth and Fifty-second regiments.

Following the plan, Pigot would enter Charlestown, come out below Breed's Hill and march directly at the redoubt. It was not an attack but a demonstration. If anything went wrong, though, he had enough troops to turn the demonstration into a serious assault.

Meanwhile, Howe, leading the flower of the British army, would deliver the decisive blow. Howe knew that the Americans had probably extended their fortifications, but he reasoned that positions that had been manned within the hour could not be strongly held. And it had already taken him so long to get in position that the day might be over before he could rearrange his forces for a sweep around the other flank.

Pigot moved out to the rattle of drums and the shrilling of fifes. He had barely entered Charlestown before snipers began felling his men. He marched out of the village and sent a message to Admiral Graves. Both the fleet and the naval batteries across the Charles River on Copp's Hill in Boston began to fire. The British guns sent both hot-shot—cannon balls heated to a glowing red—and carcasses—perforated shells filled with pitch-soaked tow—into the town. The village was an inferno as Pigot's men marched around it and lined up at the bottom of Breed's Hill.

On the British right, Howe was walking ahead of two waves of red-coated infantry, each wave three ranks deep. The towering grenadiers, the army's shock troops, formed the first wave. In the second were the regular battalion companies. Ahead of everything was a scattering of skirmishers.

"I shall not desire any one of you to go a step farther than where I go myself at your head," the general had told his troops. He was as good as his word.

Behind their breastworks, the Americans were impressed by the long, straight, crimson-and-white lines moving towards them. They could not understand why the British were moving so slowly and why the army cannons, as opposed to the naval guns, were silent.

The army cannons were silent because the gunners found that their six-pounder guns had been supplied with 12-pound shot. Howe had told them to try grape shot, but grape was useless beyond 300 yards. So the artillerymen could only watch.

The infantrymen were moving slowly because they were plowing through uncut hay, stumbling in holes and climbing over fences and stone walls hidden in the hay. Howe began to worry that the timing of his attack might be thrown off.

The light infantry were to deliver the key stroke by turning the rebels' flank and attacking the men behind the breastworks from the rear. The grenadiers would then hit the disorganized enemy from the front and rout them. Howe's force would then swing around the fort, where the rebels were being held in place by Pigot's demonstration. Seeing that they were about to be cut off, Howe believed, the entire rebel force would run like rabbits. To get the maximum effect, though, the grenadiers' attack should fall on the Americans at the psychological moment. The grenadiers were being held up in this accursed field while the light infantry had an easy jog up the beach, hidden by the steep bank from both the army and the enemy.

The light troops were jogging easily, fusils at port arms. They trotted in a column of fours, the light company of the Royal Welch Fusiliers, an elite regiment, in the lead. Behind the Welshmen came the light company of the King's Own Regiment. Howe, the old light infantryman, was going to deliver the fatal stroke with the *creme de la creme* of his favorite arm.

When the British looked at the American positions, they saw little and heard nothing. There's no contemporary evidence that Stark drove a stake into the ground in front of his line so the New Hampshiremen could fire when the Redcoats reached it. Nor is there any good reason to think that Putnam gave his "whites of their eyes" order. "Old Put" was on Bunker Hill, to the rear. The Americans were not firing, though. They were waiting as silently as Barrett's militia at Concord. This time, though, they were hidden behind the newly made stone wall and the stone-bottomed rail fence. They had stuffed grass between the rails, not for protection but for concealment.

On the beach, the Welch Fusiliers jogged to within 100 feet of a crude stone wall running into the water. They shifted their muskets to the "charge bayonets" position.

With an ear-splitting crash, a cloud of thick, light gray smoke erupted from the wall. And as a military unit, the light company of the Welch Fusiliers ceased to exist. The King's Own leveled their bayonets and sprinted forward before the rebels could reload. They leaped over the bodies of their comrades and were yelling in fury as a second volley blasted them. The light company of the Tenth Infantry hesitated for a flickering instant, then they dashed for the wall. A third volley annihilated them. Nothing human could fire so fast. The fourth company stopped dead, and the column piled up behind them. Then somebody turned around, and the whole column stampeded to the rear.

Behind the wall, John Stark's baleful eye dampened the first exuberant desire of his men to pursue the fleeing lobster-backs.

"Reload and wait," he told them. He had kept his men crouched behind the wall in three lines. Each line had fired a volley. If the fourth light company had continued and reached Stark's men before the first line had reloaded, all the New Hampshiremen would have been wiped out and the Yankee flank turned.

The grenadiers had not seen the rout of the light infantry. If they had, it would have made no difference. They came on stolidly, trying to execute the slow march over the broken meadow. They could see the heads of the rebels looking over their leveled muskets. When they were 80 yards from the rebel line, they took the muskets off their shoulders, fired a volley and charged at double-time. They covered about 30 yards. Then a blast of flame and smoke hid the Yankee breastworks. William Howe looked around and saw, in place of his lines of grenadiers, clumps of men here and there and a few individuals standing alone and bewildered. The grenadiers reloaded and fired, but their bullets hit nothing but dirt. The rebels fired again. The remnants of the grenadier line began to flow to the rear in spite of Howe's exhortations. The Fifth and Fifty-second regiments marched through the grenadiers and fired. Their volley had no more effect than those of the grenadiers. The next rebel volley opened wide gaps in their line.

Screaming, waving his sword, Howe stood in front of the wavering, disorganized troops on the hillside, but he couldn't make them go forward. The rebels had stopped volleying. Now each was firing his piece as fast as he could load it. Americans had grown up with guns. Even along the eastern seaboard, hunting was not a sport for most people but a necessary technique for putting meat on the table. The militia could not improve their smoothbores' accuracy, but they could fire them faster than veteran British officers believed possible. "An incessant stream of fire poured from the rebel lines," one officer recalled later. "It seemed a continuous sheet of fire for near 30 minutes."

The British began moving back down the hill.

As Pigot's men neared the redoubt, they had the same experience. Standing by the battery on Copp's Hill across the Charles, Henry Clinton reported: "General Burgoyne and I saw appearances on the left of the army which made us shudder—in short, it gave way." That was too much for Clinton. He rounded up the reserves and sent them over to Charlestown. Then he followed and organized the walking wounded into another unit.

Meanwhile, Howe and Pigot had reformed their troops and begun a second advance 15 minutes after the repulse. This time, there was no dash up the Mystic River beach. Pigot moved closer to Howe so they could advance in an unbroken line. The rebel skirmishers who had been burned out of Charlestown had continued to harass Pigot's men by firing from trees and stone walls. This time, the British hoped to avoid them.

Howe joined what was left of his light companies to the shreds of his grenadiers in the first wave of his advance. A frontal assault in an extended line against the entrenched Americans was not the sort of subtlety his colleagues had come to expect of William Howe. Howe, though, didn't believe the Americans could withstand a second assault immediately after the first. And, perhaps, he did not wish to have waded through blood—literally—just so Clinton could come up with the reserves and claim an easy victory. The second assault wasn't subtle, but it could be arranged quickly.

It was a quickly-arranged bloodbath.

"Most of our Grenadiers and Light-Infantry, at the moment of presenting themselves lost three-fourths of their men. Some had only eight or nine men a company left; some only three, four and five," a British officer wrote later.

Prescott recalled seeing Howe standing alone surrounded by bodies. All of his staff were dead or wounded. Howe, an inveterate gambler, had always had a deep belief in his personal luck. He was luckier than he knew. A Captain Tilley of the Connecticut militia later wrote to a friend that the Americans had detailed sharpshooters to pick off the officers. "A choice party of our best shots under cover were appointed to fire at none but the Reddest Coats."

The sight of his beloved flank companies in ruins changed Howe's feelings about his fortune. "The Light Infantry being at the same time repulsed, there was a Moment that I never felt before," he confessed. For the rest of his life, William Howe would never live down that moment.

As Pigot's main body was being scythed down by the rebels in the fort, the brigadier sent a detachment to outflank the redoubt. Once again, the fire of the American skirmishers stopped the British on the Yankee right. Pigot ordered his men to retreat. Howe didn't order his men to retreat, but they did anyhow.

At the base of the hill, Howe and Pigot joined Clinton and the reserves. This time, Howe came up with a plan that showed some imagination. When the troops advanced against the breastworks, they'd march in column, instead of in line. Such a formation would reduce their firepower, but it would also reduce their casualties. So far, their firepower hadn't accomplished anything visible, and their casualties had been unbelievable. At the last moment, the columns would deploy, fire a volley and charge.

It had finally dawned on Howe that the American militia were fighting the regulars' sort of war, and they were fighting it like the best regular troops. In spite of modern legend, soldiers defending a fort in the eighteenth century did not leave their entrenchments to volley with their opponents in the open. There was precious little chivalry in the Age of Enlightenment. Even the famous British toast at Fontenoy, "Gentlemen of France, fire the first volley," had an ulterior motive. If the French fired before the British were in maximum effective range, the British would carry their position with the bayonet before their opponents could reload.

The smoothbore musket was a powerful weapon, but its inaccuracy, magnified by the fact that the musket ball had to be undersize to make reloading easy in the soot-filled barrel, limited useful range to little more than 100 yards, and then only when firing volleys. At 30 or 40 yards, a volley from these guns was frighteningly destructive. For such short-range firing, troops usually loaded their muskets with a combination of ball and buckshot. At Breed's Hill, some militiamen who ran out of buckshot used nails and broken glass. The psychological effect of a short range volley was even greater than its physical effect. Two such volleys, fired in rapid succession, were all it took for Wolfe to gain Quebec, the key to Canada. The only reason troops did not use close range volleys exclusively was that it took either iron discipline or extreme devotion to withhold fire against an enemy advancing with 15-inch bayonets. And regular troops, unlike most of the colonists at Breed's Hill, had bayonets of their own.

Behind the American lines, there was a crisis. The militia were running out of ammunition. Further, a steady stream of desertions had cut Prescott's troops in the redoubt to about 150 before the second assault. There were fewer now. Prescott and the other American leaders broke open some artillery cartridges and distributed the powder to their men. The men chose stones, bits of glass or other hard objects to shoot when they had no more lead bullets.

Neither supplies nor reinforcements had arrived since the fighting began. To the rear, a disorganized mass milled around on Bunker Hill. On the other side of Charlestown Neck, the situation was even worse. Thousands of men, with both cannon and supply wagons, stood on the mainland side, afraid to cross the neck. The only ship guarding the neck was the armed transport *Symmetry*, which, with 18 guns, was far from being the most formidable ship in the harbor.

Below the hill, Howe was organizing his troops without the aid of a staff. He had 400 fresh troops from the Second Marine Battalion and the Sixty-third Regiment. This time, the weight of the British attack would fall on the breastworks and Prescott's undermanned redoubt. Howe detailed a few men to make a demonstration to keep the Connecticut and New Hampshire troops at the stone-and-rail fence. (Because the Americans had no overall command, it worked.) He ordered his artillery to go forward, ahead of the infantry, and take up positions close enough to the rebel lines to spray them with grape shot. Then he launched his columns.

One of the rebels in the fort later wrote that the British "advanced in open order, the men often twelve feet apart in the front, but very close after one another in extraordinary long or deep files." It was no longer possible to point a musket at a wide, solid mass and fire, knowing that you would knock a man down. The Americans had to aim now.

They did. An Ipswich, Massachusetts, militiaman recalled, "They looked too handsome to be fired upon; but we had to do it." Another rebel described the scene: "As fast as the front man was shot down, the next stepped forward into his place; but our men dropt them so fast they were a long time coming up. It was surprising how fast they would step over their dead, as if they were logs of wood."

The rebels were running out of ammunition. Already, some were hurling rocks. The British reached the parapet, climbed it and were blasted back by a volley. One of those hit was Major John Pitcairn, the marine who had commanded the light infantry at Lexington. His son, another marine officer, took him back to Boston, where he died.

The British momentarily huddled beneath the parapet, then they climbed up again. The last American volley "sputtered like an old candle," and the British were inside the fort.

Only a handful of militiamen had bayonets; not all the officers had swords. But they fought "more like Devils than Men" with clubbed muskets, a regular reported. They made their way out of the rear of the fort through a fog-bank of dust and powder smoke.

Outside, they dashed from wall to tree to ditch, firing from cover if they had ammunition. The Americans on the flank, who had been but lightly engaged in this assault, covered the retreat. The regulars fired volley after volley. More militiamen died at this stage of the battle than at any other. One of them was Dr. Joseph Warren.

Fresh men from Bunker Hill came down to cover the retreat. Some New Hampshire militiamen managed to drag two field pieces up Bunker Hill and down across the neck, fighting off British infantrymen who tried to capture them.

John Burgoyne, watching the action from Copp's Hill, said the rebel retreat was "no flight: it was even covered with bravery and military skill."

And Henry Clinton, who took part in the last of the fighting, said the battle was "A dear bought victory, another such would have ruined us."

The British never did occupy Dorchester Heights.

6

As with Malplaquet, though, "another such" victory was not needed. One was enough.

At the beginning of the rebellion, the odds against Britain's crushing it were enormous. The entire British army numbered only some 30,000 men.

There was no conscription; the idea of war in America was unpopular with the lower classes in England—the people who, though they did not rule, would have to fight. Even press gangs could not have produced enough bodies to win a war against the 13 rich, populous American colonies. The eighteenth century English economy just couldn't spare the manpower.

Economic warfare—primarily the blockade—had for a century been a major British weapon in European wars. But a blockade was ineffective against the Americans. They were already self-sufficient in food, clothing and shelter. They had been boycotting English exports already, and the impact on the British economy was at least as great as on that of America.

The rebellious colonies formed a mass a thousand miles long and a thousand miles wide. Much of it was scantily populated, of course, but it contained about two million European colonists, equal to between a fifth and a quarter of the entire population of all the British Isle. And, as the fighting so far had shown, when their homes were threatened, most of the adult males would fight. During the war that followed "the Battle of Bunker Hill," there were seldom more than 10,000 men in the Continental Army at any one time. But the militia not only controlled the countryside, constricting British control of the colonies, it outnumbered the Continentals at critical battles like Saratoga.

In America, there was no key point like London or Paris that the British could seize to defeat the rebels. Philadelphia was the second-largest English-speaking city in the world—larger than Glasgow, Manchester, Dublin or Birmingham—but its capture by the British didn't even slow the rebellion. The British were fighting 13 separate governments, and none of them depended on a capital city. Moreover, communications in America were miserable. Not only were there no decent roads; there were hardly any roads at all.

The British could always hire German mercenaries. Gage suggested that option. Gage, though, was considering only New England. All of Germany could not have provided enough shuffling military serfs to conquer the united colonies if the colonists resisted. Furthermore, a good part of Germany, including the powerful kingdom of Prussia, favored the Americans.

His Majesty's government could rely on only three things in the struggle: the American Tories, the colonists' ingrained respect for the monarchy, and the Americans' fear of the regulars.

Relying on Tories had gotten Gage into trouble in the first place. The British consistently over-estimated the number of loyalists in the colonies. Even today, the idea persists that a third of the colonists were loyal and another third were neutral. It's true that at the beginning, only a tiny

minority of those the British called "rebels" wanted independence. But the
so-called rebels, fighting for their "rights as Englishmen" were a large
majority of the colonists. The facts are that the rebels controlled all the
militia and organized a popular government that functioned everywhere not
under the direct occupation of the British Army. That is not possible for a
minority or even a small majority. After Concord, Thomas Gage had no
illusions about the the help he could expect from New England Tories
(although his colleague, John Burgoyne, would not learn the same lesson for
another two years).

American respect for the monarchy was strong even among the most
ardent rebels. It was so strong that the rebels besieged Boston and invaded
Canada in the king's name—hardly the sort of actions George III wanted
them to take. A month after the "Battle of Bunker Hill," the Continental
Congress petitioned the king to stop the war by repealing the Coercive
Acts. In reply, George proclaimed that a "general rebellion" existed and
that "the utmost endeavors" should be made to "suppress such rebellion
and bring the traitors to justice." The colonists then began traveling
headlong down the road to independence that they had really been on since
the king's troops fired on the "embattled farmers" at Lexington.

So all the British could really count on was the rebels' fear of the
regulars. At Breed's Hill, the rebels killed or wounded 1,054 of the 2,600
regulars they fought. They lost 449 killed or wounded out of the 3,200 in
the general vicinity—1,800 of whom saw action. After inflicting such
casualties on what they considered, probably correctly, the best army in
the world, the rebels had little fear of regulars. Following "Bunker Hill,"
even the dissidents of Georgia and New York decided they could afford to
join the rebellion.

It was different on the other side. After the rebel commander-in-chief,
George Washington, fortified Dorchester Heights, William Howe, who had
replaced "Blundering Tommy" Gage, called back a planned occupation of the
heights and evacuated Boston. For the rest of his career, the once-daring
Howe turned away from any move that would involve attacking entrenched
Americans. In August, 1776, for instance, he outmaneuvered Washington
on Long Island but followed the routed Americans so slowly that Washington
was able to fortify Brooklyn Heights. Instead of attacking the heights, Howe
resorted to siege tactics, and Washington again escaped. Later, Howe
hesitated to launch an all-out attack at White Plains, saying, "If I could by
any maneuver remove an enemy from a very advantageous position without
hazarding the consequences of an attack, . . . I should certainly adopt that
cautionary conduct." He even refused to attack the starving American army
at Valley Forge, while his large and well-equipped army was only a few miles

away because conditions "did not justify an attack on that strong position during severe weather."

The Revolutionary War dragged on for five more bloody years until Cornwallis surrendered on October 17, 1780 and for two less bloody years until the Peace of Paris on February 3, 1783.

As the Redcoats marched up Breed's Hill, the war was theirs to win. If the rebels had panicked, the rebellion would have been all over. After the fight, the war was for the rebels to lose. During the first two years after the fight on Breed's Hill, the colonists frequently appeared to be trying to snatch defeat from the jaws of victory by their niggardliness, internal squabbling and sometimes arrant cowardice. Their glorious "defeat" at Breed's Hill was not wasted, though. Not one town, let alone a colony, offered to submit to the crown during the most trying times. Rebel militia continued to control all the countryside. All the Americans had to do was to give their army minimal support (which is about what they gave it).

Actually, the main function of the Continental army turned out to be simply existing. It forced the British to concentrate, instead of spreading all over the colonies as an army of occupation. That wasn't intentional strategy, but it worked superbly. Whenever the British detached small units to get supplies, the rebel militia ate them up. Cornwallis, for instance, chased the Continentals all over the South, winning victory after victory before his tattered army, unable to get supplies or to care for its wounded, staggered into Yorktown and final defeat.

That defeat had already been assured in 1777, when Burgoyne collided with another armed rabble near Saratoga in the wilderness of upstate New York. His surrender convinced France—already helping the Americans, thanks to the colonies' brilliant emmissary, Benjamin Franklin, the one-time peacemaker—to declare war on Britain. Spain and Holland followed suit. The colonial rebellion turned into a world war, and Britain lost all chance of regaining its colonies.

It all began with Howe's fatal victory on the Charlestown peninsula, when the colonial militiamen proved that they could stand up to regulars.

MORE

PEOPLE,

MORE

POWER

9

1863, CHICKAMAUGA CREEK
(AMERICAN CIVIL WAR)

"You Got Into
Our Inwards"

"THE CRISIS IS UPON US," WARNED THE LEAD HEADLINE IN THE CHATTA-
nooga *Rebel*, as tattered members of the Army of Tennessee straggled
through town. Braxton Bragg, the Confederate Army's most unpopular
commander, had culminated months of retreat by falling back on the gateway
to the Old South.

It was 1863, the third year of the American Civil War. To the North,
the war begun to preserve the Union had more and more come to be
regarded as a war to end slavery—to free millions of people who had been
regarded as little more than cattle. To Southerners, though, it was a war to
defend their homes and way of life.

"Civilized" warfare in the 1860s was far different from "civilized"
warfare in the 1760s. In 1798, the French government, bankrupted by
decades of profligate royal spending and participation in a series of world
wars, the last being the American Revolution, collapsed. The French
Revolution and the wars that followed radically changed the part ordinary
people played in the fighting. In the American struggle, militia volunteers
played a key part. In the French fighting, crowds of citizens joined (and
were later impressed) into the regular army. They overwhelmed the
professional armies of their royal enemies with sheer manpower. Later,
under Napoleon, the French kept mass armies. These legions, as well
trained as earlier European armies and led by a military genius who was
also head of state, dominated nearly all of Europe. Napoleon's success
forced all continental European nations to adopt mass armies in self defense.

This social revolution coincided with the Industrial Revolution. Railroads
now made it easy to quickly move masses of troops. Iron mills made it
possible to armor ships in quantity, and both sides had fleets of iron-clads.

Rifled cannons, rifled muskets, breech-loading rifles, a few of them repeaters, and even primitive machine guns appeared on the battlefield.

The combination of mass armies and far more effective weapons was a particularly bloody mix. Generals continued to use tactics developed while the smoothbore musket and bayonet ruled the battlefield. But the minié rifle, the most widespread and most primitive of the new weapons, had ten times the range of the smoothbore. Soldiers died in heaps.

War had become hell for everyone, but particularly for the Confederate States. In order to fight the more populous North, the South had to enlist practically all free males of military age. By 1863, the future of the Confederate States of America had begun to look dim. Union forces had taken Vicksburg and now controlled the whole length of the Mississippi. They had also defeated Robert E. Lee's invasion of the North at Gettysburg.

The future, however, was far from hopeless. Although Vicksburg's loss had, in a sense, cut the Confederacy in two, there had been little important commerce between the two portions since the war began. The great bulk of Confederate resources and manpower was in the eastern section. As for Gettysburg, only hindsight could make it a decisive battle. At the time, it was no more decisive than the Confederacy's 1862 defeat at Antietam. In both cases, Lee retired with his army intact, after having inflicted approximately equal, though heavy, losses on his opponent. About all that either battle had proved was that Lee couldn't conquer the North, and he had never attempted that.

One great Confederate victory could practically reverse the trend. But few southerners looked for one from the hated Bragg, now retreating before the cool Yankee general, William Rosecrans.

For months, Rosecrans had been camping at Murfreesboro, building up supplies and gathering horses. Eventually, he had enough provisions, and although he'd never have enough horses to let him equal the enemy's cavalry, Washington had had far too much delay.

While Rosecrans sat in Murfreesboro, Bragg had held strong positions near Tullahoma. Though his numbers were reduced by men called away to help defend Vicksburg, Bragg blocked the railroad and the only good road to Chattanooga. On either side of his line stretched an expanse of waterless pine barrens without a single decent road.

Rosecrans feinted at the barrens to the east, but Bragg was not deceived. He easily repulsed Rosecrans' subsequent attack along the railroad route near Shelbyville. Then a blinding rain began and continued for 15 days, drowning out all action north of Bragg's headquarters. The Confederate general was bracing himself for a resumption of the attack when the mud-encrusted Federal army suddenly emerged from the barrens at Manchester and threatened to cut Bragg's communications. Too late, Bragg learned that Rosecrans had feinted not once, but twice—first at the barrens, then at Shelbyville. Then he led his army on a wide turning movement through the "impassable" pine barrens.

Bragg had nowhere to go but Chattanooga. By the time he entered the town, the general's popularity in the Confederacy was scarcely higher than Abraham Lincoln's.

2

A strange, black-browed prickly pear of a man was Braxton Bragg—all brains and no heart. Or so he preferred others to think. In private conversation with his surgeon, Bragg had broken down and wept at the thought of leaving a hospital full of wounded men to the advancing Yankees. Most of his subordinates, though, saw only the stern face of authority. Duty was Bragg's god; he shunned human ties as Moses had shunned the fleshpots of Egypt. Once, in the Old Army, Bragg had been both battery commander and post quartermaster. As battery commander, he turned in a requisition for certain supplies. As quartermaster, he rejected his own requisition.

A man who could not be swayed by friends—or even himself—would not be swayed by enemies, Bragg believed. Early in the war, he had demonstrated that. Don Carlos Buell, the Federal commander, had taken Nashville and advanced on Chattanooga. Instead of meeting him head-on as Buell expected, Bragg swept around the Union army and invaded Kentucky. Buell went scurrying back to protect his communications.

Against orders, Bragg's men attacked the Union army at Perryville. The unplanned battle was a gory draw, but it hurt Bragg. The man the world knew as an iron martinet had a serious weakness for a general: he hated to see soldiers die. Further, he saw no profit in staying in Kentucky. Many of the "liberated" Kentuckians were ardent Unionists and amused themselves by sniping at his campfires. Bragg withdrew to Tennessee.

Rosecrans, who replaced Buell, followed cautiously. He and Bragg met at Stone's River, near Murfreesboro. Rosecrans attempted to take Bragg in the left flank, while Bragg simultaneously attempted to take Rosecrans in the left flank. Bragg got there first with the most, but not quite soon enough with enough. The result was both bloody and confused, but Bragg was sure that he had won. The next day, however, the Rebels found the Yankees still on the field and ready for another day's blood-letting.

A good general doesn't rush at the enemy like a mad bull, trusting to the valor of his riflemen. Bragg would gladly trade miles of wilderness for a chance to trap his opponent. So, after another skirmish, he retreated from Murfreesboro to Tullahoma. To many Richmond politicians, any retreat was a disgrace to Southern Honor, but Bragg was neither a politician nor a romantic. He was a good match for Rosecrans.

3

The evenness of the match was not immediately apparent to the citizens of Chattanooga. What was apparent, on August 21, were blue-coated soldiers on Walden's Ridge, across the river and a little north of town. Rosecrans had sent Colonel John Wilder's Lightning Brigade through some more "impassable" terrain—this time, the precipitous, deserted mountains ringing Chattanooga.

No unit in either army was better fitted for the job than the Lightning Brigade. Some time before, Wilder's doughfeet had been annoyed by the hit-and-run tactics of the Confederate cavalry. They had voted to provide their own horses, so they could meet the Rebel riders on their own terms. They became mounted infantry. Wilder threw in a bonus: he bought Spencer repeating rifles for his men. Though it lacked the range of the issue muzzle-loader, for close fighting in the woods, the Spencer was as deadly as most of the rifles used in World War II.

The Lightning Brigade lived up to its name. Wilder's troops surprised the Confederate outposts and appeared on the Tennessee River before Bragg knew an attack had begun. The Yankees wasted no time admiring the view. As soon as he reached the top, Captain Eli Lilly unlimbered his rifled field guns, squinted through a perforated metal disk that served as his personal range finder and laid his guns on two steamers tied up on the Chattanooga waterfront. One sank almost immediately. The other was quickly disabled. The Confederates opened up on Lilly's four guns with 19 of their own. The Lightning gunners rammed home more charges and sent their shells right through the embrasures of the Confederate gun emplacements. By the end of the day, every Confederate gun had been silenced.

Meanwhile, the rest of the Lightning Brigade fanned out along the river bank. Some seized boats; some hacked down trees; some just pounded on empty barrels and raised an infernal din. Bragg decided that Rosecrans was going to try crossing the river north of town. He pulled in his outposts south of Chattanooga to reinforce the troops in the north.

Rosecrans then sent his whole army across the river south of Chattanooga. One corps moved on Chattanooga along the river; the other two marched inland a few miles and turned north, their movements screened by the mountains. Chattanooga had been changed from a Confederate fortress to a Federal trap.

Bragg hurriedly evacuated Chattanooga and retreated into Georgia. By now, Bragg, the career officer, recognized the skill of the peacetime industrialist who opposed him. Subtlety must be met with subtlety.

4

The Confederate general sought out volunteers who were both intelligent and brave. They had to be intelligent, because their mission was to pose as deserters and sell Rosecrans on the idea that Bragg's army was in rout. They had to be brave, because the risk of death was greater than they'd face in the hottest infantry fight—a lingering, painful death from starvation or disease in a Union POW camp.

Bragg organized his army behind LaFayette, Georgia, and sent for reinforcements. The Confederate railroad network, unbroken and operating with top efficiency, performed tasks that would have amazed Napoleon. Troops had already come from Mississippi after the fall of Vicksburg. Others arrived from Knoxville, where they had been harassing the army of bumbling Ambrose Burnside. In Virginia, Robert E. Lee agreed to send his most able subordinate, the redoubtable James Longstreet, with his corps. An army of 70,000 Confederates would close a trap on Rosecrans' 57,000 Federals when they came through the mountains. If the "deserters" did their work well, Rosecrans wouldn't even be prepared for a battle.

The "deserters" couldn't have been more successful. Bragg's past performance had convinced Rosecrans that the Confederates would fall back on another fair-size town, not wait in ambush like an Indian war party. In the last year, Washington had prodded Rosecrans unmercifully for his procrastination. He was eager to show how quickly he could move and destroy the enemy. He drank in the "deserters" story like a thirsty camel.

Rosecrans' advance shows how thoroughly he believed the rout story. Thomas's corps was to advance directly from Bridgeport, south of Chattanooga, through a pass in Lookout Mountain called Steven's Gap. Crittenden's corps was to join the Lightning Brigade and other elements in Chattanooga, then proceed around the north end of Lookout Mountain and converge on Thomas's corps. McCook's corps was to swing wide around the south end of Lookout Mountain, through the town of Alpine, and take in the rear any enemy force that Thomas and Crittenden might contact. Each corps was separated from the rest of the army by miles of mountains and woods.

Because Rosecrans' cavalry was inferior to the Confederate horse, he

ordered Thomas to substitute an infantry division for a cavalry screen as he
marched through the mountains. One division would probably be able to
handle any resistance Thomas would meet, Rosecrans believed.

And so Negley's division marched directly at the center of the Confederate army, too far ahead of the main body to receive quick support.
Rosecrans was offering his army for Bragg to destroy piecemeal. As one of
Bragg's officers said, it was a chance "which comes to most generals only
in their dreams."

It was Bragg's move. He moved his bishop—a real bishop, Leonidas
Polk, who had traded the crozier and mitre of an Episcopal bishop for the
sabre and braid of a Confederate lieutenant general. Polk was to rush
Hindman's division to hold Negley, while D. H. Hill, lately of the Army of
Northern Virginia, sent up Cleburne's division to finish off the Yankees.
Hindman took up his position but merely watched the federals while he
waited for Cleburne. It was a long wait. When he heard what was happening,
or rather, not happening, Bragg sent a courier to Hill to ask where Cleburne
was. Hill reported that the division commander was sick. Bragg spurred his
horse over to Hill's corps area and found Cleburne perfectly healthy.
Moreover, Irish-born Pat Cleburne was astounded that anyone should have
reported him ill. Bragg tried to have Hill removed from command. The
Confederate government, however, refused to side with the "cowardly"
Bragg, who had abandoned Chattanooga without a fight, against a veteran
of the glorious Army of Northern Virginia.

Before searching out Cleburne, Bragg had ordered Simon Bolivar
Buckner to take the two divisions of his corps over to join Hindman. With
their men outnumbering Negley's three to one, Generals Buckner and
Hindman refused to attack. They decided they had a better plan than the
commanding general's. While they sent couriers to Bragg for approval of
their idea, Negley pulled back to safety.

Opportunity knocked again when Crittenden, coming down from the
north, divided his Union corps. He sent two divisions to Ringgold and one
to Lee and Gordon's Mill. Bragg moved his bishop again, this time telling
Polk to take himself and his whole corps to Lee and Gordon's Mill and
attack the one Federal division. That night, Polk reported that he had taken
up strong *defensive* positions. Bragg led up Buckner's corps to reinforce
him. When the commanding general arrived, he found the bishop still holding
his "strong positions for defense." The Union division had slipped away.

Polk was a brave man. A few months later, he would die in battle. In
civilian life, though, his only superior had been God. He had no inclination
to render unto Braxton Bragg the obedience that had been the Lord's.
Bragg wanted to court-martial Polk. But the bishop, too, had powerful allies

in Richmond. Bragg's only friend in the whole Confederacy, it seemed, was that other cold intellectual, Jefferson Davis. And the President had all he could do to keep Bragg from losing his command.

Bragg's strong sense of duty, as well as his long retreat, had turned both his generals and the civilian population against him. Stories of his harshness spread throughout the Confederacy. It was said, for instance, that he had a soldier shot for shooting a chicken. The story omitted two details: one, that the soldier had been marching under orders to make no unnecessary noise so the enemy couldn't locate his column; two, that he had missed the chicken and hit a black child. Of course, the gossipers probably didn't think the child was worth mentioning.

By this time, Rosecrans had realized his danger. He issued orders to close up his array and to cover the roads to Chattanooga, so his army wouldn't be cut off in the wilderness.

5

Bragg realized his danger, too. With subordinates like his, the plan of battle must be so simple the veriest dolt could not claim he misunderstood it. If he must fight a set-piece battle, Bragg wanted the numerical odds as much in his favor as possible. He withdrew his forces to await Longstreet's corps. Rosecrans continued to concentrate.

On September 18, four days after the initial clash, the advance guard of Longstreet's corps arrived by train. Bragg resumed the initiative. He planned to move his army around the Yankee left, across Chickamauga Creek, north of the position held by Crittenden's Federal corps. The Confederates would drive in the Yankees' flank, get around their rear and force them against a bend in the creek called McLemore's Cove. There, with Bragg's army behind them, and the creek and the mountains, held by more of Bragg's men, hemming them in, they'd have to surrender.

Rosecrans had two units guarding the two crossings north of his main position. The most extreme flank guard was Colonel R. H. G. Minty's cavalry brigade, one of the few Union cavalry outfits superior to the average Confederate horse. The other guard was Wilder's mounted infantry brigade.

Minty's riders dismounted and took up positions on the east (Confederate) side of Reed's Bridge. About 7:30 a.m., a mass of horsemen wearing gray uniforms, yellow-brown uniforms, country homespuns and civilian garb of every description burst from the woods firing revolvers and sawed-off shotguns. N. B. Forrest's entire cavalry corps was trying to rush the bridge. Minty's men took cool aim with their breech-loading carbines and blasted back the charge.

Forrest's men dismounted and brought up their artillery. Their numbers and elan were too much for the Federals; Minty's men withdrew across the bridge. They continued fighting until noon. Then long ranks of Confederate infantry, complete with rifles, bayonets, banners and field artillery appeared on their northern flank. Minty's troopers withdrew to the south after being reinforced by part of Wilder's Lightning Brigade.

Meanwhile, Wilder's brigade had been holding off two Confederate infantry divisions at Alexander's Bridge. Forrest's cavalry, having done their work at Reed's Bridge, swung south. They took Wilder's skirmishers in the flank and sent them over the bridge. As the Confederate columns tried to push across the bridge, Wilder's men opened a drum-roll of fire with their Spencer repeaters. As they fired, the men of the Lightning Brigade saw the head of the enemy column disappear. The troops continued to rush forward, but when they reached a certain point, they seemed to sink into the earth.

Eventually, the overwhelming numbers on their flank and front were too much even for the Lightning Brigade. The mounted infantry moved south as darkness fell. One brigade had held up two infantry and two cavalry divisions most of the day. Bragg's army poured onto Rosecrans' flank.

The delay had given Rosecrans time for a new move. He ordered his most steadfast corps commander, George Thomas, to pull out of the center of the line and take up a position north of Crittenden's corps. McCook's corps, at the southern end of the Federal line, was to move up and make contact with Crittenden's.

That night, Thomas's men crept through woods so dense that even in daylight, a company commander rarely saw all his platoons. As day dawned, they stumbled right into Confederates who were groping their way in the opposite direction. Companies marched blindly into volleys. Artillery was hauled into the woods and never seen again. Colonels and brigadier generals gathered up scattered companies from strange commands and led them into the unknown. The battle had become a series of slugging matches that nobody, least of all the commanding generals, could control.

Some of Bragg's troops moved south, between the Union lines and the creek, looking for a way to get around Rosecrans' southern flank. One group actually got through the diminishing gap between Crittenden's and McCook's corps, but converging blue columns caught them in a crossfire. In this action, the Spencers of the Lightning Brigade again heaped up bodies as the Confederates tried to charge across a clearing. The Rebels broke, rallied and reached a drainage ditch. The Federals brought up two cannons double-shotted with canister—cans filled with musket balls—and raked the length of the ditch. When these two enormous shotguns had finished,

Wilder later said, "One could have walked 200 yards down that ditch on dead rebels without touching the ground."

As the day faded, Cleburne, Bragg's best combat commander, led one last assault against the Union left. It gained a few yards at the cost of many casualties.

When darkness ended the fighting, both armies were lined up west of Chickamauga Creek. The Confederates had access to the creek's water; the Federals were tortured by thirst. The Yankees' dryness was increased by the way they spent the night—cutting down trees and building breastworks. They were outnumbered in the wilderness, and there were worse things than thirst.

Bragg's sweep around the Union left had found soldiers were he expected only trees, and his chance for a grand slam died. The fighting had exhausted his men too much for him to try another all-night march followed by a day of attacking. He'd have to make do with what he had in place, which, aside from numbers, wasn't much.

His army had three lieutenant generals, Longstreet, Hill and Polk. Although Longstreet had a great reputation in the East, he was new to the western theater. He would command the Confederate left. Hill, also new to the West, had been no advertisement for eastern generals. After his unexplained, and unexplainable, failure to throw Cleburne against Negley's isolated Union division a few days earlier, Bragg would gladly have sent Hill back to the East. Richmond wouldn't permit that, but Bragg could at least remove him from personal contact by putting him under his third lieutenant general, Polk. Polk would command the right. And the right was the wing that would begin the day's action.

Why Bragg chose Polk for such an important command is something he never explained. Polk had been almost as insubordinate as Hill, but Bragg knew that on other occasions, the bishop-general had been as good as the best. Bragg's devotion to duty may have been a factor in his decision. Such a single-minded soldier seemed unable, in spite of all his experience, to imagine another soldier without a similar devotion. He might rate some, such as Hill, incompetent. But though Bragg used "insubordination" freely in his reports on subordinates, willful defiance was really almost unthinkable to him. Each new case surprised and shocked him.

The Confederate general was aware, though, that his fellow generals weren't Napoleon's marshals. The new plan was even less complicated than the previous day's. No one could claim he misunderstood orders. The extreme right of Polk's command, Breckinridge's division of Hill's corps, was to strike the extreme left of Thomas's Union corps. The division to the left of Breckinridge's would go into action as soon as it heard shooting, then the division to the left of that, and so on down the line from north to south. The federals would probably have to call for reinforcements from the south of their own line. Somewhere, a Confederate division might find a weak spot.

The attack was to begin at dawn. The sun rose, though hidden by a thick blanket of fog, but Braxton Bragg heard no sound of firing. Minutes, then hours, went by. Finally, Bragg sent an aide to see what had happened in Polk's wing. The officer returned with word that Bishop-General Polk was eating breakfast with his staff. Bragg uttered what a witness termed "a terrible expression" and went galloping off to the right wing. Around 10 a.m. the attack began.

Just before that, a brigade of Negley's Union division had moved through the fog to a new position on the far left of the Union line. Before the Federals could begin fortifying their area, the fog in front of them coagulated into blotches of deeper gray. Moments later, the blotches materialized into Breckinridge's Confederate infantry. The Federals were driven back before many of them could even fire their rifles.

As Breckinridge's men moved forward, the resistance got stiffer. Then they hit the section of the Union line that had been fortified during the night. At the same time, the fog lifted. Caught in the open by riflemen protected by log breastworks, they were slaughtered.

Brigade by brigade, Polk's troops took up the attack, each brigade advancing as it heard firing to the right. Soldiers formed lines and marched into the woods, crashing through brush and stumbling over roots, to be met by volleys from an enemy they couldn't see.

On the Federal side, units shuttled from point to point as each new assault reached a crescendo and died away.

"Old Pete" Longstreet was no Hannibal, but he was a good orthodox general. He knew that whatever Bragg's numerical superiority might be, these piecemeal attacks would soon eliminate it. Longstreet formed his corps into a deep column—a giant battering ram—and waited to launch it at the Union center, where there was a stretch of open ground that would let his troops form the regular lines that orthodox tactics demanded.

Then fate rode into Union headquarters with a staff officer. The officer had passed a position held by Brannan's division. The division was in the forest and the officer couldn't see it. He reported that there was a gap south of Reynolds' division.

Rosecrans was busy trying to meet the attacks on the northern portion of his line.

"Tell General Wood to close upon General Reynolds," he said without thinking twice.

Unfortunately for the Union, Rosecrans had the tongue of a mule-skinner. Earlier that day, he had severely reprimanded Wood for a supposed delay in moving his troops. So, though Wood knew the order was absurd, he carried it out to the letter. He moved his division out of the line and into a position behind Reynolds' troops, leaving a real gap in the line.

"Human factors," including pique, jealousy and self-importance, were not confined to the Confederate Army. They were, and are, considerations in any enterprise, military or civilian. They are too often ignored in history.

Just as Wood opened the gap, Longstreet launched his battering ram. It came right through the hole in the Union line.

Longstreet's column suffered heavily from the fire on its flanks. If there were Union troops in front of it, the Confederate charge might have met the same fate as Pickett's effort of a few months before. In that age of transition from the smoothbore to the rifle, even a brilliant tactician like Lee could order a long frontal advance over an open field. While an individual smooth-bore's inaccuracy made it almost harmless at 100 yards, the rifle was deadly at half a mile.

Through sheer luck, Longstreet's troops charged into a void. After passing the gap, they struck the divisions of Sheridan and Davis in the flank as they were moving up to fill the hole Wood's withdrawal had opened. Even Phil Sheridan, later to become Grant's Marshal Ney in Virginia, couldn't organize an effective counterattack.

Rosecrans left his headquarters to try to stop the panic, only to find that his whole right wing was melting away. His troops were leaving him alone on the battlefield. He followed them to Rossville, far to the rear, where the stampede lost steam, and the soldiers milled around like exhausted cattle. At Rossville, Rosecrans heard that Thomas's corp, his left wing, was "holding like a rock." He resolved to return to the front and command what was left of the army. His chief of staff, James A. Garfield, had another idea. Garfield, using all the powers of persuasion that had already made him a leading political figure, told Rosecrans that the commanding general's place was at the key base, Chattanooga, where he could arrange retreat, defense or reinforcement. The chief of staff could go to the front and make sure that orders were carried out. Garfield was later elected President of the United States, partly because he claimed that he stayed with the army while Rosecrans deserted it.

His story was backed by another political figure, Charles A. Dana, New York newspaperman and assistant secretary of war. Dana had been sent to Rosecrans' headquarters by Secretary of War Edmund Stanton to spy on the general. He had been sleeping when the thunderbolt struck, and he woke up just in time to see the right wing disintegrating. Spotting a column of Union troops that had not retreated, he galloped over to its commander.

The troops were Wilder's Lightning Brigade. The reason they hadn't retreated was that Longstreet's corps was scattered in all directions and had paused for lunch before reorganizing to continue operations. Wilder saw an opportunity to cut through the Confederates and join Thomas' corps. The Spencer-armed horsemen might even wreck Longstreet's exposed headquarters. They would certainly give the Confederates a shock.

Wilder never attacked. Dana ordered Wilder's men to the rear. Although Dana was in a babbling panic, Wilder felt that a colonel couldn't argue with an assistant secretary of war.

Some other Union troops did reach Thomas. General John Brannan had collected the regiments of his shattered division and posted them on Snodgrass Hill, a high point making a right angle with Thomas' southern flank. Other regiments began to show up, and Thomas consolidated them into a new front, bending back from the right of his old line. It was hardly enough. The Unionists had been outnumbered before the battle began. Now half of them had been driven from the field.

Longstreet ordered charge after charge against Thomas' lines. To the men on the firing line, all the charges seemed to blend together. They felt that they were fighting a continuous stream of Confederates all afternoon.

Ammunition ran low. Yankee riflemen divided the cartridges of their dead comrades. Rifle barrels grew searing hot. Cartridges dropped to a few rounds a man. Some men ran out completely.

"Fix bayonets," said "Old Pap" Thomas. The men fixed bayonets and hurled back another Rebel wave.

One Confederate division—Bushrod Johnson's, which had headed Longstreet's column—managed to get around Thomas' position on Snodgrass Hill. Just at that time, a Union reserve force under General Gordon Granger arrived and hit the Confederates, driving them back. Granger's men brought extra ammunition, enough for a handful of cartridges for each man.

Night was falling. Longstreet asked Bragg to send him men from Polk's wing, so he could cut off the Yankee force. He was told that Polk's wing had already suffered so heavily there were no men available. Longstreet had one division in reserve. Instead of swinging it behind Thomas' corps, he sent it straight up the hill in a last, desperate assault. The Yankees met it with cold steel and broke the charge. The Confederates didn't charge again.

With the pressure off, Thomas led his men back to Rossville. Longstreet wanted to renew the attack at dawn, but Bragg said the Confederate army was too disorganized to proceed. The next day, Thomas marched into Chattanooga.

6

Longstreet railed at Bragg for his refusal to move, but the stern commanding general had reasons.

Chickamauga was a Confederate victory. But for the hard-faced martinet who loved his men in secret, it was a shocking victory. Bragg had suffered a total of 20,950 casualties—a third of his army. For the number of men and the time they fought, Chickamauga was one of the bloodiest battles in modern history. And most of the casualties were Confederate.

Bragg's army had lost more than even he realized. At Perryville, the Confederates had surprised a Union force but had been fought to a standstill. Bragg, unwilling to take further losses, had retreated. Much the same thing had happened at Stone's River. At Chickamauga, the Confederates had every advantage—surprise, position and overwhelming numbers. But they couldn't destroy even a fragment of the Union army. They had to watch the northerners (under Virginian George Thomas) march off almost unmolested at a time of their own choosing. To the southern riflemen, the Yankees seemed less an army than an elemental force.

The first inkling of how far Confederate morale had dropped came when Bragg tried to invest Chattanooga. The Yankees were hemmed in on all sides by mountains and the river—the very trap in which Rosecrans had tried to catch Bragg. The Unionists attempted to force supplies in over the mountains. The Confederates attacked the convoy, strung out over a narrow trail, but they were routed. They were not routed by Yankee infantry. They fled from a few stampeding mules. Thereafter, no attempt was made to close the "cracker line."

Reinforcements poured into Chattanooga, along with a new general. U. S. Grant had been appointed overall commander in the West, and he brought with him the troops that had taken Vicksburg. Rosecrans was dismissed from his command of the Army of the Cumberland. Until he issued his fatal order to Wood, Rosecrans had been the only Union general who always won against superior odds, but that one mistake was his undoing. In his place, Grant appointed George Thomas, now called "the Rock of Chickamauga."

Grant planned to break out of the trap with a feint to the south by "Fighting Joe" Hooker and a hammer blow to the north by his most trusted general, William T. Sherman. Hooker ran into a flooded river, and Sherman ran into unmapped ground held by Pat Cleburne. Both were stopped cold. The positions Bragg held compensated for quite a bit.

No position, though, could compensate for Confederate morale.

To relieve pressure on Sherman, Grant ordered Thomas to create a diversion by rushing the Confederate skirmishers at the base of Missionary Ridge, Bragg's central position.

Missionary Ridge is a rocky, wooded mountain that an unencumbered man, able to use both hands, can climb in half a day. Once they'd taken the Confederate outposts, the Federals were exposed to fire from the top of the ridge. Without orders, they began to climb.

Grant was furious and horrified. He muttered threats of court-martial as he watched the unplanned assault through a telescope. Up and up moved the little knots of men around regimental colors. It should have been a massacre. No one should have survived to reach the top.

But Bragg's men had had enough. They dropped their rifles, abandoned their cannons and dashed down the opposite slope. Bragg himself came out to rally them.

"Stop, men! Stop!" He shouted. "Here's your general!"

"Here's your mule!" the troops jeered with what had been a deadly insult in the Old Army.

The statistics for the battle around Chattanooga are eloquent. There were 56,359 Federals and 64,165 Confederates actually engaged in the fighting. Killed were: Federal, 753; Confederate, 359. There was no bloodbath at Chattanooga as there had been at Chickamauga. The Confederates didn't wait for heavy fighting.

"No satisfactory excuse can possibly be given for the shameful conduct of the troops on the left (of Missionary Ridge) for allowing their line to be penetrated," Bragg reported bitterly. "The position was one which ought to have been held with a line of skirmishers against any assaulting column."

7

No excuse, but perhaps an explanation.

"After Chickamauga," said Lieutenant General Hill, "the elan of the Southern soldier was never seen again."

Years later, at a reunion of the troops from both sides at Chickamauga, an ex-Confederate put it more succinctly: "You Yanks got into our inwards."

They stayed there. Except for the momentary repulse of Sherman's foolish frontal assault at Kenesaw Mountain, the Army of Tennessee never won another victory. Hood, in the Atlanta campaign, had local superiority several times, but he was never able to stop the Yankees. When he slipped out of Atlanta, his whole army couldn't take a single one of the outposts Sherman had left along the railroad. Confederate troops began deserting. Confederate morale sank until "Sherman's bummers" could drive off entrenched infantry by shouting, "We're Bill Sherman's raiders, and you'd better git!"

No soldiers had fought more valiantly than the riflemen of the Army of Tennessee. But every army's morale has a breaking point. Bragg's army reached its at Chickamauga. The victory that should have given a lift to the entire South had crushed the victorious army. Chattanooga merely proclaimed the fact to the world.

Chattanooga finished Bragg, just as Chickamauga finished Rosecrans. Rosecrans, though, was able to go back to his business and even be elected to Congress.

After that insult from the troops he cherished, Bragg was a broken man.

Nevertheless, he did his duty to the end. He served as military advisor to President Davis. Just before the last shot, he was called on for the most hopeless of tasks—to stop Sherman, leading what was probably the finest army ever fielded in North America, with a ragtag corporal's guard.

He failed, as anyone would have failed. The Confederate States of America disappeared, and President Davis was imprisoned. To many, the Confederacy became a romantic lost cause, but there was little sympathy for the man who saw the southern dream evaporate before his eyes.

When the war ended, Bragg wandered through the South, lonely and unsuccessful. He tried civil engineering, selling real estate and selling insurance. He failed at everything. When, 17 years after Chickamauga, he fell over dead on a Galveston street, Braxton Bragg possessed little but his flinty integrity.

10

1881, MAJUBA HILL (FIRST BOER WAR)

Rabble and Regulars

MRS. DE JAGER WAS UP EARLY THAT MORNING, AS A GOOD AFRIKANER housewife always was, even when her man was on commando. As she was putting wood in the stove, she looked out the window at Majuba Hill—a mountain, really, rising 6,000 feet above sea level. Someone had built a fire near the top of Majuba, a signal fire. Nobody would be able to see it from the Afrikaner *laagers:* they were on the wrong side of the mountain.

Mrs. de Jager left the stove and saddled her horse. She galloped around Majuba to the nearest laager. She shouted at the first sentry she saw: "English! There are English soldiers on Majuba!"

In his tent in that laager, or camp, Commandant General Piet Joubert was writing a report when a burgher burst into the tent. The man, like Joubert, wore an ordinary civilian suit. Only the bandolier of cartridges over his shoulder and the Westley Richards breech-loader in his hand indicated that he was part of an army. He did not salute.

"General, we have a report that there are English soldiers on Majuba Hill."

Joubert left his tent and squinted at the bulk of Majuba to the south, trying to see what was moving along its flat top. The sun was just rising among the hills, and Joubert couldn't be sure.

"It might be just mountain goats," he said.

"Did you ever see goats wearing red coats?"

The general looked around and saw his wife, who had accompanied him on the campaign. She had better eyes than he.

Other people in camp had good eyes, too. Men all around him were hitching up wagons and saddling horses. If the British were on Majuba, they'd be dropping shells on the camp any minute. The burghers broke

154

camp completely and were starting to move away, ignoring Joubert and his wife, who yelled at them to stay and drive the English off Majuba.

Then someone remarked that no shells were falling, although it was broad daylight. Joubert noticed their hesitation and called an impromptu council of war. Everybody attended—commandants, cornets, corporals and ordinary burghers, for all Transvaal men were equal, even on commando.

Joubert pointed out that the whole nation depended on them. If the *rooineks* (red necks) brought cannons up on Majuba, the Transvaal would be open to them. The British garrisons now under siege would be free. The recently reborn South African Republic would be finished.

It was true that they had no artillery and that they would be attacking who knows how many regular troops on top of a mountain. But God had always stood by those who feared Him. And it was obvious the British didn't. They had moved their troops up on the Sabbath. The burghers murmured approval of the general's words. Joubert asked for volunteers. And operations got under way for a most peculiar army, which was born of a most peculiar people.

2

Their ancestors were contemporaries of the first European settlers in what became the eastern United States. Holland had established a supply station at the southern tip of Africa. There, ships bound for the Indies could take on fresh vegetables to stave off scurvy. The settlers, unlike their kinsmen along the Hudson, encountered little resistance to their occupation. There were no ferocious warriors like the Iroquois here—just a few scattered families of Bushmen, living a primitive hunter-gatherer existence. The Dutch settlers spread out and developed a strong aversion to control by the Dutch East India Company.

Britain acquired the Cape settlement after the Napoleonic Wars. When, in 1834, the British ended slavery in their colonies, some of the Afrikaners moved deep into the interior, where no European power claimed the land. This brought them into conflict with the Bantu-speaking blacks who were moving south as the Afrikaners were moving north. The horse, the rifle and the wagon-ring laager, however, were advantages the black warriors couldn't overcome.

No sooner had the trekkers established themselves in the new land, than the British government claimed that British jurisdiction applied to all British subjects (which the crown considered the trekkers to be) south of the twenty-fifth latitude in Africa. In 1842, the British moved into the Afrikaner republic of Natal. The Afrikaners fought and were defeated. The more intransigent trekkers trekked farther. The British followed them. There was another battle, and the British annexed all the land between the Orange and the Vaal rivers.

Then in 1852, the British agreed to the *de facto* independence of the Afrikaners beyond the Vaal. Two years later, they extended independence to the burghers living between the Vaal and the Orange, who immediately organized the Orange Free State.

The Orange Free Staters prospered from the start, but it took the Transvaalers four years to even write a constitution. They called their state the South African Republic, but it could reasonably be described as anarchy tempered by bankruptcy.

In 1877, when the South African Republic could no longer pay its creditors, Britain annexed it. The British softened resistance by promising the Transvaalers autonomy. But instead of representative government, they got arrogant and high-handed officials.

In 1880, the government said a farmer named Bezuidenhout owed taxes of 27 pounds and five shillings. Bezuidenhout proved in court that he owed only 14 pounds. The magistrate then ordered the farmer to pay court costs, even though he had won and even though the government had initiated the case. The court costs, the magistrate said, were 13 pounds and five shillings.

A riot followed, and the British couldn't suppress it. The Transvaalers elected a new national assembly, appointed an executive triumvirate—Paul Kruger, Piet Joubert and Marthinus Pretorius—and organized commandos to seize garrison towns or invest their garrisons.

The British had already started a column of troops to reinforce the garrison at Pretoria. As the column approached a stream called Bronkhorst Spruit, an armed and mounted Afrikaner trotted up to its commander and gave him a message signed by the triumvirate. It told the commander, a colonel named Anstruther, that any farther advance would be an act of war. It gave him two minutes to decide what to do.

"I have orders to march to Pretoria, and that's what I intend to do," Anstruther told the messenger. The messenger galloped away. The British, waiting for a reply, took no security measures. Then they noticed burghers flitting through the scrub, moving toward their rear. The soldiers began to unsling their rifles. A long, ripping volley burst out of the brush, and soldiers began dropping all along the column. In a few minutes, 120 men, including Anstruther, were dead or wounded. The Afrikaners had two killed and five wounded.

3

Bronhorst Spruit introduced the British Army to a new way of war. The British had always considered the Afrikaners, or Boers as they called them (from the Dutch word for farmer), a rather feeble foe—not to be compared with the Zulus, for example. They didn't realize that the breech-loading rifle had changed the entire military picture in South Africa.

All over the world, the Industrial Revolution, joined to the new democratic impulses in society, was creating new ways of war. Nowhere in the world, though, was the result as bizarre as in South Africa. There, the breech-loading rifle, a product of the new technology, gave new life to a society that carried individual freedom to almost anarchic extremes but at the same time was a xenophobic, slave-holding theocracy. The breech-loader allowed the Afrikaners to make the most of their strange military system.

Neither the South African Republic nor the Orange Free State ever had a regular army. When danger threatened, all males between 16 and 60 in each locality gathered to form a commando. Each man brought his own rifle, ammunition and horse. They elected a leader, called a commandant. The commando subdivided itself into groups called field-cornetcies, each of which elected a field-cornet to lead it. The men in the field-cornetcies got together in still smaller groups called corporalships, which elected corporals to lead them.

Usually, the men joined the commando from their own town or district, but if they preferred, they could ride with another commando. There was no rule about the size of these units. Each commando could have anywhere from 1000 to a couple of hundred men. Field cornetcies usually had 150 to 200 men and corporalships around 25. But a popular field-cornet or corporal could have twice as many men as one of his peers.

Even after a man had joined a unit, he felt no compulsion to follow orders. God had made all men equal—at least, all white men who belonged to the Dutch Reformed Church. (The Afrikaner sincerely believed that all dark-skinned people were descendants of Ham, cursed by God to be "hewers of wood and drawers of water" for the rest of humanity.) The burgher participated in all councils of war. In combat, he went where he felt he could do the most good. An officer's only power of command was from the personal prestige he had built up by performance in the field. That was true even of a commandant general, who was elected when several commandos combined to form an army.

Such an army, totally without discipline by European or American standards, had serious and obvious weaknesses. It also had surprising strengths. The greatest weakness, from a foreign policy standpoint, was that an army operating on Afrikaner principles could take no action that did not promise a personal benefit for each individual bearing arms. No one in the army was paid, so the only personal benefit a soldier could see was defense of his home and his homeland. An Afrikaner army would be unlikely to hold out to the last bullet, nor would it launch any banzai charges for the sake of honor. The Afrikaner considered war an unpleasantly dangerous civic duty. He studiously avoided unnecessary risk.

On the other hand, the Afrikaner system insured that blithering idiots did not long command troops. If an Afrikaner army was a poor invasion tool, it was a magnificent instrument of defense. Every man was motivated, not by fear of his officers, but by the need to defend his home.

The breech-loading rifle brought out the military potential of the Afrikaner commando. With it and the hunting skills—marksmanship and the use of cover and concealment—that life on the veldt gave every Afrikaner man, the commando was truly formidable.

When the veldt hunters had used muzzle-loading rifles, they couldn't stand against regulars. The muzzle-loader was slow to load. Between shots, the burghers were vulnerable to the bayonets of the infantry and the lances and sabers of the cavalry. They couldn't take cover, either. A man had to stand up to load a muzzle-loader.

With the breech-loader, an Afrikaner could lie concealed and fire shot after shot. The breech-loader was fast. In U. S. Army tests in 1866, the Peabody rifle fired 17 aimed and 30 unaimed shots a minute. The Peabody was the direct ancestor of both the British Martini-Henry and the Westley Richards most of the Afrikaners carried. The later guns were even faster than the Peabody, because they got rid of the Peabody's manually-cocked hammer. Some Afrikaners carried repeaters like the Swiss Vetterli and the American Winchester. With any rifle, the average burgher was a superb marksman.

The average British soldier was not. He was, however, an experienced fighting man. From the end of the Napoleonic Wars to the beginning of World War I, there were only seven years in which British soldiers were not fighting in some part of the world.

At the time Anstruther's column was shot down, the British Army had just begun to reduce the term of enlistment from 20 to six years. The army remained the same size, but experience had shown that, especially in the tropical and mountainous regions where they had been fighting, younger men made better soldiers. In Africa at this time, the British Army had both long- and short-service units. All had far more experience than the Afrikaners.

4

General Sir George Pomeroy Colley, high commissioner for South Africa, learned of the disaster at Bronkhorst Spruit on Christmas Day. He gathered about 1,200 troops, including 120 sailors, six field pieces and a rocket battery and set out for the Transvaal. In the Drakensburg Mountains, the road climbed a pass called Laing's Nek. Across Laing's Nek and on either side of it for several miles, were Afrikaner trenches held by some 2,000 burghers. Commanding them was Piet Joubert, a general who truly believed that the British had been sent by the Devil to plague God's chosen people. Colley set up an entrenched camp on a hill called Mount Prospect and looked over the situation.

The British general decided to seize the high ground above the nek, where the Afrikaner left flank was located. Five companies of the Sixtieth Rifles were to provide fire support, while five companies of the Fifty-eighth Regiment would advance up the steep hill—so steep they would be unseen from the Boer trenches until they were almost at the top. While the infantry was holding the Afrikaners' attention, Colley's cavalry would trot up a gently sloping finger to the top of the ridge and hit the Boers in the flank.

Troubles began at once. The cavalry started too soon and headed in the wrong direction. It advanced too fast: most of the horses were blown from galloping uphill. Nevertheless, a few of the horsemen rode right up to the Afrikaner trenches. The burghers shot them down, but they were so shaken that even this misdirected charge might have routed them if it had been repeated. It was not repeated, however.

The infantry plodded on. Just below the point where the steep slope becomes almost level, they formed a line, stepped over the crest, fired a volley and charged with fixed bayonets. There was a drum-roll of firing from the Transvaaler trenches, only 40 yards away, and the men went down like dominoes. The soldiers fled. Of the 480 men who went up the ridge, 150 were left there. One sentence from a newspaper report of the battle shows how the officers fared: "Sub-lieutenant Jopp now commands the Fifty-eighth Regiment."

Colley took his men back to Prospect Mountain to think of something else.

While he was thinking, the British government launched a serious peace proposal. It would give the Transvaalers autonomy and also free them from debt. President Jan Brand of the neutral Orange Free State pleaded for a truce and offered to mediate. The belligerents signed no truce, but they refrained from overtly aggressive actions.

Colley wasn't happy about the prospects of peace. He couldn't wait to get at the Boers again to erase what he considered the shame of Laing's Nek. So when an Afrikaner force ambushed a British patrol on the road to Newcastle, the general personally led a 300-man reconnaissance force.

Colley's column had just reached a plateau called Schuin's Hoogte when it saw some mounted men a thousand yards away. The column's two nine-pounders fired. The shells burst behind the burghers. The Afrikaners galloped directly at the British. They got as far as a ravine under the plateau. There, screened from the British, they opened fire and moved around the perimeter of the plateau. Colley sent a messenger to Mount Prospect for reinforcements, but the Boers drove off the new troops and got reinforcements themselves. Before long, they had completely surrounded Schuin's Hoogte. The Afrikaners, under Nicholas Smit, Joubert's chief assistant, were about as numerous as Colley's force. They fired so fast, though, the British general thought there must be 900 of them. Their fire made his artillery useless and was slowly wiping out his infantry. Nightfall stopped the Boer fire, and torrential rain began.

Colley, fearing for his camp on Mount Prospect, decided to evacuate the plateau under cover of the storm. He had to abandon both his wounded and the guns, but he saw no other way to save the army. He succeeded only because Smit was so sure the British would not try to break out that he let his men scatter to seek shelter from the storm. Only half of the 300 British soldiers made it back to Prospect Mountain. Of Smit's 300, eight were killed and ten were wounded.

Meanwhile, in London, the British colonial secretary, the Earl of Kimberly, was sending a telegram to President Brand. It was the most conciliatory message so far. A few days later, Paul Kruger replied in a letter sent to Colley. For Kruger, the letter was incredibly conciliatory. Colley transmitted the message to London. Colley also sent a telegram of his own to London, protesting the government's giving in to the Boers. If they made peace now, he couldn't wipe out the stain of two defeats.

The British government made more concessions. Kimberly told Colley that if the Transvaalers gave a favorable reply within a reasonable time, the general should agree to a cessation of hostilities. To avoid the dread outbreak of peace, Colley construed "a reasonable time" to be 48 hours. Then he framed the time offer in a way that made Kimberly's peace offer sound like an ultimatum. Colley delivered the message to Smit, who told him that Kruger had been called away and could not even be reached within 48 hours. The Afrikaners assumed that the suspension of fighting would continue until Kruger's reply reached the British.

Instead, Colley resolved to move that night. He had little time now to erase his "shame." When Kruger replied, the war would undoubtedly end. It was now or never.

5

Late at night on February 22, Colley led 600 picked men in the direction of Majuba Hill. He had been observing the big, flat-topped mountain by telescope. He knew it was unoccupied. He was traveling light. Later, when he was established on Majuba, Colley planned to bring up the artillery, enfilade the Boer line and drive the enemy away from Laing's Nek.

Once they were on the mountain, the war was as good as won, Colley believed. One of the lessons he had learned at Laing's Nek was that troops on a mountain cannot be dislodged.

Colley detached some troops to guard his rear, but he led 365 to the top of Majuba, all groping their way by starlight. Colley ordered a signal fire to be built to inform the troops on Prospect Mountain that they had arrived safely. In the pre-dawn grayness, the British saw that the mountaintop resembled a triangular saucer. It had a definite rim around its edge, and it sloped toward its center. On the southeast and west edges, there were two knobs that the Bantu tribesmen called "the breasts of Majuba." A short distance in from the northern rim was a fold in the ground deep enough to hold a crouched man. Behind that was a low ridge. There were a couple of semi-detached knolls at the northwest and south corners. The western edge of the hill dropped off steeply. About the only good ascent on that side began at the southern corner, the point from which Colley's column began its climb. The southeastern edge was also precipitous except for a couple of spurs sloping down to lower ground. The one that provided the best approach passed directly under the southeastern "breast." To the northwest, the entire slope was gentler, and it took the form of a two-tiered terrace.

Colley's staff officers asked if he shouldn't have the troops entrench. He replied that they could rest from their climb; there was plenty of time to dig.

When the sun came up, the troops could look right down on the laagers where all the dumb Dutchmen were breaking camp. Breaking camp. They were running already! Messengers took the news to Colley, who received it with a beatific smile while cautioning his subordinates to be on guard all around the rim. He had already stationed troops on both breasts, which were called after the local commanders Macdonald's Kopje (Afrikaans for knoll) and Hay's Kopje. The naval contingent took the detached southern knoll, and a group of Highlanders was stationed on the northwest knoll, which became known as Gordons' Knoll.

6

After their council of war decided to fight, the Transvaalers sent commandos out to block any British reinforcements. Then 80 young men who had volunteered to storm the hill were divided into three tiny commandos. The older men ringed Majuba to provide fire support. Nicholas Smit directed the whole operation. The storming party rode their horses up the lower slopes. Then they dismounted and, one by one, began working their way up the slope, crawling through draws and darting from bush to bush. Eighty amateur soldiers, with neither training nor experience, without bayonets or artillery, were assaulting a hill held by four times their number of regulars. And a third of those regulars, the Gordon Highlanders, were hard-bitten long-service troops, fresh from victories in Afghanistan, where they had fought the best mountain troops in the world.

So far, though, the regulars didn't even feel threatened. They noticed that the Boers below were firing at them, but staying concealed as they fired, so there was little to shoot at. The Dutch were diabolically good shots, the troops noticed, so they kept themselves pretty well concealed, too. Every so often, a soldier would look over the rim, see nothing and duck back quickly. A second or two later, a score of big lead bullets would spatter on the rocks at the edge of the saucer.

Under cover of their comrades' fire and the broken ground of the mountainside, the storming parties had worked their way to the bottom of the second step in the two-tiered northeastern slope. Here they assembled, hidden from the defenders by the sharp drop-off. One group moved southeast along the terrace, hoping to reach the group creeping up the spur under Hay's Kopje. The other burghers moved northeast and took up positions directly under the Highlanders on Gordons' Knoll. They climbed up the slope of the knoll, then stopped. At a hand signal, all the burghers stood up with their rifles in firing position. For an instant, the startled Scots thought the men had risen out of the ground.

The burghers fired a volley that sounded like a single blast. All but two or three of the Highlanders fell dead. The survivors dashed madly for the main line.

From Gordons' Knoll, the Transvaal riflemen could command the whole northern part of the British defense perimeter. The nearest part of the main line was only 70 yards away. They began firing with deadly accuracy into the Highlanders who held this sector. In a few moments, 40 of the Scots were killed. The rest wavered and started to inch back. Suddenly, they turned and ran.

They ran right into the reserves that Colley, awakened from a nap, had ordered up to their support. The fleeing Gordons struck the reserves—Highlanders, Redcoats and Bluejackets—and carried them all to the rear in a panic. The Afrikaners spread out along the rim of the mountain and fired into the fleeing mass. The British finally halted behind the low ridge that ran beside the hollow traversing the mountaintop, but they scarcely dared to raise their heads. By screaming at them and threatening them with revolvers and swords, Colley and his officers got their forces spread across the mountaintop to link Macdonald's and Hay's Kopjes.

Hay's Kopje was now coming under fire from three directions—from the northern rim of the mountain, from the northeastern slope, along which a second party had infiltrated, and from the spur directly below, which the third party was climbing. The kopje might not hold out long.

Colley saw even more danger to the front. The Boers were moving in rushes of twos and threes, making for the hollow. He had expected that 20 riflemen on Macdonald's Kopje could enfilade any such advance, but a storm of fire from the western slope was keeping everyone on the kopje pinned down.

Lieutenant Ian Hamilton approached Colley and begged him to order a bayonet charge. The Boers were just out of reach; they had no bayonets, and the only thing they knew about those wicked steel points was that they wanted nothing to do with them.

Hamilton's advice might have changed the whole situation. But Colley remembered the bayonet charge at Laing's Nek. He told Hamilton they'd wait until the Boers stood up. Then they'd give the enemy a volley and charge.

The Afrikaners had no intention of standing up. They just kept infiltrating across the mountaintop and into the hollow. It became apparent that all the Boers at the base of the mountain were now following the storming party. Soon there would be 450 Boers on top of Majuba. They didn't stand up; they didn't charge. They just poured incredibly heavy rifle fire into the British positions.

The troops on Hay's Kopje found the fire on their outpost unbearable. They dashed for the main British line.

Thomas F. Carter, a newspaper correspondent who was there, reported that at this point "a piercing cry of terror . . . rose from the line or group of infantry below the kopje." The whole British line disintegrated. Soldiers ran to the rear and threw themselves down the slope, while the Afrikaners fired as fast as they could at the fleeing backs. Colley seemed dazed. He stood up and tried to rally the fleeing men, but a Transvaal bullet struck him in the forehead.

Of the 365 British troops on top of Majuba, the Transvaalers killed, captured or wounded 280. Only 24 of the 120 Highlanders who had climbed the hill came down unscathed. The British killed one Afrikaner and wounded five others.

7

If you consider only numbers, Majuba Hill doesn't amount to a decent skirmish. But if numbers or casualties are the only criterion, the T'ai Ping

Rebellion was a thousand times more important than the American Revolution. You have to consider the results.

Majuba's results were profound in both the immediate and distant futures.

The immediate result was that it gave Kruger the strength to demand and get virtually complete independence for the Transvaal.

More important, though, was its effect on the hearts of his people. A handful of poorly equipped, untrained farmers had defeated some of the most experienced troops in the world. And the regulars had held a strong defensive position. Majuba Hill was not Missionary Ridge. Its defenders, unlike the Confederates overlooking Chattanooga, were not in awe of their foes. Not one British regular would have dreamed that a handful of dumb Dutchmen would have dared to attack them.

To the pious and provincial Afrikaners, there was only one explanation. It was a miracle. It was dramatic proof of what they had always suspected— that this tiny band of Christians, beset by both the pagans of the bush and the pagans from Europe, were truly God's chosen people.

Majuba proved that only those who strictly followed the word of God as defined by the Dutch Reformed Church of South Africa ever since the seventeenth century were worthy of paradise. It proved that the British and most other *Uitlanders* were worthy of hell in the next life. And it proved that in this life, the black tribesmen of Africa were worthy of slavery. Whatever happened, the Afrikaner would stick to his principles, because he knew that God would provide. After Majuba, this attitude spread from the Transvaal to all Afrikaners.

It transformed the Transvaal. Under Kruger, the tiny trekker republic launched an aggressive foreign policy and a repressive domestic policy—at least toward the Uitlanders living in the country. The narrowness of Afrikaner egalitarianism was about to cause its first—but not its last— crisis. The Uitlanders protested to the British. Because gold had been discovered in the Transvaal, and because its leaders thirsted to "avenge Majuba," Britain needed little urging. The British were massing troops when the Transvaal, joined this time by the Orange Free State and imbued with the "Spirit of Majuba," invaded the Cape Colony and Natal.

The Second Boer War was an utter disaster for the South African republics. In open fighting, the Afrikaners almost always inflicted higher casualties than the British, but there was no way they could stand up to the whole British Empire. The British poured an enormous number of soldiers into South Africa, dotted the veldt with blockhouses and crisscrossed it with barbed wire. When the burghers became guerrillas, the British burned their homes, slaughtered their cattle and destroyed their crops. They built concentration camps and herded the families of Afrikaner guerrillas into them. At their peak, these camps held 117,000 persons.

Because the British neglected to provide either sanitation or medical care, the death rate from disease in these camps reached an average of 344 per 1,000 in October, 1901.

The Spirit of Majuba survived even that disastrous war. A hundred years after that fantastic victory over the British, the Spirit of Majuba, manifested in apartheid, was still troubling the modern Republic of South Africa.

11

The Bee's Sting

ARCHDUKE FRANZ FERDINAND WAS IN HIGH SPIRITS AS HIS CAR ROLLED through the streets of Sarajevo, capital of Bosnia. His beloved Sophie, the woman he had married over the objections of the emperor himself, was with him, two days before their fourteenth anniversary. The weather was delightful. Jubilant crowds lined the streets. The archducal couple were among Sophie's people—Slavs. These were the people whose cause Franz Ferdinand had championed against the arrogant Germans and haughty Hungarians who dominated the Empire of Austria-Hungary. Franz Ferdinand wanted to make the Dual Monarchy a triple monarchy. If that were impossible, he'd turn it into a federal monarchy—something that would give the Slavs an equal voice with the Germans and Hungarians. There were certainly as many of them as there were of the dominant nationalities, counting the North Slavs, like Sophie, a Czech, and the South Slavs, like these Bosnians. In Vienna, Franz Ferdinand's advocacy of the Slavs led to continual quarrels, but in Slavic territory, he felt safe.

He had no idea, as he smiled and waved to the cheering crowds, that he had only minutes to live. Nor did he suspect that his violent end would touch off one of history's supreme outbursts of violence—World War I.

2

Five teenage boys were later arrested for the murder. Behind them, though, was the most experienced master terrorist and regicide in Europe—an amiable and outgoing Serbian army officer named Dragutin Dimitrijević. Dimitrievic had been scheming and organizing all his life. In high school, his busy-ness earned him the nickname "Apis," Latin for bee. He continued plotting when he joined the army. Now all his plots aimed at increasing the honor and glory of Serbia. In 1901, he organized a conspiracy to kill the unpopular and pro-Austrian King Alexander of Serbia and his equally unpopular mate, Queen Draga.

This first attempt at regicide suffered from excessive complication. During the queen's birthday ball, a group of army officers were to take over the Belgrade power plant and turn off the electricity. The officers in the ballroom would then set fire to the curtains, and in the confusion, they would poison the king and queen. But the officers who were supposed to take over the power plant couldn't get through the guard. Further, both the king and the queen stayed away from the ball.

Dimitrijević's next attempt, in 1903, had a simple plan. The army officers would just rush into the palace and gun down the king and queen. Dimitrijević was the first man through the door. The single palace guard on duty opened fire. Dimitrijević killed the guard, but absorbed three bullets in the process. He fell flat in the palace foyer while his fellow conspirators scrambled through the royal residence seeking the monarchs. They eventually cornered them in a bedroom, shot them dead and threw their bodies into the garden. Then somebody remembered Dimitrijević, more dead than alive near the palace door.

Dimitrijević eventually recovered, but he carried those three bullets in his body for the rest of his life. The Serbian parliament passed a resolution thanking the young captain and calling him "the savior of the fatherland."

The assassination was about a crude as it could be, but the preparation for it showed the subtlety that later became Dimitrijević's trademark.

In days gone by, assassins simply assassinated their targets and tried to get away. In the twentieth century, though, public opinion, even in autocracies, was beginning to be a factor in government. King Alexander was unpopular, but Dimitrijević wanted more than mere unpopularity to justify his murder.

The conspirators started a whispering campaign against Queen Draga. She was supposed to be a loose woman; to be of illegitimate birth, even to be an enemy agent. No one has ever produced proof of any of these charges, but they served to inflame the public and prepare them to substitute the Karadjordjević family, descendants of a Serbian national hero, for the ruling Obrenović dynasty.

Those who met Dimitrijević in his office in the army general staff building came away impressed with his extraordinary intelligence and his pleasant manner. They were also impressed with his influence over officers of equal or superior rank.

"Although there was nothing despotic about him, his suggestions and wishes were treated as commands," wrote a friend, Milos Bogicević. "One saw him nowhere, yet one knew that he was doing everything."

In spite of his obvious courage, intelligence and personal magnetism, promotions came slowly to Dragutin Dimitrijević. One reason was his outspoken criticism of corruption and backwardness in the Serbian Army. More important, his superiors feared him. They didn't want to give him any more power than he had.

Dragutin Dimitrijević was one of the founders and the moving spirit of a secret organization named *Ujedinjenje ili Smert,* "Union or Death." It was better known as the Black Hand. In the Black Hand, Dimitrijević was known by his schoolboy nickname, Apis. Among the nine other members of the Black Hand's Central Executive Committee, anything following the words "Apis says . . ." were taken the same way medieval Japanese received whatever followed "the Shogun suggests . . ." At two or three levels below the Central Executive Committee, even Black Hand members never heard of Apis. The Black Hand itself was so secret that most Serbs and the Austrian intelligence services confused it with *Narodna Odbrana,* or National Defense, which at one time was a militant anti-Austrian organization. *Narodna Odbrana* remained anti-Austrian but had ceased to be militant by the eve of World War I.

Many people who had no connection with the Black Hand, though, knew there was something about Dimitrijević that demanded respect—and caution. Again, Bogicević: "There was no minister of war who did not have the feeling of having another, invisible minister next to him."

Even those who thought there was something sinister about the jolly officer had to admit that he was a good soldier and a patriot. Whenever he could, Dimitrijević traveled abroad, to places like Germany and Russia, so he could learn the latest developments in the military art. In addition to his general staff work, he was appointed Professor of Tactics at the Serbian military academy. Serbia's victories in the Balkan Wars of 1912 and 1913 owed much to strategy Dimitrijević had planned.

The first Balkan War began with a revolt against Turkey in Montenegro. Serbia, Greece and Bulgaria came to Montenegro's aid. The Serbs contributed both their regular army and Serbian-led guerrilla bands, recruited from mountain clansmen all over the Balkans. Just before open fighting broke out, Dimitrijević disguised himself as a simple partisan, made his way behind Turkish lines and got the most powerful Albanian chieftains to agree to cooperate with Serbia.

In Albania, Dimitrijević contracted a rare disease known as Maltese fever. He almost died when he returned to Serbia and was unable to take further part in the war.

After Dimitrijević's mission to Albania, even those who feared Apis knew that the country could not afford to waste the talent of Dragutin Dimitrijević. In June 1913, the Second Balkan War broke out. Bulgaria was opposed by its former allies. Just before it started, the government appointed Colonel Dragutin Dimitrijević head of Serbian Military Intelligence.

While the Bee was gathering intelligence about the Bulgarian enemy, he also busied himself setting up a highly professional spy network in Austria-Hungary. To Dimitrijević, Austria-Hungary was the chief obstacle to achieving the dream of his life—the union of all the South—or Yugo—Slavs in one country. The reason for that went back a generation.

3

In 1875, a revolt against Turkish rule had broken out in Bosnia. All the Balkan nations joined in, then Russia entered the war against Turkey. Turkish rule ended in most of the Balkans, but the Great Powers, unwilling to give Russia a free hand in the Balkans, allowed Austria to administer Bosnia and Herzegovina. In 1908, Austria-Hungary unilaterally annexed the two provinces. Russia, which had posed as the protector of all small Slavic nations, took no action to prevent the annexation. Just as the Balkan Slavs shook off one colonial master, and before they could unite in a great South Slavic nation, another alien government had stepped in.

To patriots like Dimitrijević, Serbia was the Yugo-Slavs' only hope. Serbia was the only independent Serbo-Croatian nation, and the Serbs were the most numerous of the Serbo-Croatians. Their brothers, the Croatians and the Slavic Moslems of Bosnia and Herzegovina, lived under the yoke of Austria-Hungary. They all spoke Serbo-Croatian, although the Croats used a Latin alphabet instead of the Cyrillic letters used by Serbs. There were differences of religion. Religion, though, did not look to Apis like a barrier to union. The Bee was a devout member of the Serbian Orthodox Church, but to him, faith and politics were entirely separate matters. Why wouldn't the Roman Catholic Croats or the Moslems want to be with their brothers? The union should also extend to their cousins who spoke slightly different languages, such as the Slavonians (already largely absorbed by the Croats), the Slovenians and the Montenegrans. About the only South Slavic group excluded (for the present) were the Bulgarians.

Serbia had fought two hard wars in two years. It was not ready for a third, especially against a giant like Austria-Hungary. Apis kept the cause alive by fomenting, planning and supplying anti-Austrian terrorism in Austria-occupied Slavic territories. At the same time, he was engaged in a behind-the-scenes struggle with Nikola Pasić, the Serbian prime minister.

Pasić wanted territories Serbia had conquered in the Balkan Wars placed under civilian control. The Army, Apis and the Black Hand wanted them governed by the military. Pasić, once a strong supporter of the Black Hand, began opposing the society at every turn. No slouch at intelligence himself, Pasić proved to be extremely well informed about Black Hand activities. Evidence indicates that his source in the organization was a certain Milan Čiganović, a fairly high-ranking Black Hander.

4

When, in 1913, a young journalist named Danilo Ilić came to Apis for support in a plot to kill Gen. Oskar Potiorek, governor of Bosnia, the Bee readily agreed. Ilić recruited a Moslem named Muhamed Mehmedbašić to kill Potiorek with a poisoned dagger. At the last moment, though, Mehmedbašić lost his nerve. Meanwhile, Apis had been studying the Bosnian situation. He learned that Archduke Franz Ferdinand, heir to the throne of Austria-Hungary, would come to Sarajevo June 28.

One thing that both Dimitrijević and Pasić agreed on was that the crowning of the pro-Slavic Franz Ferdinand was Serbia's greatest danger. As emperor, he might make life in Austria-Hungary so attractive to the Yugo-Slavs they'd have no desire to join in a Greater Serbia. In a rare moment of candor, Pasić once confided to an Italian friend that he had feared for the future of his country only once—when he first learned of the Austro-Hungarian heir-apparent's plans to make the Slavs the equals of the Germans and Hungarians.

Apis canceled all plans to murder Potiorek. The new target would be Franz Ferdinand.

The Bee recognized that war was a possibility if the Austrian heir were murdered. He discussed the project with his close associate, Col. Victor Artamonov, the Russian military attache. After conferring with Moscow, Artamonov assured Apis that Russia would back Serbia if Austria-Hungary attacked first. If that happened, the Bee believed, Austria would be checked. Dimitrijević knew almost everything that was going on in Serbia and the Slavic portions of Austria-Hungary. He had no idea, however, how the leaders of the great powers would react to a single incident in the Balkans. He was sure Russia's backing would give Serbia the insurance it needed.

Dimitrijević remembered Russia's inaction during the 1908 annexation. He knew that if the Austrian archduke were assassinated, there must be no credible evidence connecting the Serbian government with the assassins.

5

Apis selected Major Voja Tankosić, a fellow member of the Black Hand Central Executive Council, to organize the assassination. Tankosić began researching the denizens of Belgrade's coffee houses. At that period, coffee houses from Dublin to Moscow were the natural habitat of desperate, intelligent young men dedicated to overthrowing the existing order. Tankosić wanted native Bosnians who were willing to lay down their lives to advance the Yugo-Slav cause. He zeroed in on three men and learned all about them before anyone in the Black Hand approached them. All three were 19 years old, all three had advanced tuberculosis, all three were ardent nationalists and proven radicals, but none had any serious police record.

The men were Gavrilo Princip, Nedjelko Čabrinović and Trifko Grabež.

Gavrilo Princip began preaching nationalism while still in school in Bosnia. Before finishing high school, he came to Serbia and joined the Black Hand. He enlisted in the Black Hand's school for partisans, hoping to fight in the Balkan Wars. Because of his poor health and frail build, he had been rejected by the partisans. Tankosić cared little about the youth's physical condition. He was impressed with Princip's spirit. He saw a man much like himself or like Apis—intensely patriotic, brave, incorruptible, intelligent and utterly ruthless in advancing the cause of Greater Serbia. Of all the assassins, only Princip understood the real reason Franz Ferdinand had to be killed.

Nedjelko Čabrinović was less impressive. He was the son of an Austrian police spy, with whom he quarreled continually before coming to Serbia. He was a man of many enthusiasms. He had been, in turn, a socialist, an anarchist and a passionate nationalist. He also had a tendency to talk a little too much. He was never admitted to the Black Hand.

Trifko Grabež, son of a Serbian Orthodox priest, was expelled from school in Bosnia for striking a teacher. He came to Serbia to finish school and proved to be a brilliant student. He joined the Black Hand and spent most of his time in coffee shops talking with former partisan veterans of the Balkan Wars.

To direct the prospective assassins, Tankosić chose a native Bosnian member of the Black Hand. He was Milan Čiganović, the man who, unknown to Takosić or Apis, was passing Black Hand secrets to the prime minister, Pasić. Čiganović obtained weapons for his charges—Browning Model 1900 automatic pistols and Serbian Army hand grenades. The Browning 1900 was a Belgian-made gun that was extremely flat and easily concealed. Dimitrijević had purchased a quantity of them for just such occasions as this. The hand grenades, rectangular and rather flat, topped with a screw cap and looking like a whiskey flask, were also easily concealed. They appear to have been designed more for clandestine use than open warfare— grenades were not the major infantry weapon they were to become in just a few months. Čiganović led the young men to believe that they were part of a cache of weapons he had acquired during the Balkan Wars. Each man was also to receive a vial of cyanide to take after killing the archduke.

Using the Black Hand's "underground railway" between Serbia and Bosnia, Čiganović smuggled the three youths and their weapons back into Bosnia. In the meantime, Ilić, the journalist, who would join the assassination team, was taking steps to reduce the possibility that the assassination would be seen as a Serbian plot. He summoned Mehmedbašić, who had failed to kill Potiorek, and recruited two Sarajevo high school boys, Vaso Cubrilović and Cvijetko Popović. The three new recruits were not expected to add any necessary firepower. They were to draw attention from the fact that Princip, Čabrinović and Grabež were Bosnians of Serbian descent who had spent time in Serbia. The two boys, though of Serbian descent had spent all their lives in Sarajevo. Mehmedbašić was, of course, the token Moslem, the only representative of a group that made up around a third of Bosnia's population. Ilić sought, but couldn't find, a Croat candidate for the assassination team. Croats made up another third of the population.

6

Archduke Franz Ferdinand, the man whose death Apis was trying to arrange, was not unlike the Bee himself. He was honest, patriotic, brave and far from a fool. He had, almost single-handedly, modernized Austria-Hungary's creaking army. Largely through his efforts, too, Austria-Hungary had its first decent navy since Don John of Austria. He laughed at death threats, disliked bodyguards and forbade local authorities bringing in a military bodyguard while he was in Sarajevo.

Where he was unlike Apis was in his personality. The Bee could charm a mixed audience of snakes and birds. Franz Ferdinand repelled almost everyone. He was a man of violent hatreds. His most violent hatred was directed against one of the dominant peoples of the empire, the Hungarians. The Hungarians were trying to Magyarize all the Slavs in their half of the empire, a policy that made the archduke furious. The Hungarians returned his hatred with interest. He was easily the most unpopular man in Budapest.

He wasn't much more popular in Vienna. He once told his friend (he had a few), Conrad von Hotzendorf, "You think every man is an angel at the outset, and have unfortunate experiences afterwards. I regard everyone I meet for the first time as a scoundrel, and wait until he does something to justify a better opinion in my eyes." His personality approached the paranoid, but there was some reason for it.

Like the men waiting to kill him, he was afflicted with tuberculosis and almost died from it twice. The last time, while he waited at death's door, newspapers and influential Viennese were openly rejoicing at the prospect of his replacement as heir-apparent by his handsome and outgoing younger brother, Otto. Even while he was recovering, an active lobby at court was trying to persuade the emperor to have succession passed to Otto. A man of Franz Ferdinand's gargantuan pride did not take such behavior lightly.

Even more galling was the court's treatment of his wife. Countess Sophie Chotek von Chotkova und Wogum was a noble descended from some of the oldest noble houses of Europe, but she wasn't royal enough to marry a Hapsburg, certainly not a Hapsburg who would one day sit on the imperial throne. It took a year of agitation before Emperor Franz Joseph consented to his nephew marrying a mere countess. And then he could do it only if he renounced any right to the throne for his children. Sophie was not permitted to sit with her husband at state dinners or ride with him in imperial processions. While he led the grand march at formal balls, she had to bring up the rear of the procession. Although the emperor eventually raised her rank to duchess, she was still separated from her husband at all official functions.

In Sarajevo, far from the imperial court, Sophie sat next to Franz in a car borrowed from Count Franz Harrach, who rode in the front seat with the driver. Across from them in the jump seat sat General Potiorek, the governor of Bosnia. In the car ahead of them was the mayor of Sarajevo and local officials. The caravan was bound for the city hall.

The assassins were lined up along the Appel Quay. As the archducal car approached him, the first, Muhamed Mehmedbašić, felt a familiar watery feeling around the knees. He let the car go by. The next team member in line was gabby Nedjelko Čabrinović. Ilić hadn't trusted him enough to give him a pistol, so Čabrinović took out the grenade, unscrewed the top protecting a percussion cap and struck the cap against a lamp post to ignite the fuse. Then he threw the bomb right at the archduke's green-plumed helmet.

The exploding cap made a sharp pop, and the driver instinctively stepped on his accelerator. At the same time, the archduke saw something he took to be a brick flying toward Sophie. He threw up his arm and deflected the bomb, which landed on the street and exploded. A fragment scratched Sophie's cheek, and several bystanders were wounded. Franz Ferdinand stopped the car and got out. Satisfied that the wounded were receiving medical treatment, he got back into the car, and the whole caravan raced to the city hall.

Immediately after throwing his grenade, Čabrinović swallowed his cyanide and jumped into the river. The cyanide only made him sick, and the river was but a few inches deep. The police arrested him and took him away before the mob could lynch him.

The other conspirators had heard the explosion, saw the police dash to the site and assumed Čabrinović had fulfilled his mission. When they saw Franz Ferdinand ride by, they weren't prepared to act.

Fehim Effendi Čuričić, the mayor, was so worried about his speech of welcome he hadn't even heard the bomb. Franz Ferdinand ran up to him and shouted, "Mr. Mayor, one comes here for a visit and is received with bombs! It is outrageous!" Duchess Sophie calmed her royal husband, who recovered his manners. He listened politely to the mayor, who began, "Our hearts are filled with happiness over the most gracious visit with which Your Highnesses are pleased to honor our capital city of Sarajevo, and I consider myself happy that Your Highnesses can read in our faces the feelings of our love and devotion, of our unshakable loyalty. . . ." The archduke replied to the mayor's speech in a similar vein in both German and Serbo-Croatian.

Sophie went upstairs to attend a reception for her by the most prominent Moslem women in Sarajevo. She and Franz Ferdinand had been scheduled to visit a museum, but the archduke wanted to visit the bomb victims in the hospital. Potiorek said the best way to the hospital was back along the Appel Quay. No one told the drivers of the change in route.

Franz Ferdinand asked an officer to gather a guard of soldiers and drive Sophie directly to the governor's residence. He would visit the hospital alone, just in case there were any more assassins.

Sophie refused to leave her husband.

"As long as the archduke shows himself in public today I will not leave him," she said.

Downstairs, Franz Ferdinand himself begged Sophie to leave.

"No, Franz," she said. "I am going with you."

Count Harrach, the owner of the car, insisted on standing on the left running board to shield the archduke and duchess. Harrach assumed that any threat to the royal couple would come from the same direction as Čabrinović's bomb.

The mayor's car, again leading the procession, turned off the Appel Quay onto Franz Joseph Street, following the original route. Franz Ferdinand's car started to follow.

Potiorek leaned over the seat and screamed at the driver, "What's this? This is the wrong way! We're supposed to take the Appel Quay!"

The driver stopped right in front of Schiller's food store and tried to back up. On the right side of the car, standing in front of Schiller's, quite by accident, was Gavrilo Princip. He drew his Browning and fired twice at a range of about five feet. Potiorek was surprised at the weak reports from the pistol. He looked at the archduke and duchess and saw that both were sitting straight up. He thought the assassin had missed. He wanted to get out of the area. As the crowd surged around Princip, Potiorek told the driver to back up and drive across the river.

Franz Ferdinand tried to say something, and a stream of blood poured out of this mouth.

"For heaven's sake, what's happened to you?" Sophie cried. Then she slumped to the car floor. Princip had not missed her, either.

"Sophie dear! Sophie dear! Don't die! Stay alive for our children," the archduke sobbed.

Harrach asked the archduke if he was in pain.

"It is nothing," he whispered several times. Those were his last words.

Princip managed to swallow his cyanide, too, but as it did to Čabrinović, the poison merely made him sick. Eventually, the police were able to get enough information to arrest all of the assassins but Mehmedbašić. They knew the hand grenades had been manufactured in the Serbian state arsenal, but that was hardly conclusive proof of Serbian involvement. Ever since the Balkan Wars, with their extensive partisan activity, caches of government issue hand grenades, rifles and pistols were to be found all through the Balkans. In spite of intensive interrogation, there was little mention of Čiganović, a Bosnian in any case. The name of Dimitrijević, Serbia's chief of intelligence, never came up. Nor did the words Black Hand. Of the assassination team, only Ilić was over 20. He was sentenced to death, the others to life in prison. A number of accomplices were hanged with Ilić.

Austria sent Serbia an unacceptable ultimatum, and when Serbia refused, invaded the smaller country. Russia, thanks to Apis's discretion, saw the invasion as unjustified and declared war.

The result was not what Apis expected. World War I began.

7

World War II killed more non-combatants, but World War I resulted in the greatest slaughter of military personnel in history. In one day, for instance, July 1, 1916, the British Army suffered 60,000 casualties—more than the total casualties suffered by both sides in some wars lasting years. And the British were just one of more than a dozen combatant armies.

Serbia was destroyed. The Serbian government under Pasić and what was left of the Serbian army was forced into exile in Greece. Apis, of course, went with the army. In Greece, Pasić decided on a final solution to the Black Hand problem. He had Dimitrijević and his closest associates judicially murdered in 1916. Among them was Mehmedbašić, the failed assassin. Apis and the Black Hand were convicted of plotting to assassinate Alexander, the prince regent. All evidence indicates that Dimitrijević, a die-hard supporter of the House of Karadjordjević, was framed. Nevertheless, he accepted the sentence as necessary for the future of Serbia.

At the execution, a Serbian official related:

"When he saw me, Dimitrijević asked if I had come on behalf of the court, and when I replied that I had and that I was obliged to read the sentence to him, he said in a bantering tone: 'Understand what has happened to me; I assure you that I am innocent.' "

The official told Apis that "according to the law he was guilty, and he might find consolation in the certain knowledge that his death was necessary for the country and for public order. He seemed to be pleased to hear these words, for he said: 'I beg you, tell my friends that I do not regret dying under Serbian bullets, since it is for the welfare of Greater Serbia, which I hope with all my heart will soon come about. . . . Relations [with Pasić's government] had become too strained through my fault, and that is why it is necessary that I go.' "

Just before the volley was fired, Dragutin Dimitrijević cried, "Long live Greater Serbia!" then, "Long live Yugoslavia!"

8

Yugoslavia, the dream of the Bee, did come about. But the dream proved to be a nightmare.

Just 18 years after Dimitrijević died, there was a real plot to kill Prince—now King—Alexander. He was shot to death in a car during a state visit to France.

The assassin was a Croat. Things did not turn out as Dimitrijević and Princip expected. Croats did not want to be assimilated with Serbs, and Moslems didn't want to be dominated by either of them. Guerrilla bands, the Serbian Četniks and the Croatian Ustaše, conducted continual warfare against their rival ethnic groups. Communal warfare continued even after the Croats got a semi-autonomous state.

When Hitler invaded Yugoslavia in 1941, the South Slav kingdom should have been a tough nut to chew. Most of it was covered with high, rugged mountains crossed by a few very primitive roads. It was not blitzkrieg country.

Nevertheless, the Germans conquered the country in 11 days.

The government had stationed Croatian army units in Serbian areas and Serbian units in Croatian and Slovenian areas. When the invasion began, civilians cut the communication lines needed by army units of the rival ethnic group. Behind the Yugoslav lines, chaos reigned. Partisan warfare, Serb against Croat, blazed with new fury, while the Germans advanced almost unopposed.

During the German occupation, Ante Pavelić, the leader of the Ustaše, became head of a Nazi puppet state, and devoted his energies to killing Serbs. Draža Mihailović, a Serbian officer, built up a Četnik army, and fought the Germans, the Ustaše and Croat civilians, mostly the latter. He was eventually overcome and executed by the partisan army of Josip Broz, known as Tito, a Croat communist. After the war, the charismatic Tito was able to hold Yugoslavia together while he lived. After he died, Yugoslav ethnic violence again came to the attention of the world. Serbs gained control of the government, and Croatian terrorists began bombing planes and hijacking trains.

The breakup of the Soviet Union seemed to send a signal to the mutually hostile republics of Yugoslavia. Slovenia, Croatia and Bosnia-Herzegovina declared their independence of Serb-dominated Yugoslavia. The result is a savage war in which "ethnic cleansing," which used to be called genocide, is an acknowledged objective of the Serbian side.

There have been many fatal victories, but few have been so fatal in so many ways as Dimitrijević the Bee's victory in Sarajevo.

12

1916, DUBLIN (EASTER UPRISING)

Easter Egg

EASTER MONDAY WAS WARM AND SUNNY, UNUSUAL FOR APRIL 24 IN DUBLIN. It had rained for 13 of the last 14 days, so there was a fair number of people strolling on Sackville Street, enjoying the holiday and the fine weather.

The Irish Volunteers and the Citizen Army marching down the street excited no interest. They were always marching. They seemed to think that marching would somehow intimidate the English. The sight of them hardly intimidated the strollers. Only half of the marchers had uniforms, either the dark green of the Citizen Army or the light green of the Volunteers. They carried old rifles—some looked as if they'd been looted from museums—cheap shotguns, pistols and revolvers, pikes and even pickaxes. Some marchers were women.

The paraders may have had some effect on the British, many Dubliners allowed. Conscription had not yet come to Ireland. That old whale, John Redmond, chairman of the Irish party, had urged the Volunteers to join the British Army, but few had done so. Indeed, many a boy had joined the Volunteers in the hope of avoiding conscription, should it come. In theory, the Volunteers had formed to defend Ireland in case of invasion, so service with them might count as service with the armed forces. The Ulster Volunteers, which had been founded first by that renegade Dubliner, Sir Edward Carson, had the same theoretical reason for being. Both, though, really existed to persuade Mother England to see one side or the other of the Home Rule question, using the only argument Mother seemed able to understand.

Carson's men, the Dubliners knew, had modern arms—Colt-Browning and Maxim machineguns, Mannlicher and Mauser rifles—that Carson's friends in the military and police had helped him smuggle in. The Irish

Volunteers had only Howth Mausers—single shot rifles that fired a great, heavy lead bullet with a cloud of smoke. The Volunteers said they had been made in 1871 for the German Army and had become obsolete 13 years later. The Kaiser, that old fox, had been about to turn them into horseshoe nails when the Irish Volunteers came along and offered him good money for them. Not even the most benighted Englishman could take the Volunteers seriously, the average Dubliner thought.

The Citizen Army might be different, although it was only a tiny force. It might be different because it belonged to James Connolly. Connolly, head of the transport workers' union, was a violent Marxist socialist. In 1913, he and James Larkin organized a crippling strike that middle-class Dubliners still remembered with a shudder.

It was Connolly himself, a heavyset man with a bushy mustache, who was leading the column, along with that nationalist poet, Padraic Pearse. Suddenly Connolly shouted, "Left turn. The GPO—CHARGE!" The ragtag army dashed under the Ionic portico of the General Post Office and into the building. Minutes later, two flags fluttered over the portico. One, a green flag with a gold harp, was like the traditional flag of Ireland (a nation that never had an official flag) except for one thing: on it, in white and gold letters, were the words "Irish Republic." The other flag was new—a green, white and orange tricolor.

The strollers collected around the post office building to see what would happen next. Connolly came out with Pearse, a big, good-looking man with a squint in one eye. Pearse was the founder and headmaster of a nationalist school, a poet, a lawyer and a leading orator. He read from a paper proclaiming an Irish republic. For a speaker of his reputation, it was a disappointing performance, but perhaps he was reacting to the crowd's reaction. One or two persons had given a faint cheer; several had smiled; most just drifted away.

A few blocks away, some armed men began building a barricade. They dragged rolls of newsprint from the *Irish Times* into the street and wedged furniture and merchandise from nearby stores against it. Someone broke the window of Keating's cycle shop, and the barricade builders, a detail of Volunteers, began fitting bicycles and motorcycles into the barrier.

"Jesus, isn't that a lovely bike?" a bystander asked.

"The bloody idiots are throwing it away," another said.

A boy dashed into the street, grabbed the bike and pedaled away. The onlookers surged forward to help themselves, pushing back the Volunteers. A couple of insurgents fired into the air. The crowd moved back sullenly.

It was not an auspicious beginning for what was supposed to be a rising of the Irish people. Perhaps the times were not right.

2

There was a time, after the Tudors began the conquest of Ireland and Cromwell finished the job, when an Irish Catholic could own no land and no weapons, could not practice his religion or educate his children, could do nothing for a living except slave for an English landlord. It was a long time—centuries long.

There were risings, of course. The Irish joined James II when he was ousted from England. They rose again—Catholics in Wexford and Mayo, Protestants in Ulster—in 1798. These were the big risings, and the English put them down savagely. Hanging, drawing and quartering, which involved disembowling the living victim, was a favorite treatment for captured rebels, although burning alive was also used. Flogging every man in a village, sometimes until the victim died, was the usual way of gathering information about rebel movements. Another method, introduced in 1798, was the pitch cap. A mixture of pitch and gunpowder was slathered on the prisoner's head and ignited. The prisoner was usually too busy screaming to give any information before he died, but his example encouraged others to tell what they knew.

Because the Irish Catholics had no weapons and no experience in using any they were given, the risings caused no grave problems for the British. During what was known in England as "the Glorious Revolution," the French war minister, Louvois, summed up the situation in Ireland for Louis XIV: "Whatever good intentions the Irish may have for the preservation of their country and their religion, if they fight with three-foot sticks against the troops of the Prince of Orange, which will have swords and muskets, they will soon be killed or forced to fly."

"There never was a country in which poverty exists in so great a degree," said the Duke of Wellington about his native land. Although a reactionary of legendary proportions, Wellington was appalled by the conditions he saw in Ireland. Ireland presented, according to a nineteenth century visitor "the extraordinary spectacle of a country in which wages and employment, practically speaking, did not exist. There were no industries; there were very few towns; there were almost no farms large enough to employ labour . . . greens were unknown, bread was unknown, ovens were unknown. The butcher, the baker, the grocer, did not exist; tea, candles and coal were unheard of."

No Irish Catholic could own any property worth more than five pounds. If a Protestant coveted a Catholic's horse, he could buy it for five pounds regardless of the real value of the animal or whether its owner even wanted to sell it.

Progress came slowly to Ireland. Until 1782, Catholic clergymen were forbidden under pain of death to set foot in Ireland. In the late eighteenth century, Irish Protestants began to chafe under British commercial restrictions. Seeking allies, the Irish Parliament gave Catholics the right to vote, but not to hold office. Britain abolished the Irish Parliament in the Act of Union after putting down the rising of '98. The British Parliament gradually gave Catholics the right to maintain schools, join the professions and vote at parliamentary elections. They eventually got the right to hold some minor offices, but they couldn't sit in Parliament until 1829.

In the 1820s, Daniel O'Connell, a Catholic lawyer, organized the tenant farmers to vote for candidates he thought would help Ireland, instead of the candidates favored by their landlords. In 1828, the small farmers of County Clare elected O'Connell to Parliament, even though he could not take his seat. The British government responded to the pressure by passing the Catholic Emancipation Act of 1829. The emancipation of most of Ireland's citizens was a giant step forward, but centuries of oppression had left the country miserably poor.

Between 1779 and 1841 the population of Ireland increased 172 percent. Families tried to exist on plots of an acre or a half acre for which they paid an exorbitant rent and were liable to eviction without notice. The only crop that could support such a densely packed agricultural population was the potato.

In 1846 and again in 1848, a blight ruined the potato crop. An estimated million and a half persons starved to death. Another million emigrated, mostly to the United States. A steady stream of emigrants followed them. For a long time, these emigrants remained poor by American standards but were rich by Irish standards. From the beginning they were able to finance revolutionary movements in Ireland. In the 1880s, a British home secretary complained that a portion of the perennially rebellious Irish nation was "out of reach."

Charles Stewart Parnell, a Protestant politician with a Catholic constituency, assumed leadership of the Irish MPs. With the aid of his associate, Michael Davitt, he was able to change the vicious land tenure laws and was almost able to get "home rule"—an Irish parliament independent of the British but owing allegiance to the crown. Because of a domestic scandal, though, Parnell fell from power and home rule fell with him.

There was a new rising—the Fenian revolt—which the British put down with ease. The government did, however, take the economic handcuffs off Ireland and encourage British investment in the island. A middle class began to develop, and to British politicians, it looked as if Ireland had finally been pacified. The Irish, that is, would accept the idea that they were part of the same country as the English.

It didn't quite work that way. The rising middle class spawned a literary revival which became ardently nationalistic. Meanwhile, poverty, especially in the west, remained grinding by any but Irish standards, and Dublin wage earners remained among the most poorly paid in Europe.

3

Instead of assimilating, many of the middle-class intelligentsia—poets like Padraic Pearse, Joseph Plunkett and Thomas MacDonagh and professors like Eoin MacNeill and Eamon de Valera—made common cause with labor leaders like James Connolly. Revolutionary organizations began to grow.

Revolutionists were a minority, though. Most Irish followed John Redmond, chairman of the Irish Party, which included all of the Irish contingent in Parliament. Redmond got a home rule bill through the House of Commons twice, only to have it killed by the House of Lords. The third time, it would have become law no matter what the Lords did. At the last minute, Sir Edward Carson stepped out of the wings with his armed Ulster Volunteers and threatened civil war if home rule became law.

Prime Minister Herbert Asquith lost his nerve. He decided to introduce a new bill, amended to exclude six of the nine counties of Ulster. Redmond said he and the Irish MPs would vote against it and bring down the liberal government. In the meantime, an unknown man named Gavrilo Princip shot and killed a well-known man named Archduke Franz Ferdinand.

The government was deciding what to do next when an Irish nationalist named Conor O'Brien and an English convert to Irish nationalism named Erskine Childers landed a load of German rifles at Howth, a Dublin suburb. The rifles, single-shot, black powder-burning Model 1871 Mausers, were a poor answer to Carson's arsenal. The Howth shipment, though, was the only substantial number of weapons the nationalists ever got. Two days later, July 28, Austria-Hungary declared war on Serbia.

Asquith finally proposed to enact a home rule bill at once, but coupled with a suspensory act that would prevent it from coming into force until the end of the war. Then Parliament would have the opportunity of "altering, modifying or qualifying its provision in such a way as to secure the general consent of Ireland and of the United Kingdom."

Redmond caved in. He decided that Ireland's best chance was in demonstrating amity with Britain. He urged the Irish Volunteers to enlist in the British Army and "account yourselves as men, not only in Ireland itself, but wherever the firing line extends, in defense of right, of freedom, and of religion." Few did.

The very last thing most Volunteers wanted to do was fight for England. They had enlisted to fight England. As a group, they were far more militant nationalists than the majority of the Irish people. To keep peace with the Irish Party, they had admitted Redmond's nominees to their ruling council. Even before Redmond had made his recruiting speech, though, a militant minority of Volunteers perceived that the chairman was getting too close to England for their liking. They split off from the main body. The main body, known as the National Volunteers, began to lose membership. The dissidents retained the name Irish Volunteers and elected Eoin MacNeill chairman and Michael O'Rahilly (known as The O'Rahilly, because he was the chief of a County Kerry clan) treasurer and Thomas MacDonagh director of training.

The Redmondites and the English denounced MacNeill and O'Rahilly as radicals, but they were actually front men for the real radicals, a clique headed by Padraic Pearse, director of military organization. Pearse's group, which eventually included MacDonagh, belonged to the Irish Republican Brotherhood, a secret society. No one outside of the top circles of the IRB knew the extent to which it had infiltrated the Volunteers. The typical IRB member knew only the IRB people in his own cell or "circle."

This sort of organization foiled that bane of Irish rebels, the informer. It led, however, to other problems, which became apparent shortly before Easter, 1916.

James Connolly was not a member of the IRB, although he was even more impatient than they for a republic. His Irish Citizen Army, formed to protect strikers from the Dublin police, was armed with a variety of weapons, and Connolly had begun training his troops in urban warfare. A man like Connolly, controlling a private army, would be invaluable to the IRB. Outside of the organization, he was a menace. By early 1916, his editorials in the *Workers' Republic* had become so belligerent that the IRB chiefs, Thomas Clarke and Sean MacDiarmida, were afraid Connolly would stage a premature uprising with his miniscule Citizen Army.

On January 19, three IRB men kidnapped Connolly and brought him to the brotherhood's supreme council. There Connolly learned that Clarke had been arranging for arms from Germany through Sir Roger Casement, an Ulster Protestant but an ardent nationalist. When the arms arrived, MacDiarmida said, Irish Volunteers all over the country would rise, and he hoped that the Citizen Army would rise, too. Connolly said they would.

The IRB leaders told Connolly their secrets, but they were so obsessed with security that they didn't tell MacNeill or The O'Rahilly that the organization they headed was about to begin a rebellion.

Pearse had chosen Easter Sunday as the day for uprising. With Mac-Neill's approval, he set Easter as the day for nationwide maneuvers. Orally, Pearse told brigade commandants who were IRB members what they should do when maneuvers began.

Word arrived at the IRB supreme council that Casement and the guns would arrive on Good Friday. Pearse had second thoughts. If the arms arrived too early, the British might find them and be warned of the impending uprising. He asked that the Germans delay their arrival until Easter. The request was garbled, and there was no way to correct it, because the German freighter had no radio and was in parts unknown evading the British blockade. And Pearse neglected the elementary precaution of having people on the beach in case the ship arrived early. To further complicate matters, the British had broken the German code. Casement got off a submarine and was arrested the next day because there was no one to take him to a safe house. The freighter, like Casement, arrived at its destination the night of Holy Thursday. But there was no sign of life on shore, and the ship's captain knew the British patrols had spotted him and would suspect that the supposedly disabled Norwegian freighter was up to something. He tried to run for the open sea, but was intercepted and scuttled his ship. Instead of reaching the rebels, the 20,000 captured Russian rifles and ten machineguns went to the bottom of the sea.

The same night the German submarine arrived, Bulmer Hobson, an IRB member who had not been informed of the plot, learned that secret orders had been passed. He told MacNeill, and they got Pearse out of bed and demanded to know what was going on. Pearse admitted that orders had been passed to begin an insurrection. MacNeill immediately issued countermanding orders. Shortly after that, some IRB men kidnapped Hobson to keep him out of trouble until the rising.

On Good Friday, Pearse, MacDonagh and MacDiarmida told MacNeill about the arms shipment. They also showed him a forged document ordering crown forces to disarm the Volunteers and to arrest their leaders as well as the Catholic archbishop of Dublin.

Saturday evening, The O'Rahilly learned about Casement's arrest and the loss of the weapons. Further, he had proof that the "Castle document" was a forgery. He also heard of Hobson's kidnapping and was furious. He confronted Pearse with a drawn revolver and told the Volunteer leader that anyone who planned to kidnap him had better be a faster shot. Pearse said nobody planned to kidnap The O'Rahilly and tried to talk him into joining the rising.

O'Rahilly refused and went to see MacNeill. Confronted with the facts, MacNeill joined O'Rahilly in again confronting Pearse.

Pearse refused to see O'Rahilly (he remembered the revolver), and he told MacNeill, "We've used your name and your influence for all they're worth. Now we don't need you anymore. It's no use your trying to stop us. Our plans are laid, and they'll be carried out."

In 1798, they would have been. In 1916, all MacNeill had to do was find a telephone and some automobiles. He sent out the countermanding order: "Volunteers have been completely deceived. All orders for action are hereby canceled, and on no account will any action be taken." The O'Rahilly, a pioneer automobilist (he had built his own car from scratch) carried the orders through six counties from 9 p.m. to 1 a.m. MacNeill followed up with a newspaper notice: "Owing to the very critical position, all orders given to the Irish Volunteers for tomorrow, Easter Sunday, are hereby rescinded."

Sunday, the insurrectionist leaders in Dublin met and agreed to begin the rebellion Monday at noon, when, they hoped, orders countermanding the countermanding orders would have been distributed.

The Dublin rebels voted that an Irish republic was now in existence and that they constituted the Irish Republican Army. They elected Pearse president of the republic and commander-in-chief of the army.

None of these men was stupid. They all knew that the odds against them, never good, were now almost impossible. But they were eager to fight.

Some had brooded so long on the centuries of injustice Ireland had suffered that they could think of nothing but driving the occupier out.

Others, like the practical mathematician, Eamon de Valera, saw that after Casement's arrest proving that a rebellion was in the works, the British would crush the Volunteers. Fighting was their only option.

Pearse, like his fellow poets, MacDonagh and Joseph Mary Plunkett, was caught up in the idea that a "blood sacrifice" was necessary to free Ireland. The poets had meditated on the old Catholic proverb: "The blood of the martyrs was the seed of the Church." Even the hard-boiled Connolly, who had not seen the inside of a church in years, shared this belief.

Marching out of Liberty Hall, his headquarters, on the way to the General Post Office, Connolly stopped to greet an old friend. In a half-whisper, he said, "Bill, we're going out to be slaughtered."

"Is there no hope at all?"

"None whatever," Connolly said with a cheerful smile. He slapped his friend on the shoulder and marched on.

As Connolly's column prepared to march up the street, a car pulled in behind it. Looking back, the rebels saw the smiling, mustached face of The O'Rahilly, who had worked so hard to prevent the rising. He was leaving an inherited fortune, a successful business and a devoted family to join a rebellion he considered hopeless. His car was loaded with rifles.

"Because I helped to wind the clock [he was one of the founders of the Volunteers]" he was quoted later, "I came to hear it strike." The truth was that neither the poets nor the socialist believed as firmly as this well-to-do engineer in the blood of martyrs.

4

The rebels planned to begin by blowing up the powder magazine in Phoenix Park at high noon. Then they'd march from battalion rallying points to seize the strongpoints north and south of the River Liffey, establishing a fortified ring in the center of the city.

The headquarters group would take the GPO and the surrounding buildings. The First Battalion, under Edward Daly, would occupy the Four Courts of Justice, a few blocks up the Liffey from headquarters, and set up barricades on Cabra and North Circular roads, in the northern part of the city. South of the river, due south of Daly's area, MacDonagh's Second Battalion would take over Jacobs' Biscuit Factory and its surroundings. The Third Battalion, under de Valera, would occupy the Westland Row railroad station, Boland's Bakery and houses near the Beggar's Bush military barracks, in the southeast part of Dublin. Between the Second and Third battalions, on St. Stephen's Green, would be the Citizen Army under Michael Mallin. Here, too, would be Countess Constance Markievicz, a member of the Irish ascendancy who had supported the Transport Workers' strike and become a commandant in the Citizen Army. On the southwest corner of the city, Eamonn Ceannt's Fourth Battalion would seize the South Dublin Union, a combination poorhouse and madhouse the size of a village.

The plan had been drawn up by Joseph Plunkett, a wealthy poet of aristocratic lineage and no military experience. One of the strong points was to be St. Stephen's Green, a flat park overlooked by tall buildings on all sides. Each of the strong points was vulnerable to being cut off from the others. The rebels would surround, but not capture Dublin Castle, the highly vulnerable and weakly guarded seat of British rule in Ireland. And the ring of rebel strong points would be immediately under siege by the six military bases on the fringes of Dublin. (The Irish notion of their capital as an occupied city was not entirely fanciful.)

Among the plan's many flaws was that the selected strongpoints did not completely block off the center of the city. As it turned out, the battalion commanders had barely enough men to hold their assigned positions. De

Valera, for instance, was supposed to hold several square miles straddling a canal and including a railroad station and a large bakery with only 120 men.

If the rising had happened as planned, there would have been more men in Dublin holding the British in place while the main Volunteer force rallied across the Shannon and drove east toward Dublin. As it turned out, there was no main force, and only a small minority of the Dublin Volunteers showed up. If Pearse, Clarke and MacDiarmida had not tried to deceive MacNeill, it might have been different. There would not have been the blizzard of orders and countermanding orders that left all Volunteers confused. If the leaders of the rebellion had exercised a little common sense and prepared to receive the arms shipment early, there might have been a main Volunteer force in the west. Outside of Dublin, there was no rising worth considering. In Dublin, Pearse's Irish Republican Army included about a thousand Volunteers, one hundred fifty Citizen Army troops, a score or two of Countess Markievicz's combat-trained Boy Scouts (the *Fianna na hEireann*), and fifty to seventy-five Irishmen who left England to avoid conscription. Before the end of the rising, some 600 more Volunteers joined in. On Easter Monday, the British forces outnumbered the rebels two to one, with almost 2,500 troops. A week later, there were many times more British than insurrectionists.

5

The lack of manpower brought serious trouble at the very beginning of the rising. IRA men cut the cables to Belfast and Britain and destroyed the Castle's private lines to London and strategic centers in Ireland. But the men who were to destroy the vault containing local cables failed to show up.

Connolly then detailed a party to capture the telephone exchange itself. In those days, all connections were made by operators. By occupying the exchange, the rebels would control the city's communications. As the IRA men approached the telephone building, an old woman leaned out of a window and shouted, "Go back, boys. Go back! The place is crammed with military!"

The men went back to the General Post Office. Later the military actually did occupy the exchange.

As a result of these fumbles, the British Army enjoyed instant communication with any part of the city, while the IRA, unable to place a call through the government-controlled exchange, had to use foot couriers.

The Phoenix Park explosion didn't work out as planned, either. An all-battalions task force led by Garry Holohan got into the fort, wounding and disarming a sentry who tried to resist. Inside, the rebels found a few soldiers and the family of the fort's commander, a Colonel Playfair, who was on duty in France. Holohan gave the civilians six minutes to leave, saying he was going to blow up the fort. Then he learned that the acting commander had taken the keys to the powder magazine with him to the horse races. Holohan placed his gelignite against the wall of the explosive storeroom, lighted the fuse and escorted the disarmed soldiers out of the fort, telling them to "clear off." They needed no urging. The IRA men started back to their own unit rallying spots.

Holohan, pedaling his bike, saw Playfair's 17-year-old son running down the street. For some reason, he decided that the boy had to be stopped, although young Playfair could tell no one anything that all Dublin wouldn't know in a minute or so when the charge went off. Holohan rode after the boy, who sprinted to a nearby house. Holohan shot the boy dead before the terrified eyes of the woman of the house.

Then the charge went off with a dull thud. It hadn't detonated the stored explosives.

A few minutes later, there was another killing on St. Stephen's Green. Mallin's Citizen Army troops had occupied the park and put the few British servicemen present into a comfortable sort of captivity. Then Constable Michael Lahiff tried to enter the park. CA men told him to go away, but Lahiff pushed in. Connie Markievicz aimed her huge Mauser 1896 pistol at him and fired. Lahiff went down with three bullets in his chest. The countess squealed like a delighted school girl. "I shot him! I shot him!" she cried.

Mallin detailed men to occupy buildings in the neighborhood. He made no attempt, though, to take over the massive Shelbourne Hotel overlooking the Green.

Captain Sean Connolly (unrelated to James) led one Citizen Army company to establish outposts north of the Green and adjoining the area held by Thomas MacDonagh's Volunteer Second Battalion. Connolly decided to make the Dublin City Hall his main base, and he detailed groups to occupy nearby stores. He sent a squad under Thomas Kain to the Castle, which almost adjoins the City Hall. The object appears to have been to prevent soldiers at the entrance to the Castle from giving the alarm before Connolly had established his positions.

Kain's men shot a policeman who attempted to close the gates of the Castle then rushed in. An army sentry fired a shot. The rebels threw a homemade grenade into the guardhouse. The explosion stunned the guards, but as the bomb was made of gelignite in a tin can, there was no fragmentation and no serious injury. The rebels tied up the guards. Then they hesitated. After the explosion, hundreds of soldiers would be pouring out at any moment. The insurgents dashed back into the City Hall.

As a matter of fact, there were only two officers and 25 enlisted men in the whole Castle. Connolly could easily have captured Sir Matthew Nathan, undersecretary for Ireland and, at that moment, Britain's top administrator on the island. He could also have netted Major Ivor Price, the army's chief of intelligence, and A. H. Norway, head of the post office.

The first serious military engagement took place on the bank of the River Liffey near the Four Courts of Justice. A party of cavalry, escorting five carts of rifles and grenades, rode along the quays, past Liberty Hall, Connolly's union headquarters, the GPO outposts, and right into a barricade Daly's men were building. The rebels fired in panic, and several troopers were knocked off their horses. The soldiers scattered; some tried to find refuge at the Four Courts, but another rebel volley drove them away. One soldier fired and hit a little girl, killing her instantly. Finally, the cavalry holed up in a nearby building and unloaded their carts. The rebels made no attempt to follow up and capture the weapons.

Immediately after the attack on the Castle, the Dublin Metropolitan Police telephoned military headquarters. Colonel H. V. Cowan, assistant adjutant general, began calling up the soldiers.

A troop of lancers arrived at the head of Sackville Street, looking down on the GPO area. All that was needed was to give the rabble a look at real soldiers, they seemed to think. They trotted down the street, looking neither right nor left, backs as straight as their lances. One hundred forty-one years before, William Howe had exactly the same idea as the lancers.

Unlike the militia on Breed's Hill, few of the IRA men had ever fired a weapon before. Someone got nervous and fired too soon. The other volunteers fired. Four troopers were killed, and the rest fled. Their performance confirmed the Volunteers belief that this was the way regulars would fight: charge the rebel positions with cold steel.

There was one other tragicomic incident before the battle settled down to grim slaughter. A group of Irish veterans of the British Army, mostly well-to-do professional men, had formed a home guard unit that was really a combination drill team and social club. From the legend Georgius Rex on their armbands, Dubliners called them the Gorgeous Wrecks with the amused affection they bestowed on all their city's eccentrics.

On Easter Monday, the Gorgeous Wrecks donned their khaki uniforms and shouldered their empty rifles for a route march that took them right into de Valera's position. Seeing the khaki uniforms, the Volunteers opened fire. They killed several of the veterans before they realized that the middle-aged marchers were not carrying ammunition. The Gorgeous Wrecks ran back to the Beggar's Bush barracks and joined the few soldiers there in sniping at the IRA outposts.

Meanwhile, Sean Connolly's troops at the City Hall were sniping at the Castle. Colonel Cowan ordered all available troops to make their way to the Castle. Most of the British troops had no trouble filtering through the porous IRA defensive ring without coming under fire.

The route chosen by the troops of the Royal Irish Regiment from Richmond barracks, however, took them right by the South Dublin Union. Ceannt's men, bracing for the bayonet charge that all IRA commandants expected, were hit by a hail of machinegun and rifle bullets. Moving by rushes in small groups, the British troops got into the Union after two attempts and pushed the IRA troops into one corner of the compound.

By nightfall, the British leaders decided that they had enough men in Dublin Castle. They detailed 200 men to push the IRA (or Sinn Feiners, as the British erroneously called them) out of the City Hall. That was seven times as many men as Sean Connolly had in all his outposts. After three machinegun-supported assaults by grenade-throwing troops, the British got into the building and fought from room to room and from floor to floor. They captured some women and wounded men. When they broke into the City Hall guard room, the last rebel stronghold, the British found it empty. The rebels had pried out a grating and escaped into the city's sewers.

Early on Tuesday, Brigadier General W. H. M. Lowe arrived at the Castle with 840 infantrymen of the Fifteenth Irish Reserve Brigade.

Lowe immediately saw what had to be done. He would secure the south bank of the Liffey, cutting off the rebels in the GPO and the Four Courts area from their comrades, then move on the GPO, where his intelligence had located the rebel high command. He sent for more troops and an artillery battery from Athlone, and he called on the Royal Navy for assistance. He also found troops who were skilled at metal working and set them to work armoring a pair of trucks.

Lowe, who was stationed at Curragh, had learned of the rising in Dublin because a young Castle officer had changed to civilian clothes and bicycled to Kingstown. From there, he was able to notify not only other parts of Ireland, but England as well. In London, Lord John French, who had been "kicked upstairs" from his Western Front command, alerted all the troops he could find and ordered them to Ireland.

In the GPO, Tuesday began for James Connolly with the shattering of an illusion. He heard artillery fire from North Dublin. A dedicated Marxist, Connolly simply could not believe that a capitalist government would destroy private property belonging to its own ruling classes. He was sure the British would never use artillery in Dublin. But that was what he heard.

Four 18-pounders had come from Athlone. Two of the four guns were towed to the barricades Daly's men had set up on Cabra and North Circular roads and blasted them to pieces. Then they opened fire on the houses where Daly's men were waiting for the bayonet charge. The rebels fled.

At the GPO, things had been quiet ever since the cavalry charge was shattered. The police were afraid to venture on to Sackville Street, and Dublin's impoverished slum-dwellers took the opportunity to loot all the stores in this swank shopping district. There was no way, short of shooting them, the IRA could stop the mob.

Into this chaos stepped Frank Sheehy-Skeffington, perhaps Dublin's best-known eccentric. "Skeffy" was a nationalist, a pacifist, a vegetarian and an advocate of the vote for women. When the looting began, he was torn between his hatred of chaos and his commitment to non-violence. He finally went out with an armload of walking sticks to recruit a citizen peace-keeping force armed only with sticks. A British soldier asked him if he favored the nationalists. Skeffy replied that he sympathized with their aims, but not their methods. That was enough for the soldier. He arrested Sheehy-Skeffington as a rebel.

At his first opportunity, The O'Rahilly accosted Sean MacDiarmida. O'Rahilly was convinced that MacDiarmida was behind the disappearance of his friend, Bulmer Hobson. MacDiarmida coolly admitted that he had had Hobson kidnapped for the good of the cause. However, he said, Hobson was safe and would not be harmed.

"If he is not free tonight," said The O'Rahilly, "I cannot guarantee the same for you." He walked away. MacDiarmida called an aide. "Go up to Michael Conlon's house in Cabra Park and release Hobson," he said.

British troops were pouring into Dublin from the north and west. General Lowe now had 5,000 men under his immediate command, most of them Irish Catholics. Troops in the Castle were filtering out through the city streets, concentrating on the rebel targets Lowe had picked. The rebels remained rooted in position. Pearse had no communications to inform him of what the British were doing or to let him order troop movements.

Moving in small parties, the British drew closer and closer to the GPO. Their sniping intensified, but the Irish Republicans seldom saw a khaki uniform.

The British showed themselves only when ready. At 2 p.m., almost 2,000 troops of the Royal Fifth Dublin Fusiliers moved against the 30 survivors of Sean Connolly's company barricaded in the *Mail & Express* office. Three times the British charged the newspaper building before they could get a foothold. After bitter room-to-room fighting, the crowd outside saw a few insurgents leap from the windows and run toward the river. Inside the building, the British troops counted the bodies of 22 rebels.

That day, the Citizen Army people on St. Stephen's Green came under machinegun fire. The British had brought several machineguns into the Shelbourne without being seen. The next morning, as soon as the sun came up, they opened fire, shooting down into the tops of Mallin's trenches. Two rebels were killed in the first burst of fire, one a boy of 16. The Citizen Army troops tried to return the fire, hitting most of the windows of the hotel, but the British had superior weapons and position. At 7 a.m., Mallin ordered a retreat. The Irish left their dead and wounded and fled to the Royal College of Surgeons.

Along the Liffey, the British also massed overwhelming numbers at the Mendicity Institution, a poorhouse held by a handful of young teenagers, recent graduates of the *Fianna na hEireann*. Early Wednesday morning, the Mendicity surrendered. The British held the line of the Liffey.

Left to themselves, Lowe and the British troops now in Dublin could have put down the rebellion easily. They were not to be left to themselves. In Kingstown Tuesday night, the troops Lord French had dispatched from England landed. They were teenagers, not even half trained and wholly confused. The soldiers hailed passing Irish girls with "Bonjour, mademoiselle." In French's haste to do something, the troops had been sent out without hand grenades, machineguns or artillery. Those, however, proved to be minor disadvantages compared to the leadership the newcomers received.

Wednesday morning, the new arrivals, the Sherwood Foresters, formed up along Northumberland Road and marched to Dublin. British headquarters knew the rebels were guarding the road and that there were safer routes. But the high command wanted to destroy the insurgent outposts en route to central Dublin. The Sherwoods were told they were in Ireland and could expect snipers to shoot at them all the way into the city. But as the troops marched through the prosperous southern suburbs, both maids and their mistresses brought them tea and cakes.

Then, before they reached the Beggar's Bush barracks, they came under fire.

Shooting at them were Lieutenant Michael Malone and Section Commander James Grace of the IRA, who had barricaded themselves in the house at 25 Northumberland Road. Grace had the long Lee Enfield he had stolen from his Canadian reserve battalion. It was a rifle that could fire as fast as the short Lee Enfields the troops carried. Malone had a Mauser 1896 pistol, a large automatic sometimes called the "broom handle Mauser" in the United States and known as "Peter the Painter" in Ireland. It had a wooden holster that could be attached to its grip to make it a carbine. The Mauser was powerful for a pistol and weak for a carbine, but it could be fired as fast as its user could pull the trigger.

Malone demonstrated what a low-recoil, semi-automatic carbine could do. With their first burst of fire, he and Grace felled ten Sherwood Foresters.

The young soldiers dropped and fired back. Then their commander, Lieutenant Colonel Cecil Fane, stood up, drew his sword and shouted "Charge!"

Grace and Malone fired as fast as they could. Fane ducked for cover, and seven other rebels, across the Grand Canal in Clanwilliam House, joined in with a collection of modern and antique rifles. The British tried to take cover in gutters and behind garden walls.

Fane ordered Major H. Hanson to flank the rebels in 25 Northumberland Road while the rest of the Sherwoods sprayed the area with rifle fire. Hanson set out.

At the bathroom window of Number 25, Mick Malone fired his Peter the Painter as fast as he could pull the trigger and strip in fresh clips. He cut down most of Hanson's company.

In front of the house, Fane was hit by a Howth Mauser slug fired from Clanwilliam House, but he continued to direct his forces. He ordered another charge on Number 25. Malone's Mauser and Grace's Lee Enfield piled up another heap of victims. Angling fire from Clanwilliam House was also heavy, but Fane thought the shots were coming from a school up the street from Number 25 rather than from the big house across the Mount Street Bridge. When his men neared the school, which was empty except for the caretaker and his wife, they came under fire from the other direction—across the street, where four IRA men held St. Stephen's Parochial Hall.

The remnants of Hanson's company, still trying to turn the rebel flank, became visible to the IRA men in the big house and on the roof of a shed in its yard. A hail of bullets finished the company off. Fane told Captain H. C. Wright to take his company around the other flank. Wright stumbled into de Valera's main position and was sent reeling back.

Fane sent in more men. They dashed through Malone's barrage, losing ten men, and got into positions concealed from 25 Northumberland. They were not, however, concealed from Clanwilliam House and other rebel positions. The IRA men poured heavy fire on them, pausing only when residents waving white sheets ran out to help wounded British soldiers.

From Dublin Castle, Lowe telephoned an order to the Sherwoods to stop procrastinating and launch a frontal attack on the handful of rebels holding them up. Every 20 minutes, a wave of troops dashed for the bridge and were cut down.

Late in the afternoon, the British troops got a machinegun, grenades and explosive charges. Covered by exploding grenades, Corporal H. Hutchinson and Private J. E. Booth crawled up to the door of 25 Northumberland and blew it in with guncotton slabs. The men of B Company raced for the door, but a storm of bullets drove them back. Malone and Grace continued to fire, but the British drew closer. Finally, the Volunteers retreated to the cellar as the British were about to get in. Soldiers appeared at the head of the stairs and fired. Malone fell dead. Grace hid behind a boiler as the troops threw grenades down the stairs. When the battle moved on, he sneaked out.

When the soldiers took 25 Northumberland, the IRA men in the parochial hall tried to get away, but they ran right into a British company and were captured.

The troops turned to Clanwilliam House, having finally identified it as a rebel position. Grenades began exploding everywhere in the house, but the defenders kept on firing. They fired so fast some soldiers thought the rebels had a machinegun. Eventually, three of the insurgents were hit. As the British broke in, the four remaining Volunteers wriggled out through the back garden, where they joined the man in the adjoining yard and fled. A final British grenade broke a gas pipe in Clanwilliam House and ignited the fuel. The house burned to the ground.

In this utterly unnecessary fight, 17 rebels held off two battalions of British soldiers for more than eight hours. The clash was conducted with extraordinary valor on both sides. But on the British side, it was conducted with monumental stupidity as well. The Sherwood Foresters lost 230 men killed and wounded. The IRA lost eight.

At the GPO, a strange vehicle slowly chugged up Sackville Street. It looked like a huge iron box on wheels, with a tiny armored hood in front. There were 16 loopholes, some real, some dummies, on each side. At the right front of the box was a narrow slit.

As he watched bullets bounce from the contraption, Joseph Sweeney concluded that there must be a driver behind the slit. He fired at it and heard his bullet ricochet away. He fired again with the same result. The third time he fired, he heard no whine of a ricocheting slug. The armored truck stopped and didn't move again that afternoon.

The armored truck, however, was never more than a minor threat. The real problem was the British artillery. This consisted of four 18–pounders, two nine-pounders from the Officers Training Corps at Trinity College and a fisheries patrol boat, the *HMS Helga*. By 1916 standards, this hardly rated the term artillery. To the IRA, which had nothing heavier than rifles, though, the British field pieces and naval guns were the Ultimate Weapon.

Wednesday morning, *Helga* began firing on Liberty Hall. (The British believed it was still occupied.) Next the field guns began dropping incendiary shells on the GPO's outposts.

The rebels could only wait. Connolly dictated orders to his devoted secretary, Winifred Carney, who had followed him into the GPO. Pearse spoke little, usually to a few intimate friends. Joseph Plunkett, who had left a hospital bed to join the rising, was dying. He could do little but lie down. Within the British cordon around central Dublin, no business was open; there was no postal service; there was no food.

Out by de Valera's position, the Sherwood Foresters had been relieved by the South Staffordshire Regiment. The South Staffs borrowed a one-pounder from *Helga,* put it on a carriage and prepared to bombard Boland's Bakery. De Valera had an inspiration: he sent a man to plant an Irish flag on top of an unused tower of a distillery some 400 yards away. As he expected, the shells were aimed at the empty tower rather than the IRA strongpoint.

By 10 p.m. Wednesday, the whole center of Dublin appeared to be on fire. Connolly took out a party to occupy the offices of the *Irish Independent* and block a possible British move up Abbey Street. As he was returning, a bullet struck him in the leg above the ankle, shattering the bone and leaving his foot attached only by strips of flesh. The British were later to make much of the supposed inhumanity of the lead bullets from the Howth Mausers. Their own metal jacketed service bullet, though, was designed to tip over on impact, inflicting even ghastlier wounds. Connolly was carried back to the GPO, where he was treated by a prisoner of war, Lieutenant George Mahoney of the Indian Army medical corps, who had blundered into an IRA barricade while on leave.

For most of the week, the British had left Edward Daly's First Battalion alone. Now the cordon began to close on the Four Courts. The Sherwood Foresters and the Royal Irish used the armored trucks to transport troops from one strategic spot to another.

At the GPO, the situation became impossible by Friday evening. All the surrounding buildings had been burned, and the British were lobbing their incendiary shells into the IRA headquarters. Connolly was out of action. Plunkett was almost dead. Although Mahoney, the Indian Army doctor, said Pearse looked like a born leader, there was little he could do.

Over the protests of the women, the IRA evacuated them and left them at the presbytery of the pro-cathedral. Mahoney and a priest, with volunteer stretcher bearers, took the seriously wounded past the British barricades to a hospital. Connolly, though wounded, refused to be evacuated. Miss Carney, though a woman, refused to leave him. The boss would still be needing typed orders and dispatches. The 13 British servicemen held as

POWs were led out to Princes Street, where The O'Rahilly shook hands with each of them before they left for the British barricades.

While the British soldiers headed back to join their own people, the rebels filed out of the now uninhabitable post office building. Pearse hoped to get them through the British cordon to a factory on Great Britain Street. The O'Rahilly led 30 volunteers through the IRA barricade on Henry Street. He divided them into two parties and explained that they would move up Moore Street, gliding through the shadows from doorway to doorway, until they reached the British barricade crossing Moore Street at Great Britain Street, two blocks away. Then they would charge the barricade and open a breech for the rest of the battalion.

As the assault party dashed across Moore Street to reach the shadows, the Sherwood Foresters behind the barricade opened fire. Even by doorway hopping, the Irish got no more than 25 yards up the street. Hit repeatedly, The O'Rahilly hid in a doorway for a few moments. Then he yelled to his men and, waving his Peter the Painter, ran for Sackville Lane, a side street that would give them cover from British fire. Only a few of his men were able to follow, and when they started, the British cut them down. The O'Rahilly, hit again, staggered into Sackville Lane, sat on the sidewalk with his back against a wall, scribbled a last note to his wife, and bled to death.

The rest of the GPO garrison scattered to seek shelter as best they could. Some were shot down at the barricades; some were captured; some hid in nearby tenements. Connolly and Pearse were the last to leave the GPO, along with Winifred Carney, Connolly's secretary, and two Red Cross nurses, Elizabeth O'Farrell and Julia Grenan. They made their way to a grocery store on the corner of Moore Street and Henry Place. Pearse went back to make sure that everyone was out of the GPO, then he rejoined the others. They got a few doors up the street, then British fire drove them into a fish store.

Meanwhile, General Sir John Maxwell, the new commander-in-chief of British forces in Ireland, found that he had two battalions of South Staffs in Kingstown that were doing nothing. He sent them to attack the Four Courts garrison on North King Street. The fight was as bitter and unnecessary as the fight around the Mount Street Bridge on Wednesday. The IRA occupied houses all around the rebel barricades and fired on the English from every side. The British hardly gained any ground. The armored trucks again proved useful for transporting troops, but in no way were they armored fighting vehicles.

"Every bullet clanged and jarred through your head," recalled Sergeant Sam Cooper of the South Staffs. "It wasn't possible to fire back, either. You couldn't discharge a rifle in that confined space."

Back in Moore Street, as the sun came up Saturday, the headquarters battalion tried digging through walls, but there were too many walls between them and Great Britain Street. Pearse and the other leaders discussed linking up with the Four Courts garrison, but as they were talking, a civilian named Robert Dillon, his wife and their daughter, tried to leave the combat zone. Waving a white flag, they walked up Moore Street. The British soldiers shot them down.

A sickened Pearse turned away from the window and decided that to save the city, he'd have to surrender.

Elizabeth O'Farrell, wearing her Red Cross uniform, took Pearse's surrender offer to the British under a white flag. The British terms were simple: unconditional surrender. Pearse accepted and ordered the Dublin battalions to march to the appointed place and lay down their arms.

6

The uprising was over. More than 3,000 persons had been killed or wounded. According to official British figures, 132 soldiers had been killed and 397 wounded. Fifty-six insurgents were killed, as were 262 civilians. The number of insurgents and civilians wounded was 2,217, all but about 120 of them civilians. The heart of Dublin had been shattered and burned; supplies had been exhausted; jobs annihilated, and millions of pounds worth of property destroyed.

As the IRA prisoners were led away, mobs thronged the streets to shout insults. They threw stones and garbage at their would-be liberators. On one or two occasions, they actually tried to lynch the IRA men.

Augustine Birrell, the chief secretary for Ireland, returned to Dublin at the height of the uprising, but martial law continued with General Maxwell in charge. Maxwell ordered the prisoners to be tried by secret court martial. On May 3, three days after the end of the uprising, Castle authorities released the news that Padraic Pearse, Thomas MacDonagh and Thomas Clarke had been shot. Some Dubliners expressed satisfaction. But many of those who had demanded Pearse's blood on April 30 were not so sure.

Nothing could remain secret long in a city like Dublin, and some recent events had Dubliners taking second thoughts. There was the Sheehy-Skeffington affair, for instance.

The pacifist had been arrested Tuesday evening, but the British could find nothing to charge him with. Before they could let him go, Captain J. C. Bowen-Colthurst, scion of the ascendancy family that owned Blarney Castle, took Sheehy-Skeffington into his personal custody. Skeffy was to be a hostage while Bowen-Colthurst fought a war of his own. Leading a party of soldiers to enforce the martial law proclaimed two hours earlier, the captain accosted two boys on the way home from church. One of them, a youth named Coade, tried to run.

"Bash him!" Bowen-Colthurst ordered, and a soldier clubbed the boy with his rifle butt. Then Bowen-Colthurst shot young Coade to death. After that, he threw a hand grenade into a pub and arrested the four men still alive—all Unionists, incidentally.

The next day, Bowen-Colthurst had Sheehy-Skeffington shot by a firing squad, along with the survivors of his pub bombing. He murdered at least two more people Wednesday. Though Castle authorities knew what Bowen-Colthurst was doing, they made no attempt to stop him. Finally, Sir Francis Vane, a Castle officer, went to London and persuaded the Army commander-in-chief, Lord Kitchner, to have Bowen-Colthurst confined to his barracks.

At the time of the executions, the main action the government took with regard to Bowen-Colthurst was to try to hush up the story of his murder spree. For daring to bring up the matter, Maxwell had Vane dismissed from the service.

Worse than the Bowen-Colthurst murders were the North King Street massacres. During the fighting Friday, eye-witnesses reported that members of the South Staffordshire Regiment shot and bayoneted in cold blood at least 15 men whose only crime was living on North King Street.

British authorities denied the stories as complete fabrications. Then the bodies of two of the men were dug up. Autopsies established that they had been shot in the back with a military rifle while bound. The British colonel in charge of the North King Street operation still rejected the charge, because he could not "discover any military witnesses."

The British went right on with their secret trials and executions. On May 4, they shot four rebels, including Willie Pearse, who held no command, and Joseph Plunkett, the dying poet. When the story got out about how Plunkett had married his fiance in jail the night before his execution, the romantic Irish began calling the British commander Bloody Maxwell.

Dubliners began to compare the heroism of Mick Malone and The O'Rahilly with what now seemed to be the inhuman efficiency of "Britannia's sons with their long-range guns." Even Sir Edward Carson pleaded for clemency for the prisoners. The British did nothing to improve their popularity by arresting thousands of Irishmen—radicals, moderates and some conservatives—and holding them without trial.

Executions continued on May 5 and May 8. On May 12, the British shot Sean MacDiarmida. Then they carried James Connolly out in front of the firing squad and tied him in a chair, as his now-gangrenous wound left him too weak to sit up. Connolly was concerned that his socialist colleagues would not understand his taking part in a nationalist uprising, he told his daughter. "They all will forget that I am an Irishman."

His countrymen remembered that they were Irish. Protests from all Irish leaders rained on London. The Catholic hierarchy, which previously had taken notice of rebels only to excommunicate them, protested. The bishops threw their support to the radical Sinn Fein party, which stood for complete separation from Britain. The British stopped the executions, but by then, it was too late. In each election, Sinn Fein, previously a despised, lunatic-fringe party, scored bigger victories.

In show business slang, the Easter Rebellion seemed to have laid an egg. It had, but in another sense. In 1919, three years later, the egg hatched.

In the elections at the end of 1918, Sinn Fein controlled the entire Irish parliamentary delegation except some MPs from Ulster and one from Trinity College. It set up a separate Irish government. The British attempted to subdue it by military means. This time, the entire country supported the rebels.

Using a combination of guerrilla war and propaganda, Ireland showed the world that a weak and tiny nation can free itself from a great power. (At least from a great power that, unlike Nazi Germany or the Soviet Union under Stalin, cared about world opinion.) The American Revolution was, of course, the first war of independence, but the power of the 13 colonies in relation to Britain was many times that of Ireland relative to the same country. The same could be said of Mexico and most of the Latin American countries relative to Spain or Portugal. It was not Ireland's military power, but its appeal to world opinion that made independence possible. And Ireland, unlike many countries that copied its war-and-propaganda campaign, became a democratic republic.

13

1941, PEARL HARBOR (SECOND WORLD WAR)

A Single Miscalculation

"IF WE ARE ORDERED TO DO IT," THE ADMIRAL SAID, "THEN I CAN GUARAN-
tee to put up a tough fight for the first six months, but I have absolutely no
confidence as to what would happen if it went on for two or three years. It's
too late to do anything about the Tripartite Pact now, but I hope you'll at
least make every effort to avoid a war with America."

The admiral was Isoroku Yamamoto, commander-in-chief of Japan's
Combined Fleet. The man he was asking to work for peace was Prince
Fumimaro Konoye, then premier of Japan. The Tripartite Pact was the
treaty better known in the United States as the Rome-Berlin-Tokyo Axis.
Yamamoto had nothing but contempt for the treaty, which tied Japan to
European powers that could give her no additional help. And even the Pact's
most vociferous Japanese supporters would not commit themselves to any
action to help their European "partners." U. S. leaders, though, took a
serious view of the treaty. They thought it meant that Japan had submitted
to Hitler's leadership. It was another addition to the growing number of
grievances between the two Pacific powers.

The conference between the admiral and the prince took place in late
September, 1940. While he was exhorting Konoye to avoid war, Yamamoto
was already working on a plan that would let him "put up a tough fight"—a
very tough fight. The plan was so daring he had confided it to only one or
two close friends.

He would attack the U.S. Pacific Fleet at its home base, Pearl Harbor.

2

Not many years before this, Americans had looked indulgently, if rather
patronizingly, on everything the Japanese did. The "plucky little Japs" had

defeated China, a nation for which the majority of Americans had somewhat amused contempt, and then autocratic Russia, which was hardly most Americans' favorite European country.

The Japanese, though, resented the United States prohibition on Japanese becoming U. S. citizens. They saw American racism beneath the supposed friendship. (The Japanese, one of the world's most racist nations, knew racism when they saw it.) They saw racism, too, in the Washington Naval Treaty after the First World War. That treaty, designed to prevent a ruinous naval arms race, assigned quotas on naval tonnage and capital ships among the major powers. The United States and Britain were assigned the largest quotas, followed, in order, by Japan, France and Italy.

Japan, the Japanese pointed out, was like Britain, an island country which had to import everything, even food. Like Britain, it had a far-flung empire. The United States was largely self-sufficient: imports for the Americans were more of a luxury than a necessity. And the U.S. overseas empire was hardly more far-flung than that of Japan, which had taken over much of Germany's Pacific empire. The United States, in the Japanese view, would have one of the world's two largest navies under the treaty simply because it could afford one.

Britain couldn't. In 1941, Britain had 12 battleships and three battle-cruisers to Japan's 10 battleships, but the British battleships were, on the average, older, smaller and slower than Japan's. The United States had 17 battleships and, like Japan, had none of the thin-skinned, vulnerable battle-cruisers. Japan had 10 aircraft carriers, generally smaller and slower than their seven American counterparts but comparable to the seven British carriers. The Japanese, like the Americans, had 18 heavy cruisers while the British had 15. The British led the world in light cruisers, with 47 compared with 18 for Japan and 19 for the U.S.A. The Americans had the largest number of destroyers (171), with the British second (159) and the Japanese third (113). In submarines, Britain trailed all other major naval powers with 38, while Japan had 63, fewer than Italy or France. The United States had 112, the largest number in the world at that time, including the vaunted German U-boat fleet.

For many years, Japanese and American naval men looked on each other as the greatest threat to their respective nations. Popular magazines in both countries speculated about the outcome of a war between the two Pacific powers. Relations became strained in 1931, when Japan occupied Manchuria and set up the puppet state of Manchukuo. The strain grew stronger after the start, in 1937, of what Japanese called "the China incident."

The invasion of China had been engineered by the jingoistic officers of

Japan's Kwantung Army Group. It became apparent rather rapidly that fighting China was like trying to dig a ditch in quicksand. Japanese men, equipment and resources were sucked into the China war and disappeared. At the same time, the army grew increasingly powerful in the government. If Japan withdrew from China, the officers would be admitting they had made a mistake. The army would lose its credibility and, therefore, its power. (One difference between Japan and the other Axis countries was that losing power was nothing Hitler and Mussolini—or Stalin, for that matter—had to worry about.) On the other hand, Japan couldn't afford to continue the war without additional resources, especially oil. All Japan's oil had to be imported. About 90 percent of it came from the United States.

Looking south, the Japanese cast envious eyes on the oil-rich Dutch East Indies. Suddenly, in 1940, events in Europe provided what looked like a golden opportunity. Germany overran Holland, defeated France and left Britain hanging on the ropes like an exhausted boxer. The Japanese government signed the Tripartite Pact. Now the colonial powers could be considered enemies and Japan had a reason for snatching their possessions. Except for one thing.

The United States.

The Americans warned against any move to the south. When Japan occupied French Indo-China under an agreement with Vichy, the Americans froze Japanese assets and imposed an embargo, cutting off the flow of high-grade steel and oil to Japan. War became a distinct possibility. And, from the Japanese point of view, unless the American sanctions could be lifted, the sooner the better.

Japan had begun to increase its naval strength. Two new battleships, *Yamato* and *Musashi* were nearing completion. Both displaced 64,000 tons and carried nine 18.2 inch guns—the most powerful guns ever put on the water. But then the Americans adopted a naval construction program. Under the Two-Ocean Naval Expansion Act of 1940, the United States began building seven battleships, 18 carriers, 27 cruisers, 115 destroyers and 42 submarines. That would be in addition to the 130 warships of various kinds then under construction. There was no way Japan could match the production of its giant rival across the Pacific. The longer the war was delayed, the weaker Japan would become relative to the United States.

On the other hand, few senior Japanese naval officers thought Japan could decisively defeat the Americans at sea with the present balance of power. Certainly Yamamoto was not one of them. On January 26, 1941, in response to the clamor for an immediate war with the United States, he wrote to an ultra nationalist named Ryoichi Sasakawa:

Should hostilities break out between Japan and the United States, it would not be enough that we take Guam and the Philippines, nor even Hawaii and San Francisco. To make victory certain, we would have to march into Washington and dictate the terms of peace in the White House. I wonder if our politicians, among whom armchair arguments about war are being glibly bandied about in the name of state politics, have confidence as to the final outcome and are prepared to make the necessary sacrifices.

This was a very unsubtle jab at the army command, which had for years been bogged down in China, a country of approximately the same area as the United States and by no means 6,000 miles away. Japanese nationalists published an altered version of the statement with the last sentence deleted to make it sound like a promise by Yamamoto to dictate peace terms in the White House. When it was published, though, Japan was already at war and Yamamoto feared he could not dispute the inaccurate version without spreading dissension.

Yamamoto never seriously believed it would be necessary for Japan to send an army across the Pacific and then across thousands of miles of mountains, deserts and plains. It might be possible, he thought, to neutralize the U.S. long enough for Japan to conquer the resources it needed in Southeast Asia. Perhaps Japan could even induce the United States to negotiate a peace on acceptable terms. His overall objective was the same as that of the standard Japanese strategy in case of war with the United States.

The traditional Japanese plan was essentially defensive, featuring something the Naval General Staff liked to call the Great All-Out Battle. It relied on airplanes, surface ships and submarines based on the Japanese-occupied islands in the mid-Pacific to whittle down the U.S. battle fleet when it tried to approach Japan. When the American fleet was small enough, the Japanese fleet would engage it in a Jutland-type battle and wipe it out. After that, the United States could be expected to make peace on terms favorable to Japan.

In 1941, and for many years before, both American and Japanese naval doctrine held that because of the difficulties of refueling at sea, the inevitable need for repairs and dispersal to hold strategic spots, a fleet lost 10 percent of its effectiveness for every 1,000 miles it operated away from its base.

If that were true, the traditional Japanese strategy made sense. And Yamamoto's plan was nonsense.

Yamamoto thought the equation of distance and effectiveness was nonsense. The American fleet was too big to whittle down to a size where it could be handled. He would strike directly across the Pacific—non-stop from Japan—and attack the Americans in their lair. Then, having crippled their Pacific Fleet with a single stroke, the whittling down strategy might work.

3

Yamamoto had no business making plans. That was the business of the Naval Operations Department of the Naval General Staff. Yamamoto was commander-in-chief of the Combined Fleets. His duty was to see that the plans were carried out. Yamamoto, however, was the proverbial 600-pound gorilla. His prestige, based on his performance, his brains and his strength of character, was so great that nobody dared to tell him anything. Still, he kept the plan quiet, telling only a few associates he respected. One was Rear Admiral Takijiro Onishi, one of the few admirals in any navy who was also an experienced flier.

An air attack on Pearl Harbor! The concept took Onishi's breath away. He summoned Commander Minoru Genda, the most brilliant aerial torpedo expert in the Japanese Navy. One expert had already told Onishi an aerial torpedo attack in Pearl Harbor was impossible. Pearl Harbor was shallow—less than 40 feet deep at its deepest. Standard practice in all navies was dropping the torpedo from around 250 feet above the surface of the water, after which it plunged to a depth of 60 to 75 feet before returning to its programmed depth. Further, Pearl Harbor was not large. A torpedo had to run at a minimum length to arm itself. That greatly limited possible approaches.

"Difficult," Genda said of the plan for a torpedo attack, "but not impossible." Japan already had the world's best ship-launched torpedo, the "Long Lance." An improved aerial torpedo could no doubt be developed. And techniques for launching could also be improved. In November 1940, a group of British torpedo bombers attacked an Italian fleet moored in Taranto Harbor. The British flew only 35 feet above the water and severely damaged three Italian battleships. The low-level attack kept the torpedoes from burying themselves in the mud. Taranto Harbor was deeper than Pearl Harbor, but it was shallower than what most sailors believed was the necessary depth for aerial torpedoes. Genda set to work on a detailed plan for the attack on Pearl Harbor.

He torpedoed one Yamamoto idea at the start. The commander-in-chief had toyed with the idea of making the attack a one-way trip. The planes would leave their carriers from a distance too far to allow them to return. After dropping their bombs and torpedoes, the pilots would ditch their planes in the water and be picked up by waiting submarines. Considering the difficulty of picking up a large number of men floating in a wide expanse of ocean, it was obvious that most of the fliers would never return to Japan alive.

Yamamoto saw three advantages to the plan: (1) the carriers would be so far from Pearl Harbor that bombers from Hawaii would be most unlikely to find them; (2) the Americans could not follow the Japanese planes back to the carriers; and (3) after this sort of attack, the American people might consider the Japanese such a fearless race that it would be useless to fight them.

That Yamamoto, who studied at Harvard and had spent a lot of time as a naval attaché in the United States, could even consider the third point shows that racial stereotypes were prevalent on both sides of the Pacific. While Americans cherished the notion of the short, bucktoothed Japanese who lacked the imagination to do anything but slavishly copy Western models, the Japanese "knew" that the Americans were a soft race whose "warrior spirit" had been leached out by a plethora of creature comforts. As he worked on the Pearl Harbor plan, Yamamoto became convinced that the loss of several, or maybe even one, battleships would be such a blow to the American public that they would ask for peace.

As his words to Konoye show, Yamamoto desperately wanted to avoid war with the United States. He saw the attack on Pearl Harbor as a chance to do that: the Americans, he hoped, would be so disheartened by their losses they'd immediately make peace on terms favorable to Japan.

In protesting the proposed one-way attack, Genda turned Yamamoto's morale argument against him. Such an attack would represent a defeatism utterly alien to the Japanese warrior spirit, he argued.

"To obtain the best results," he wrote, "all carriers must approach as close to Pearl Harbor as possible. Denuding them of planes and departing the scene of the action minus their scoring punch would invite disaster in case the Americans launched a counterattack." Further, the one-way plan would make repeated attacks impossible. "To secure complete success, we must stay within effective bomber and fighter range until we accomplish our mission."

Genda's plan emphasized nine points:

(1) The attack must catch the Americans by surprise. If they expected it, they might set a trap.

(2) The prime target should be the U.S. carriers. Genda, Japan's top aerial strategist, was convinced that air power would decide all naval battles of the future.

(3) Along with the U.S. carriers, the Japanese should attack the land-based military planes on Oahu.

(4) Every available carrier in the Japanese Navy should participate. The attack was the key to any successful war with the United States, so Japan must use all its strength.

(5) The attackers should use all types of naval bombers. Torpedo

planes were the most potent weapon, but Pearl Harbor was far from an ideal spot for that type of attack, and the Americans might have installed anti-torpedo nets. Horizontal bombers would be the next most potent, but ships made poor targets for bombs dropped from a high altitude. Dive bombers were the most accurate, but a bomb dropped from a diving plane could never gain the momentum of one free-falling from a great height.

(6) There should be a strong fighter element to escort the bombers, strafe airfields and to fight off any counterattack.

(7) The attack should be made in the early morning. The attack would be difficult enough without trying to do it in the dark. Early morning would catch the Americans asleep or just waking up.

(8) Refueling at sea would be necessary. Most of Japan's navy was composed of short-range ships designed for defensive warfare in or close to home waters, in accordance with the Great All-Out Battle plan.

(9) All preparations must be conducted with the strictest secrecy.

Yamamoto accepted the plan even though its author was a very junior commander. The admiral knew that rank does not necessarily indicate talent. He set to work on the many problems the plan posed, and he did it without getting the consent of the Naval General Staff.

Training commenced immediately, supervised by Lieutenant Commander Mitsuo Fuchida, a highly talented flier Genda had recruited. Torpedo plane crews trained continuously in a southern Japanese harbor that resembled Pearl Harbor. They concentrated on approaching targets at the minimum height. Meanwhile, officers involved in Yamamoto's plot worked with torpedo manufacturers to get a shallow-running torpedo that didn't need a long run to stabilize its path and arm itself.

At the same time, horizontal bombers worked to improve their accuracy. They found their hit ratio greatly improved when they dropped their bombs from only 3,000 feet. The trouble was that none of the standard bombs could penetrate the deck armor of the largest American ships. The Japanese solved that problem by putting fins on 16-inch armor-piercing shells for battleship guns. These were heavy enough and hard enough to pierce the deck armor of any American battleship from 3,000 feet.

Accepting Genda's fourth point, Yamamoto created the First Air Fleet—a concentration of Japan's six best carriers, escorted by a couple of battleships and a number of cruisers and destroyers. That was the force that would deliver the blow to Pearl Harbor if negotiations with the United States broke down.

The negotiations were on the point of breaking down several times. The Japanese wanted an agreement of some kind by October 15, 1941. The fall of 1941, their military planners believed, would be the optimum time for an invasion of Southeast Asia, the land flowing with, not milk and honey, but oil. The Americans had broken several of the Japanese diplomatic codes—and probably the military "JN 25" code as well—and knew the southern move was in the cards. They wanted time to strengthen their military position by increasing forces in the Philippines.

The Japanese military decided that Prince Konoye was wasting time. If he were not ready to lead the nation into war, they'd have to get a premier who would. On October 12, three members of the cabinet called on Konoye. They were Foreign Minister Teijiro Toyoda, an admiral; War Minister Hideki Tojo, a general; Navy Minister Koshiro Oikawa, another admiral. Four days later, Konoye resigned and was replaced by Tojo, a spokesman for the army, but not its sole leader.

The Tojo government did not immediately break off relations. The Pearl Harbor plan had not yet received the approval of the Naval General Staff, so Tojo wasn't continuing negotiations at this point so Yamamoto could surprise the Pacific Fleet. He didn't even know what Yamamoto was planning. But Tojo believed that surprise was always good. While the American were talking, they wouldn't be preparing to disrupt the "Southern Operation."

Yamamoto was preparing to move south, too, but not the way Tojo expected. He planned to move the First Air Fleet to a base in the Kurile Islands, in the far North Pacific. His intelligence sources had informed him that the Americans did not patrol the area north of Hawaii effectively, probably because the stormy North Pacific was the least inviting route any fleet could take. The First Air Fleet would first steam due east, then turn sharply south in the direction of Hawaii. For the Japanese, the route would mean refueling in windy, heaving seas that, in the cooler months, coated everything they touched with a layer of ice. While the airmen were practicing their bombing runs, Yamamoto had his ships practicing refueling.

Yamamoto's preparations for the attack were almost complete when the Naval General Staff nearly destroyed the commander-in-chief's still almost-secret plan for the Pearl Harbor raid. They ordered three of his six carriers to take part in the operation in Southeast Asia. Yamamoto had already demonstrated to them that land-based planes could provide sufficient air cover as far as the Philippines. Faced with this opposition, Yamamoto delivered an ultimatum to the Naval General Staff.

If the Pearl Harbor operation didn't get six carriers, he would resign from the navy along with the whole staff of the Combined Fleet.

The general staff was stunned. Yamamoto got his six carriers. In early November, the Pearl Harbor operation was incorporated into Combined Fleet Operation Order No. 1. Yamamoto's brain child finally had official approval.

4

Yamamoto's problems with Tokyo were nothing to those his opposite number, Admiral Husband E. Kimmel, had with Washington. Kimmel's official title was commander-in-chief of the U.S. Fleet. Actually, he was commander-in-chief of the Pacific Fleet. Since the beginning of the Second World War, the Navy Department had been siphoning off ships from Kimmel's fleet to increase the American presence in the Atlantic, where they reported to Vice Admiral Ernest J. King. In late 1941, Kimmel's forces were considerably inferior to Yamamoto's.

Washington had adopted a "Europe first" policy. Secretary of War Henry L. Stimson was even lobbying for sending all naval units to the Atlantic. Stimson saw no need to keep "the fleet in the Pacific, where it is well known that we don't intend to use it actively against the Japanese and to keep it from its real function in the main theater of operations."

A report generated by an Anglo-American military conference prior to the U.S. entry into the war declared, "Since Germany is the predominant member of the Axis Powers, the Atlantic and European area is considered to be the decisive theater. The principal United States military effort will be exerted in that theater, and operations of United States forces in all other theaters will be conducted in such a manner as to facilitate that effort."

The American leadership was convinced that the Japanese, those slavish imitators, were slavishly serving Germany. Even after the Pearl Harbor attack, Stimson could say, "We know from interceptions and other evidence that Germany had pushed Japan into this." The code interceptions showed no such thing, nor did any other evidence. But Stimson and many others were convinced that the Japanese didn't have the initiative to strike Pearl Harbor, deep in American waters. Some still thought they didn't have the skill, either. There were reports that Germans piloted the planes.

In late 1941, the British were hard pressed by Germany's vastly expanded submarine fleet. They and the Americans would continue to be hard pressed through 1942. Warships were needed to convoy merchantmen. But the need was mostly for destroyers and small, specialized escort vessels, including light escort carriers. There wasn't much need for such giant carriers as *Yorktown*, and none at all for most of the U.S. battleships, including the newest and fastest. But Kimmel was left with eight aging battleships—nine, counting a decommissioned target ship—and three carriers. The Pacific C in C asked for two new battlewagons about to be completed, *North Carolina* and *Washington*. Admiral Harold R. Stark, chief of naval operations, replied that the need for them was "far greater in the

Atlantic than in the Pacific." He added, "I believe that, in all probability, the Pacific Fleet can operate successfully and effectively even though decidedly weaker than the whole Japanese Fleet."

The air element of the navy fared no better than the surface element. Rear Admiral Patrick N. L. Bellinger, commanding the navy's aerial patrols, wrote to Stark in 1941, "I was surprised to find that here in the Hawaiian Islands, an important naval advanced post, we were operating on a shoestring and the more I looked, the thinner the shoestring appeared to be.

" . . . As there are no plans to modernize the present patrol planes comprising Patrol Wing TWO, this evidently means there are no plans to replace the present obsolescent type. . . . This, together with the many existing deficiencies, indicates to me that the Navy Department as a whole does not view the situation in the Pacific with alarm, or else is not taking steps in keeping with their view."

Lieutenant General Walter C. Short, commander of the Army and Army Air Forces in Hawaii, had similar troubles.

On April 23, 1941, Stimson told General George C. Marshall, army chief of staff, that President Franklin D. Roosevelt believed some ships should stay at Pearl Harbor for the islands' defense. Marshall "indicated his strong dissent," Stimson wrote later. He said that "with our heavy bombers and our fine new pursuit planes, the land forces could put up such a defense that the Japs wouldn't dare attack Hawaii."

In a memo to Roosevelt, Marshall wrote:

The Island of Oahu, due to its fortification, its garrison and its physical characteristics, is believed to be the strongest fortress in the world. . . .

Air Defense. With adequate air defense, enemy carriers, naval escorts and transports will begin to come under air attacks at a distance of approximately 750 miles. This attack will increase in intensity until when within 200 miles of the objective, the enemy forces will be subject to attack by all types of bombardment closely supported by our most modern pursuit.

Hawaiian Air Defense. Including the movement of aviation now in progress, Hawaii will be defended by 35 of our most modern flying fortresses, 35 medium range bombers, 13 light bombers, 150 pursuit of which 105 are our most modern type. In addition, Hawaii is capable of reinforcement by heavy bombers from the mainland by air. With this force available a major attack against Oahu is considered impracticable.

Actually, *when the Japanese attacked,* Short had only 12 B-17s—six of which could fly. For most of the year, his shortage of long-range patrol planes was so great the army turned over to the navy the long-range patrol task—to the "shoestring" force Bellinger complained about. It should be further noted that the flying fortress was designed to bomb stationary, relatively large targets from a very high altitude. It was not designed to attack small, fast-moving ships. And in fact, its record when it did so was resoundingly unspectacular.

Marshall concluded: "In point of sequence, sabotage is first to be expected and may, within a very limited time, cause great damage. On this account, and in order to assure strong control, it would be highly desirable to set up a military control of the islands prior to the likelihood of our involvement in the Far East."

Hawaii had some 160,000 residents of Japanese ancestry. Of these, though, only 37,500 were born in Japan. The rest were American citizens. All through the war, not one of them, Nisei or Isei, committed an act of sabotage. Nevertheless, Marshall's view powerfully influenced Short, who took measures against sabotage and little else.

The military commanders at Pearl Harbor could make a good case for the contention that they were hamstrung by Washington. But it was also true that they could have done far more with what they had. Radar and other warning posts were not manned continuously: Short considered them training tools rather than operational installations. The navy was short of planes, and those they had were obsolescent, but they could have done more patrolling than they did. There had been talk in both Hawaii and Washington of barrage balloons. Barrage balloons would have seriously hampered the Japanese attackers, but none were sent. Kimmel refused to install torpedo nets around his ships because, he said, an aerial torpedo attack in Pearl Harbor was impossible. On Sundays, both army and navy facilities were manned by skeleton crews. Ship movements in and out of the harbor followed such a rigid routine that even the hard-working Japanese spy, Ensign Takeo Yoshikawa, was disgusted by the lack of security.

The much-criticized two-by-two mooring of ships beside Ford Island in the middle of the harbor was probably not an important factor in the battle. It did not make the ships a larger target for the torpedo planes. In fact, the outboard ships protected those moored beside them from torpedoes. The double mooring did not hamper ship movement. It normally took 3½ hours for a battleship to get up steam to move, and none of them were prepared to move when the attack came.

There were things that should have alerted both the Pearl Harbor commanders and their superiors in Washington that something might happen. The distance-effectiveness formula, however, was still strong in the military mind. It was also reinforced by the Western stereotype of the Japanese. So nobody took the warning signs very seriously.

After the war, some "revisionist" writers claimed that Franklin D. Roosevelt knew about the attack and refused to warn the Pearl Harbor commanders that it was coming. His aim, they claimed, was to get the United States into the war. There are several things wrong with the thesis.

No matter how much he might have wanted to stop Hitler, Roosevelt was not such a fool that he'd put a large segment of America's military might in danger of annihilation to achieve that end. An attack on a Pearl Harbor prepared to receive it would have aroused the American people as effectively as one that succeeded. Further, Roosevelt himself did not have all the code intercepts his intelligence people had gathered. Rear Admiral Richmond Kelly Turner did not trust some of Roosevelt's advisors, whom he considered pro-Communist, so he gave Roosevelt oral summaries instead of the actual intercepts. Roosevelt eventually learned he was being blacked out, and from then on, he got the full messages.

Turner further denied much of the gathered intelligence to Kimmel and Short. Rear Admiral Edwin T. Layton, intelligence officer for the Pacific Fleet at the time, detailed in his book, *And I Was There*, how Turner refused to disseminate intelligence. One glaring omission was what intelligence people later called the "Bomb Plot" message. The Japanese foreign office had signaled its consulate on Oahu to mark the position of each ship in Pearl Harbor on a grid it sent. The obvious reason—which seemed to escape the intelligence people—was to help Japanese bombers select targets.

Another was the "winds execute" message, which also went out in diplomatic code. The Japanese government notified its representatives around the world that it would signal whether it had broken off relations with various countries by a code phrase in the daily weather report. "East wind rain" would mean the United States; "west wind clear" would mean Britain, and "north wind cloudy" would mean the U.S.S.R. Intelligence people called this promised information the "winds execute" message. Layton and two British intelligence experts, James Rusbridger and Eric Nave, present evidence that the "winds execute" message was received in both Washington and London. It was not sent to Pearl Harbor. Rusbridger and Nave also report that the British learned that the First Air Fleet was in the Kuriles, after U. S. intelligence had lost track of them. The British did not notify Washington. If so, it may have been because, as Rusbridger and Nave charge, Winston Churchill wanted to get the U.S. into the war. As for the "winds execute" message, if it were lost, there seems to be no other reason than ineptitude. When the navy's most senior operations and intelligence officers could testify later that they didn't consider the "bomb plot" message important enough to send to Pearl Harbor, ineptitude is not hard to believe.

Still, on November 27, Naval Operations sent a "War warning" message to Pearl Harbor that did not specify, however, where an attack might take place. On December 1, the Japanese Navy changed its call signs—the second time in one month, a most unusual development. And on December 3, Lieutenant Colonel George W. Bicknell, the chief investigative officer for the army Hawaii command, learned that the Japanese consulate staff was burning its code books. Those messages alone should have been enough to end the "business-as-usual" atmosphere at Pearl Harbor. Another message that could have alerted Pearl Harbor was intercepted by the Hawaii Naval District Intelligence Office December 2. From the Japanese foreign office to the consulate, it read:

> In view of the present situation, the presence in port of warships, airplane carriers and cruisers is of utmost importance. Hereafter, to the utmost of your ability, let me know day by day. Wire me in each case whether or not there are any observation [probably a garble for obstruction (barrage)] balloons above Pearl Harbor or if there are any indications that they will be sent up. Also please advice (sic) me whether or not the warships are provided with antimine [anti torpedo?] nets.

This message was *mailed* to Washington on December 11 and was translated December 13.

5

During the first days of December, Japan's First Air Fleet, under the command of Vice Admiral Chuichi Nagumo was bearing down on Hawaii. Nagumo was a battleship admiral who had little faith in the aerial attack on Pearl Harbor, but he was doing his duty.

While Nagumo was approaching Hawaii from the north, a fleet of Japanese submarines, five of them carrying two-man submarines on their decks, took up positions south of the islands. The midget subs were to enter Pearl Harbor and torpedo the ships there, while the full-size boats were to wait for American ships trying to leave the harbor. Several more ships, designated the Guam Invasion Force and the Midway Neutralization Force, were approaching those islands.

The biggest Japanese ship movement, though, was the Southern Operation invasion fleet. That was spotted soon after it took to sea. American intelligence officers watched it with a kind of horrified fascination that made it easy for them to miss Nagumo's fleet.

At 0400, December 7, the minesweeper *Castor* saw a midget submarine. It notified *Ward*, a destroyer, which failed to locate the midget. There was no report to Pearl Harbor. One and a half hours later, at 0530, two cruisers in the First Air Fleet launched float-equipped Zero fighters to see if there was any activity at Pearl. There was none. The Air Fleet could not wait for the seaplanes' return, however. At 0550, the six carriers, now about 220 miles from Pearl Harbor, started launching their planes.

At this time in Washington, Ambassador Kichisaburu Nomura and his associate, Saburu Kurusu, were decoding a note to deliver to the U.S. Secretary of State. They had no idea what was going on in the Pacific.

At 0702, Privates Joseph Lockard and George Elliot at the radar station on Opana, the most northerly point on Oahu, were about to close down the station when they noticed blips on their radar screen indicating a large number of aircraft. "More than 50," they reported later. Actually, there were 183. Lockard notified Lieutenant Kermit Tyler, who knew that a flight of B-17s was due. Lockard made one mistake; he didn't tell Tyler there were more than 50 planes. No B-17s would be coming in numbers like that. Tyler told the two privates not to worry and to shut down the station.

Meanwhile, *Ward* sank two of the midget submarines. The use of two-man submarines was not Yamamoto's brightest idea. Of the five midgets, four were sunk very quickly along with one of the full-size subs. The fifth midget hit a coral reef and grounded. One of her crew survived to become the first U.S. POW of World War II.

At 0735, the seaplane from the cruiser *Chikuma* reported on the ships in Pearl Harbor. There were no carriers. *Saratoga* was undergoing repairs in Bremerton, Washington; *Lexington* was taking planes to Midway, and *Enterprise* was ferrying another batch of planes to Wake Island.

At 0749, Mitsuo Fuchida, leading the Japanese attack, looked down on the U.S. Pacific Fleet and said "To, to, to" into his radio—the signal to attack. Four minutes later, he gave the signal the Japanese fleet had been waiting for, "Tora! Tora! Tora!" ("Tiger! Tiger! Tiger!"), the code meaning the Americans had been taken completely by surprise.

Fuchida intended the torpedo bombers to lead the attack, followed by the horizontal and the dive bombers. But the leader of the dive bomber group misunderstood the signal and attacked at once. The faster, but less lethal, dive bombers reached the target first. The Americans got a few seconds warning, but it didn't do much good.

Aboard *Oglala*, a minelayer, Rear Admiral William R. Furlong saw a plane drop a bomb near the edge of the harbor. He first thought an American plane had had an accident. Then he saw the red Rising Sun symbol on its wings.

"Japanese! Man your stations!" he yelled. Then he had *Oglala* signal: "All ships in harbor sortie."

The ships didn't have time to start their engines, let alone leave the harbor before torpedo bombers swept over the rooftops of Pearl City, north of the harbor, and over the U.S. naval station, south of the harbor. The cruiser *Raleigh* was hit by one torpedo and old *Utah*, the target ship that looked like a battleship, by two. Skimming over Ford Island in mid-harbor, the southbound flight fired a torpedo at *Oglala*, Furlong's flagship, which passed under it and struck the cruiser *Helena*. The concussion of that explosion burst the seams of *Oglala*. Two torpedoes from the northbound flight also passed under the repair ship *Vestal* and hit *Arizona*, moored beside it. *Oklahoma*, moored outboard of *Maryland*, and *West Virginia*, outboard of *Tennessee* were hit several times.

On the fleet, some sailors at first thought the raid was a training exercise by the Hawaiian Air Force. Others tried to man anti-aircraft guns. Most of the ammunition was locked up, and the sailors had to break the locks off with hammers and chisels.

By controlled flooding, *West Virginia's* crew was able to keep her upright as she settled on the mud, her superstructure above water. *Oklahoma* capsized, trapping many of the men aboard her. *California*, moored alone, went down after only two hits, because all her manholes were open in preparation for an inspection Monday. A quick-thinking ensign, Ernest M. Fain, directed prompt counter-flooding so the ship didn't capsize but sank like *West Virginia*, with her superstructure above the surface. *Nevada*, also moored alone, was hit by one torpedo and two bombs, which severely damaged it. The attack on *Pennsylvania*, Kimmel's flagship, was unsuccessful because the big battleship was in dry dock, but two destroyers in dry dock with her were almost destroyed. Within minutes after the start of the attack, all the battleships except *Maryland* and *Tennessee* had been sunk or severely damaged.

The horizontal bombers took up where the torpedo planes left off. *Maryland* and *Tennessee* were hit with two bombs each, and more bombs fell on the already damaged *Nevada* and *West Virginia*.

Then a bomb penetrated *Arizona's* deck and exploded in her magazine. The concussion blew the men on *Vestal's* deck into the harbor, among them the ship's captain, Commander Cassin B. Young. The explosion also blew out the fires that other bombs had ignited on the repair ship. *Arizona*, though, was an inferno. About 1,000 men, half of all the navy men who died at Pearl Harbor, and almost half of *all* those who died there, died aboard *Arizona*. The heat from *Arizona* was so great that some officer on *Vestal* ordered "Abandon Ship," even as the crew was fishing survivors from *Arizona* out of the water. As the first crewmen started to leave, an oil-covered figure just hauled out of the harbor demanded: "Where the hell do you think you're going?"

"We're abandoning ship."

"Get back aboard ship! You're not abandoning ship on me!" roared Commander Young, *Vestal's* skipper.

Some skippers couldn't get to their ships. On *Nevada*, Lieutenant Commander J. F. Thomas and Lieutenant Lawrence A. Ruff shared command, Ruff managing topside while Thomas worked below decks. Thomas performed a near-miracle by getting up a head of steam in the damaged battleship. She moved away from her mooring, slid past the blazing *Arizona*, and headed for the harbor mouth. *Nevada* became a magnet for all the Japanese planes. Hit repeatedly, it looked as if she might sink in the channel, blocking the harbor. Thomas and Ruff reluctantly grounded her. *Vestal*, too, moved away from *Arizona*, but she, too, had to be grounded. *St. Louis*, a cruiser, moved out, tearing up the channel (eight knots speed limit) at 22 knots. She cleared the harbor.

While the torpedo planes and horizontal bombers were working on the fleet, the dive bombers and fighters were attacking airfields, both army and navy. At the height of the attack, the flight of B-17s Lieutenant Tyler had been expecting arrived, unarmed, low on gas, and manned by skeleton crew. Somehow, all of the big bombers managed to land, although they were scattered all over Oahu.

Another 19 planes from *Enterprise* landed at Pearl. The carrier had dispatched 24 planes while it was still at sea. The pilots knew nothing of the attack. Zeros shot down four of the U.S. dive bombers and U.S. anti-aircraft gunners mistook another for a Japanese plane and shot it down.

Because of Short's fear of sabotage, the army planes were not in bunkers prepared for them but lined up wingtip to wingtip, guns unloaded and ammunition locked up. Ammunition for anti-aircraft guns was also locked up out of harm's way. When the Japanese bombed the hangars, they destroyed most of the ammunition.

Lieutenant Stephen G. Salzman of the Coast Artillery heard a plane pulling out of a dive. He snatched a Browning Automatic Rifle and a couple of clips from an enlisted man nearby and ran outside. He was joined by Sergeant Lowell V. Klatt with another BAR. They saw a Japanese dive bomber. As the bomber pulled out of his dive, both soldiers emptied their BARs at it. The Japanese plane flew over their building and crashed on the other side. Of the four planes in the first wave of attackers that were shot down by army guns, all had been hit at low levels by either BARs or machine guns. Ammunition for heavier guns never reached the gunners.

Few of the American pilots managed get into the air. Lieutenants George S. Welch and Kenneth Taylor were exceptions. They had just finished an all-night poker game when they saw the Japanese. They raced to Haleiwa, got a couple of P-40s and attacked the first Japanese planes they saw. Before the attack ended, they shot down seven enemy planes.

The Japanese had inflicted tremendous damage to the American forces, but that was only the beginning. Now a second wave of attackers—fighters, horizontal bombers and dive bombers—swept in. In Pearl Harbor itself, flak was far heavier than it had been earlier, and the damage the attackers inflicted was minor compared to what had been done by the first wave. One reason, of course, was that there wasn't as much left to damage.

There were still more targets on shore, especially at airfields. But there, too, resistance had increased. The Japanese remained determined, though. Before take-off Lieutenant Fusada Iida told his shipmates that if his plane were so damaged he couldn't return, he'd crash it into an enemy installation.

Iida led his nine-plane group against Bellows Field, where they destroyed one of the B-17s that had landed that morning. They moved on to the naval air station at Kaneohe.

They were swooping down on the field when an aviation ordnanceman named Sands stepped out of the armory building with a BAR. Sands emptied his automatic rifle at the attackers then yelled to his mates, "Hand me another BAR! Hurry up! I swear I hit that yellow bastard!"

Iida saw the sailor, turned and swooped in again to kill him. Sands again emptied a Browning. This time, as Iida pulled out of his shallow dive, sailors on the ground saw gasoline spray from his plane. The Japanese flier reached his mates and pointed to himself, then to the ground. He wheeled around and headed for the armory.

A sailor saw him and yelled, "Hey Sands! That sonofabitch is coming back."

Sands grabbed the nearest weapon, a bolt-action Springfield rifle. Ignoring the bullets kicking up dirt around him, Sands got off five shots with the hand-operated rifle. On the fifth shot, the Zero ceased firing. It sailed over the field as if it were out of control and crashed into a road climbing a low hill. Japanese veterans of the raid later told the story of Iida's heroic self-sacrifice. The truth, though, is that Iida was killed by a .30 infantry rifle wielded by a sailor who didn't care that what he was doing was supposed to be impossible.

Even if Iida's end were not exactly as they told it, the Japanese fliers had nothing to be ashamed of. They had sunk or crippled every operational battleship in the U.S. Pacific fleet. Three light cruisers, three destroyers and four auxiliary craft were either sunk, capsized or severely damaged. The U.S. Navy also lost 46 patrol bombers, 21 scout bombers, five dive bombers, 13 fighters, three utility planes, two transport planes, one observation plane and one trainer. Even Yamamoto had not expected such a heavy blow to the U.S. Navy.

The U. S. Army's Hawaiian Air Force lost four B-17s, 12 B-18s, two A-20s, 32 P-40s, 20 P-36s, four P-26s, two OA-9s, and one O-49. The Japanese also damaged 34 bombers, 88 pursuit planes and six reconnaissance planes. They had caused extensive damage to all of the air bases.

Killed were 2,008 U.S. sailors, 109 marines, 218 soldiers and 68 civilians. Wounded included 710 sailors, 69 marines, 364 soldiers and 35 civilians.

Japan lost 29 planes, five midget submarines and one large sub. The attack had succeeded beyond Nagumo's wildest dreams. Fuchida assured him that the U.S. Pacific Fleet wouldn't be able to venture out for six months. Nagumo decided to leave while he was ahead.

It was the worst defeat ever suffered by the U.S. Navy. And its location was such a surprise that Secretary of the Navy Frank Knox, receiving the first report of the attack, said, "My God, this can't be true. This must mean the Philippines."

6

Admiral Kimmel and General Short were retired almost immediately after the attack, with a provision that they might be court-martialed at a later date. The provision was pure public relations. Neither officer could be reasonably charged with any offense that would warrant a court-martial.

Proving the value of public relations was Douglas MacArthur, the U.S. Army commander in the Philippines. A relentless self-promoter, MacArthur was probably better known than anyone in American public life except Roosevelt. *Seven hours* after the Pearl Harbor attack, MacArthur's planes were still lined up wingtip-to-wingtip on Clark Field when the Japanese planes came over and destroyed them on the ground. Instead of being dismissed, MacArthur was made commander of all U.S. forces in what the Pentagon called the "Southwest Pacific."

Admiral Stark was replaced as chief of naval operations and sent to England as commander of U.S. naval forces in Europe. Admiral Kelly Turner, who, according to Admiral Layton, really ran naval operations, was sent to the Pacific Fleet where he reported to Admiral Chester Nimitz as chief of amphibious operations. While there, he was discovered by the press and, like all other foul-mouthed, bullying old men in uniform, described as "colorful."

And the war went on.

On January 7, 1941, Yamamoto had written to Admiral Koshiro Oikawa, the Japanese navy minister, that he would "fiercely attack and destroy the U.S. main fleet at the outset of the war, so that the morale of the U.S. Navy and of her people" would "sink to the extent that it could not be recovered."

Instead of sinking the morale of the American people, the attack on Pearl Harbor roused them to fury. Differences between isolationists and interventionists were forgotten. All Americans had one feeling in common: they wanted to destroy Japan.

Ironically, Yamamoto showed them how to do it.

Pearl Harbor emphatically demonstrated that the aircraft carrier was the new capital ship. The Japanese First Air Fleet became the model for the new basic U.S. naval formation—the carrier task force. American officers were even more convinced than their Japanese counterparts that battleships were, at most, of secondary importance. With that attitude, conducting the war without battleships was no particular problem. The vital repair facilities at Pearl Harbor and the enormous tank farm of fuel had not been touched. The United States still had all its carriers, all its heavy cruisers, almost all its light cruisers and destroyers and—most important—all its submarines. There were 112 in service and 65 more nearing completion.

Before the war, Japan sustained itself with goods carried in 10,000,000 tons of merchant shipping. Only 6,000,000 of those tons were Japanese. When it went to war, it lost the use of 4,000,000 tons, most of which were American ships plying the trade with Japan. The Empire of the Rising Sun was able to capture 1,250,000 tons of shipping, but that still left it short of supplies. Japan now faced an all-out attack on its shipping by the U.S. submarine fleet, the second largest and probably the most efficient in the world. Japanese shipyards, working at top speed, couldn't begin to make up the losses from submarine sinkings. Of the 8,000,000 tons of Japanese merchant shipping sunk during the war, submarines accounted for 60 percent, aircraft for 30 percent and mines and surface ships for 10 percent. In four years, Japan had little more than a handful of sampans on the Inland Sea. Before V-J Day, both its navy and its air fleet had virtually ceased operations because there was no more oil.

In spite of a respectable Japanese submarine fleet and the immensely long lines of supply to U.S. forces in the Pacific, Japanese submarines were almost a negligible factor in the Pacific war. Japanese submarines were designed to attack warships. Under *Bushido*, the code of the warrior, warships were a far more honorable foe than merchantmen.

The U.S. undersea fleet did not put as much emphasis on merchant shipping as the German, which seldom attacked a warship. U. S. submarines attacked warships. Lots of them. Of the 686 Japanese warships sunk during the war, 201, almost a third of them, were destroyed by submarines.

Right after Pearl Harbor, Japan had a slight edge in the number of carriers—10 to seven. The thing that had worried Yamamoto when he talked with Prince Konoye, though, was the U.S. ability to produce more of everything, including carriers. Half a year after the Pearl Harbor raid, even before American production could change the balance of power, the Japanese had another encounter with the U.S. Pacific fleet near Midway and lost four of their carriers. From that point, things could only get worse for Japan. Two years later, at the "Marianas turkey shoot" in 1944, Saburo Sakai, Japan's leading air ace, could only marvel at the power of "the American war machine" as 15 carriers in a single task force made mincemeat of Japanese air power. The pessimistic part of Yamamoto's prediction to Konoye was right on schedule.

Yamamoto had calculated American production as carefully as he calculated the odds for an attack on Pearl Harbor. The one place his calculations were wildly off the mark was his calculation—based on the prevalent Japanese stereotype—of American morale. Instead of discouraging his enemies, Pearl Harbor united them as nothing else could.

14

The Year of
the Monkey

THE LEADERS OF THE DEMOCRATIC REPUBLIC OF VIETNAM, MORE COM-
monly called North Vietnam, had always laid great stress on staying in touch
with the peasants of their country—with peasant culture, thinking and
activities. That's why, in 1967, a certain former history teacher probably
devoted some thought to one of the activities of people in backwoods
Vietnam.

The backwoodsmen in Vietnam and other southeast Asian countries
used to catch monkeys for foreign zoos and pet shops. The monkey hunter
needed only a coconut with a hole bored in it and a shiny bead. The hole
would be large enough to let a monkey put its open hand in, but too small
for it to take its clenched fist out. When a monkey saw the bead, it would
reach in to take it, but it couldn't withdraw the hand while holding the bead.
It wouldn't let go of the bead. As a small monkey can't move very fast when
attached to a large coconut, the hunter easily caught his quarry.

The former history teacher was not interested in catching monkeys.
He had bigger game in mind. His name was Vo Nguyen Giap, and he was
the defense minister of North Vietnam.

Giap would need a better lure than a shiny bead, but the trap he planned
would work on the same principle as the monkey trap. The reward would
not be a few coins but all of South Vietnam. It would take a little time to
place the lure, but if all went smoothly, his quarry should be caught by the
new year, which in the lunar Calendar of the Twelve Beasts, was the Year
of the Monkey. The lure would be constructed on a plateau near the village
of Khe Sanh.

2

For Giap, success would mean the end of an armed struggle he had directed since 1941. It would also mean the culmination of a dream that was far older.

The dream went back to 1916, when a photographer's assistant in Paris became aware of what started in Ireland on Easter Monday. The photographer's assistant was a Vietnamese named Nguyen Ai Quoc. When the uprising was crushed, he studied the growth of Sinn Fein. After the war, he joined Sean O'Kelly, a veteran of the GPO fight, and other unauthorized delegates in their vain attempt to get a hearing for their "small nationalities" at the peace conference.

Nguyen traveled around Europe and helped found the French Communist party. Later, he returned to his home, Vietnam, then part of French Indo-China, and organized a Communist party there, too. The party joined in an uprising in the 1930s, which the French crushed. Nguyen fled into exile, and a French court sentenced him to death in absentia. When Giap, also in exile, met Nguyen in China, Nguyen had organized a group called Viet Nam Doc Lap Dong Minh (League for the Independence of Vietnam), or Viet Minh for short. He had also taken a new name, Ho Chi Minh. To Vo Nguyen Giap, Ho gave the task of organizing the Viet Minh's fighting forces.

In 1941, the Viet Minh reentered Vietnam. The Japanese had occupied the country, but they allowed Vichy officials to front for them. The French, in turn, used officials of the puppet Annamese Empire as their front men. Giap and Ho fought the Franco-Japanese combination until 1945. On March 9 of that year, the Japanese deposed and jailed their French stooges. Then, as the war was about to end, they granted independence to the Annamese Empire. Ho immediately proclaimed a Vietnam republic and grabbed all the levers of power before Emperor Bo Dai knew where they were.

Then the British helped the Free French back into Indo-China. The French at first agreed to accept a Republic of Vietnam as part of the French Union, but negotiations broke down when they started discussing details with the Viet Minh.

Fighting broke out in 1946. Over the years, Giap's forces grew stronger steadily. They progressed from local guerrillas supplemented by platoon-size flying columns to a fully equipped field army, backed by a reserve of guerrillas. Finally, on May 7, 1954, after 56 days of battering French forces with 105 millimeter howitzers and surrounding them with concentric trenches and saps worthy of Vauban, Giap's men took the fortress of Dien Bien Phu. The first Vietnam War was over.

The next day, a peace conference, which had already been arranged by the French, Vietnamese, Laotians, Cambodians, Americans, British, Chinese and Russians, opened in Geneva. The agreement eventually reached provided for a military partition of the country between French and Viet Minh forces, the French holding the south and the Viet Minh the north. There would be a demilitarized zone between them, and neither side could import foreign troops or military aid. Cambodia and Laos became fully independent countries, pledged to hold general elections in 1955.

As for Vietnam, Article 7 of the final declaration of the conference stated:

> The Conference declares that, so far as Vietnam is concerned, the settlement of political problems, effected on the basis of respect for the principles of independence, unity and territorial integrity, shall permit the Vietnamese people to enjoy the fundamental freedoms, guaranteed by democratic institutions established as a result of free general elections by secret ballot. In order to ensure that sufficient progress in the necessary conditions obtain for free expression of the national will, general elections shall be held July, 1956, under the supervision of an international commission composed of representatives of Member States of the International Supervisory Commission, referred to in the agreement on the cessation of hostilities. Consultations will be held on this subject between the competent representative authorities of the two zones from July 20, onward.

The representatives at Geneva were not school children. It is inconceivable that they did not understand, first, that the Viet Minh would never agree to what the western signatories regarded as the most basic of "democratic institutions"—multi-party government—or, second, that the puppet empire the French sponsored would dare risk its existence in an electoral confrontation with the Viet Minh. What the Geneva signatories did was pass the buck back to the French. France wasn't buying. Just before the deadline for the election, the French withdrew entirely.

And just before the French left, Ngo Dinh Diem, premier of the puppet empire, overthrew Bao Dai and proclaimed the Republic of Vietnam. Under the Geneva agreement, which the United States did not sign, Britain and Soviet Union had the responsibility to see that a free election was held. Neither nation lifted a finger. No country-wide election was held.

The United States government, which was unalterably opposed to the spread of Communism in Asia, then began supplying the Diem regime with military and other aid. For a short time, the Diem government was able to suppress various guerrilla groups and bandit gangs. By 1960, though, a Communist-led guerrilla movement was launching small-scale, but coordinated attacks on government personnel. Diem began losing control. On

November 21, 1960, Vietnamese paratroopers mutinied. Diem's government crushed the revolt, but then the high-handed Diem became increasingly dictatorial. Most of the popular support he'd retained began to disappear.

In January, 1961, Major General Edward Lansdale of the CIA, who had helped Diem become president of the republic in 1955, returned to Vietnam. As one result of Lansdale's subsequent report, the first hundred U.S. Special Forces troops were sent to Vietnam in 1961. They were to instruct Diem's army in counter-insurgency techniques.

For three weeks, Lansdale headed a task force set up to shape U.S. policy toward Vietnam. Then chairmanship of the task force passed to Sterling Cottrel of the State Department. Under Cottrel's leadership, and against Lansdale's advice, the United States advisors endorsed a "strategic hamlet" program. The British had used a similar program to suppress Communist insurgency in Malaya, and the Americans imported Robert Thompson, a British expert, to help them in Vietnam.

No one but Lansdale seems to have noticed the profound difference between the Malayan and Vietnamese situations. In Malaya, the insurgents were all Chinese, a despised minority. What Malaya's "new village" program did was to incarcerate almost the entire rural Chinese population in comfortable concentration camps. The new villages were surrounded by barbed wire and guarded by troops and cooperative villagers. Villagers went out to work as usual, but they were locked in the village at night. That deprived the guerrillas in the woods the community support they needed. But what worked for a minority in one country could not be applied to the entire population of another. This was especially true because in Vietnam, the strategic hamlet program involved moving people away from their ancestral lands, where they believed the spirits of their forebears lived.

Not surprisingly, the war against the guerrillas did not go as well as the American advisors expected. They blamed Diem, who had become increasingly autocratic, and his relatives, who were becoming increasingly corrupt. In 1963, a military junta overthrew Diem in a coup instigated by the Americans. Then they murdered him on their own initiative.

The war continued to go poorly. The U.S. advisors now blamed the inability of the South Vietnamese to wage a war properly. They told correspondents that if they had American troops they could finish the job. Little by little, the number of American advisors and other forces in Vietnam increased, but they conducted no operations on their own.

In July, 1964, in response to a reported attack by North Vietnamese torpedo boats on two United States destroyers, Congress passed a resolution authorizing the use of American forces in a direct combat role.

In February, 1965, in retaliation for guerrilla raids on U.S. air bases, President Lyndon Johnson ordered raids on "supply routes and staging areas" in North Vietnam that were used by the enemy. On March 2, the United States began regular daily air strikes in North Vietnam. At first, these strikes hit mostly supply routes, but this was not a particularly profitable enterprise. First, up to that time, the guerrillas, or Viet Cong, as they were called, got most of their weapons from South Vietnamese troops who had abandoned them or sold them. Second, the so-called Ho Chi Minh Trail was only a complex of paths through the jungle. While a bomb can wreck a railroad or a paved highway, it can't do much to a dirt footpath. Defense Secretary Robert McNamara, testifying before a congressional committee in 1967, admitted that the bombing had cost the North Vietnamese no more than two percent casualties as they moved south.

The air strikes shifted to more destroyable targets. They began hitting ever deeper in North Vietnam. By mid-April, they were bombing 50 miles from Hanoi. There was a pause in May to see if the North Vietnamese would be amenable to peace talks. But the North Vietnamese were no more susceptible to softening from the air than the British had been in World War II. The bombardment of North Vietnam, a largely pre-industrial nation, had, in fact, considerably less potential than the bombardment of Britain.

Meanwhile, on March 6, two battalions of marines had arrived in Vietnam to guard the air base at Danang. They were the first regular U.S. combat troops in Vietnam, the beginning of a swelling stream. In response, the North Vietnamese sent their own regulars to the south and greatly increased their aid to the Viet Cong.

By 1966, the North Vietnam and Viet Cong forces in the south came to 221,000, but the Americans alone numbered 200,000. By the end of the year, U.S. forces amounted to almost 400,000, and by the end of 1967, there were more than half a million American fighting men in Vietnam. Presiding over this concentration of military power was a handsome, soldierly-looking general named William C. Westmoreland. He had set no records for academic achievement at West Point, but Westmoreland had held a number of important staff jobs, including superintendent at the Point. He was one of the first generals with experience in "air mobile" tactics— the large-scale use of helicopter-borne infantry, artillery and armor. If he lacked the brilliance of a MacArthur or a Patton, he also lacked their vast abrasiveness. Westmoreland was a good organization man.

Westmoreland aimed to occupy important population centers, then spread out with both American and South Vietnamese troops. He would bring the villages under a spreading "oil slick" of pacification. The trouble was that the South Vietnamese troops, or ARVN (Army of the Republic of

Vietnam) did not do well against the NVA (North Vietnam Army). The ARVN even had trouble with Viet Cong main force units. Westmoreland modified his tactics. The South Vietnamese protected villages in the rear while the Americans fought the NVA and regular Viet Cong units.

This took more U.S. troops than figures on Communist strength would indicate. The NVA fought a semi-guerrilla war, moving like guerrillas and fighting like regulars. So did the Viet Cong main forces. To restrict their movements and force them to fight, the Americans had to have many more men than their enemy. President Johnson had set a limit of 525,000 troops in Vietnam. Westmoreland would have liked at least 200,000 more.

Neither the president nor most congressmen wanted to call up reserves or increase draft quotas. Demonstrations against the war were increasing. Most were on college campuses, as they held the largest concentrations of people liable to be sucked into the war.

Early in 1967, Westmoreland launched Operation Cedar Falls, a sweep through a forested area 25 miles from Saigon. Calling in air strikes at the slightest resistance, the Americans "generated" 7,000 refugees, but found only one company and a couple of independent platoons of Viet Cong troops. Next came Operation Junction City, 50 miles northwest of Saigon. This time, the Americans destroyed large VC and NVA forces.

"Whereas in 1965, the enemy was winning, today he is certainly losing," Westmoreland said on November 21. He said the war could be divided into four phases. The first, from February of 1965 to the summer of 1966, was when "we came to the aid of South Vietnam, prevented its collapse under the massive Communist threat, built up our base and began to deploy our forces." The second phase, from the summer of 1966 through 1967, was when the U.S. and South Vietnamese forces drove the enemy's divisions back to their sanctuaries or into hiding, destroyed his supplies and inflicted heavy casualties. Westmoreland expected the third phase to begin in 1968, during which the ARVN would take on an increasing share of the war effort. In the fourth phase, lasting "probably several years," the United States would be able to start withdrawing its forces.

The NVA seemed to prove Westmoreland's assertion that it had been driven back to its sanctuaries. Its next attack was on U.S. bases in Quang Tri Province, the fartherest north in South Vietnam. Most NVA attacks were near the demilitarized zone (DMZ) and the Laotian border. Heavy fighting took place at outposts with names like Con Thien and Dak To. Fighting would rage for days or weeks, then the NVA would disappear, leaving the Americans in position. The U.S. forces would claim to have inflicted enormous casualties on the enemy, and the NVA would proceed to attack another U.S. base.

Westmoreland began concentrating his troops in the north. Operation Junction City was the last big sweep through the jungles in 1967.

3

By the beginning of 1968, even the war in the north seemed to have slackened. On January 17, Westmoreland told reporters that he expected a renewal of enemy activity, although the enemy forces "seem to have temporarily run out of steam."

That same day, a marine patrol from the base at Khe Sanh, near both the DMZ and the Laotian border was ambushed. Patrols on January 19 and 20 became involved in new skirmishes.

On January 20, a North Vietnam lieutenant appeared at Khe Sanh waving a white flag. He told the marines that he had decided to surrender because after 14 years of service, he had been refused a promotion. He also told them that an attack on Khe Sanh was imminent.

None of the dedicated fighting men who interrogated the lieutenant, it seems, found anything odd about a soldier who had served his cause for 14 years going over to the enemy because of a missed promotion. That may have been because aerial reconnaissance backed up the lieutenant's story of an impending attack. The planes had discovered two new roads from Laos that ended 14 and 27 miles from Khe Sanh. They gave access to trails leading to the Khe Sanh area. On January 21, North Vietnamese troops attacked an outpost of the Khe Sanh base, and the NVA began shelling the base itself. The marines pulled outlying platoons back into the main defensive perimeter and hurriedly evacuated civilians from the area. Then North Vietnamese troops overran Khe Sanh village.

On January 25, Westmoreland's headquarters told the press that the "largest battle of the war" was shaping up at Khe Sanh. The enemy had concentrated his largest single force in the area, and the United States was shifting its forces north to meet the threat. Briefing officers described Khe Sanh as a roadblock on enemy infiltration routes, although they did not explain how a single base could block an army that moved mainly on footpaths. Nor did they explain how the enemy managed to surround the "roadblock" with 20,000 troops. If Khe Sanh were surrounded, some 10,000 enemies were presumably behind it, and, therefore, had not been blocked.

In addition to the 20,000 men he was supposed to have around Khe Sanh, U.S. intelligence believed Giap had 20,000 more within 20 miles of the base. The United States had 6,000 within the defense perimeter, but they were not alone. Within a short distance of the base were 40,000 more, briefing officers said. Actually, according to Michael Herr of *Esquire,* there were a quarter of a million.

Meanwhile, the NVA had been digging concentric trenches around Khe Sanh and inching saps toward its barbed wire perimeter. Planes approaching the Khe Sanh airstrip had to run a gauntlet of machine gun fire. There were undoubtedly a lot of enemy troops around Khe Sanh. American casualties began to mount. The newspapers of the world began comparing Khe Sanh to Dien Bien Phu. The influential London *Economist* ventured that the North Korean capture of the *U.S.S. Pueblo* was part of a concerted Communist attempt to divert American attention from the decisive battle to take place at Khe Sanh.

Westmoreland remained supremely confident that he could hold Khe Sanh. He pointed out that the United States forces had incomparably more air support than the French; the firepower of the ground troops dwarfed that of the French soldiers; Khe Sanh was within artillery range of other U.S. bases, and the helicopter-equipped Americans were infinitely more mobile than the French.

He was right on every point, but the press continued to talk about Dien Bien Phu. Everyone agreed that a major battle was shaping up in the north. U.S. President Lyndon Johnson had a sand table model of the Khe Sanh area built at the White House and studied it religiously as reports from Westmoreland came in. Most of Vietnam had been freed from enemy forces. The coming battle on the northern border could end the war. And for most of Vietnam, the war was already a long way off.

4

It arrived suddenly. The war came to Saigon with the Year of the Monkey, while Westmoreland was holding on to Khe Sanh with his enormous military fist.

The first night of Tet, the Vietnamese lunar new year celebration, was over. A cease-fire was in effect in Saigon and everywhere except the I Corps area in the north, where the U.S. command had canceled it because of the NVA build-up around Khe Sanh.

About 3 a.m. on January 31, a man named Nguyen Van Muoi slowly drove a black Citroen sedan toward the U.S. embassy. He glanced at his watch, leaned out of the car window and yelled, "Tien! Tien!" ("Forward! Forward!"). Nineteen young men suddenly appeared out of the shadows and dashed at the building. Simultaneous explosions blasted the early morning stillness from all directions. Rockets and mortar shells, fired from somewhere outside the city, were landing in Saigon.

One of the youths rushing the embassy paused a second and aimed a Russian-designed RPG-7 anti-tank weapon, a combination recoilless gun and rocket launcher that fired a large, shaped-charge missile. The RPG missile struck the ten-foot-high wall around the embassy and blasted a gaping hole in it. Some of the Vietnamese, members of the Viet Cong C-10 shock troop battalion, dashed into the hole. Two U.S. Army MPs by the side gate opened fire at the attackers and killed the first man though the hole. Seconds later, a burst of automatic fire from one of the attackers' Kalashnikov assault rifles killed the guards. An unarmed Vietnamese chauffeur who impulsively rushed forward to stop the raiders was their next victim. The VC commandos then shot the lock off the side gate and let in the men waiting outside.

Marine Sergeant Ronald Harper heard the shooting and shut the embassy door. As he and another marine were locking it, the VC fired an RPG-7. The shaped charge of the weapon (somewhat slightingly called a "rocket propelled grenade" by army public information people) was designed to concentrate its force into a narrow jet. It could cut a hole through the thickest tank armor known and fill the interior of the tank with flame and molten metal. Against the thick cherry wood door of the embassy, though, it merely punched a hole, wounding one of the marines. The wood did not shatter like masonry.

The VC fired more RPGs, but the $2,600,000 embassy was designed to resist a siege. The terra-cotta sunscreen that surrounded the building doubled as an anti-bazooka device. Shaped-charge rockets striking would explode and expend their lethal jet blasts on air.

A "reaction force"—eight marines and MPs—arrived. Two were killed instantly. But the three marines inside the embassy kept up a steady fire. Small groups of MPs and marines began arriving. The VC returned their fire from behind pillars and plant urns in the compound.

Shortly after 7 a.m., Private First Class Paul Healey led a counterattack that reached the embassy building from the front gate, Healey killing five of the enemy personally. Around 8 a.m., two platoons of the 101st Airborne Division landed on the embassy roof by helicopter. Moving into the grounds, the relief troops saw the bodies of Viet Cong commandos sprawled in every direction. Some wore western clothing; some wore peasant pajamas; but all were marked with red armbands.

One of the raiders broke into the home of the mission coordinator, retired army Colonel George Jacobsen. As the Americans prepared to flush the raider out of Jacobsen's house with tear gas, the colonel leaned out of an upstairs window and asked for a weapon. An MP threw up a pistol. Jacobsen heard the raider moving around on the first floor, then heard him start up the stairs. When the Viet Cong commando appeared, carrying his automatic assault rifle, Jacobsen fired three times and killed the last of the embassy raiders.

The embassy raid, though, was only the most spectacular event of the Tet Offensive. Viet Cong and North Vietnam troops seemed to be everywhere in Saigon. And not just in Saigon. The offensive simultaneously struck 100 places in South Vietnam, including 38 cities and towns. Attackers appeared from Duong Dong, on Phu Quoc Island, south of the mainland, to Quang Tri, just below the DMZ. They struck coastal cities and places like Pleiku, deep in the Central Highlands.

During the fighting, Radio Hanoi exhorted the people to rise in revolt.

Compatriots, the revolution we waited and yearned for has broken out. . . . Everybody must stand up and launch attacks against the hideouts of the Thieu-Ky clique. . . . We exhort the officers, soldiers and police forces of the Saigon regime to side with the ranks of the people. . . . We exhort the American troops [to] end their military activities. . . . We exhort the American people [to] side with the South Vietnam revolution.

There was no uprising. Most civilians tried to stay clear of the fighting, although that wasn't always possible. In the old imperial capital, Hue, an estimated 3,000 VC and NVA troops took over the whole city. They killed 1,000 government employees, some by burying alive. And in Hue, Saigon and other towns, U.S. troops used the tactics they had learned in the field— advance until resistance appears, then call in air strikes. Civilian casualties were high.

Westmoreland was determined not to be fooled by the Communists. On the evening of January 31, after the first day of fighting, "Westy" inspected the damaged embassy, then called a press conference to explain that the fighting was a VC diversion to take the Americans' attention away from Khe Sanh, where the enemy expected to fight their decisive battle. Then he sent more troops north.

The VC and NVA were able to get established in Hue because Westmoreland wouldn't send his nearest troops, two brigades of the First Air Cavalry, to aid the government forces. They were on standby to relieve the defenders of Khe Sanh when the big attack developed, and the general couldn't spare them to root out the enemy guerrillas in Hue.

Saigon and Hue were the scenes of the strongest VC-NVA effort. NVA Major General Tran Do commanded the Saigon operation. To prepare it, he smuggled 4,000 men, both VC and NVA, into the city. Some wore civilian clothes; some, the uniform of the South Vietnam police. Rifles and RPGs entered the city in empty gasoline trucks, inside hollow logs ostensibly being shipped to lumber mills, and under truckloads of watermelons and flowers marked for the Tet festivities. Inside the city, the arms were placed in empty coffins and buried in cemeteries or hidden in houses the Viet Cong underground had rented for the purpose. Outside the city were more troops with mortars and large rockets.

Tran Do established his headquarters in the middle of the city so he could direct the action. But as his communications were by courier, there wasn't much directing he could do after the fighting started.

Tran's plan was nothing if not bold, but nothing seemed to work out. His men did not take the embassy. U.S. Ambassador Ellsworth Bunker was whisked away to a secret hiding place. Another of Tran's units failed to capture South Vietnam Premier Nguyen Van Loc. The troops were supposed to take him to a radio station and force him to broadcast an order requiring all South Vietnam troops to cease firing. Still another group of attackers, wearing ARVN uniforms, was supposed to have previously captured the station. The Viet Cong Sixth Battalion seized the Phu Tho Racetrack, but it failed to open the prison.

Most of Tran Do's failures could be blamed on overly ambitious objectives. One, however, resulted from an intelligence error of heroic proportions. The VC Sixth Battalion, which failed to open the prison, was also supposed to take over the ARVN armor school north of Tan Son Nhut airport. It would then use half the tanks and armored personnel carriers there to attack the airport and half to assault the U.S. military headquarters, where Westmoreland was trying to coordinate the American reaction from his windowless bunker. The Sixth Battalion took its objective. But then it learned that the armored vehicles had been moved out two months before.

Tran Do achieved fantastic surprise. Half the ARVN personnel in the Saigon area were home with their families, and the nearest U.S. mechanized force was 38 miles away. But the VC-NVA forces failed to take any of their key objectives. They didn't even manage to blow up the bridge between Saigon and that American mechanized force. Some of the attackers fled to the villages surrounding Saigon. Others made a bloody last stand against the American helicopters, tanks and fighter-bombers, fighting from densely packed houses in Cholon, the Chinese section of Saigon.

American operations in the villages outside Saigon followed the same pattern as those in the city. It was during the fighting outside Saigon, in the Mekong Delta, that the anonymous American major made his comment about the village of Ben Tre: "We had to destroy it in order to save it."

According to American intelligence officers, the chief Communist error in Saigon and other cities was that too many local commanders were too stingy with their manpower. They used platoons for tasks that required battalions and held back most of their strength for a reserve.

The attackers created tremendous havoc. They destroyed 100 planes and helicopters, practically wiped out the South Vietnam "revolutionary development" (pacification) program, opened jails in a number of towns and killed hundreds of allied military and civil service personnel. But after the first week, the attackers were on the defensive everywhere and, except in Hue, losing ground rapidly. In the old imperial capital, the NVA and VC put down deep roots and had to be blasted out inch by inch. They held out for 25 days in the old walled citadel of Hue. When they were gone, the best part of the city had been destroyed.

United States forces, which had lost an average of 140 men a week in 1967, had 973 men killed in the first two weeks of the Tet Offensive. In the same period the ARVN had 2,119 dead. U.S. headquarters estimated that 30,975 Communists were killed in the first two weeks. One was General Tran.

The figure, like most estimates of enemy casualties, was probably too high. But there is no doubt that the VC and the NVA had suffered heavy losses. Worse for them, the mass revolt the offensive was supposed to touch off never happened.

In Washington, an unnamed official said, "This is the Viet Cong's Bay of Pigs. The Vietnamese people did not arise and otherthrow their government as Hanoi had predicted." In Saigon, Westmoreland told his troops, "You have destroyed more of the enemy in seven days than the U.S. has lost in seven years."

5

By any conventional measurement, the United States forces had won a resounding victory. But conventional standards do not apply to unconventional warfare. The victory was fatal to all American objectives in Vietnam.

First, there was the reaction of the Vietnamese. The devastation caused by the American reaction won few "hearts and minds" to the American point of view. Further, according to *Newsweek's* Saigon bureau chief, Everett G. Martin, "The statement by U.S. Ambassador Ellsworth Bunker that last week's attacks will be resented by the Vietnamese population and will hurt the Viet Cong politically is extremely wishful. Things just don't work that way in South Vietnam. The Saigon government has as yet failed to provide the people with any reason to support it, and there is even less likelihood that such support will be forthcoming now." Robert Shaplen of *The New Yorker* found evidence of a growing disaffection for American policy among Vietnamese, both important and unimportant.

For a long time, though, no Vietnamese public opinion had been really important in the conduct of the war. The only civilian opinion that counted was the American.

And the Americans were stunned. How could the Tet Offensive have happened in the first place? Westmoreland later said it wasn't a surprise: American headquarters knew an offensive was coming. But if that were so, why were half the ARVN relaxing with their families when Giap's men struck? Why had the guard at the embassy been increased only from four men to five? Why was most of the American army up north looking at Khe Sanh?

The military seemed totally oblivious to the shock the Tet offensive had delivered to the American people. They didn't understand that their credibility had been completely wiped out.

According to *Time*, General Earle Wheeler, chairman of the Joint Chiefs of Staff, "is, moreover, determined to hold Khe Sanh, for he believes that the loss of the outpost would allow the Communists to roll from the mountains of Laos right down to the South China Sea." This was a month after Giap had sent 84,000 men all along the South China Sea in the Tet Offensive. A little later, an unnamed general told *Newsweek*, "If you give up Khe Sanh, you are surrendering the western anchor of our defense line. The enemy could then turn our flank and two or three provinces would be in serious jeopardy." Six weeks before that, the entire country had been in serious jeopardy.

Westmoreland still clung to the notion that the "greatest battle of the war" would be fought at Khe Sanh. It was a comforting notion to him—the idea that the enemy would face American troops in the kind of big, standup battle that American troops were organized and equipped to fight. One crushing defeat of the NVA would wipe out all the ill effects of the Tet Offensive. Westmoreland had grounds for his belief in the coming battle of Khe Sanh. In mid-February tank-driving NVA troops had overrun a U.S. Special Forces base at Lang Vei, the first time the enemy had used mechanized forces. And Radio Hanoi continued to promise a great slaughter at Khe Sanh.

U.S. bombers delivered a fantastic tonnage of explosives on the trenches that ringed the marine camp. They even dropped armor-piercing bombs that could destroy the tunnels everyone was convinced the NVA was digging.

On April 1, troops of the First Cavalry Division (Air Mobile) launched Operation Pegasus, history's first large-scale assault by helicopter-borne ground troops. It was a textbook operation, observers said. The Cav troopers set up fire bases and leap-frogged them to set up new bases deep in enemy-held territory. By April 6, they landed around Khe Sanh with a secure supply route extending back to friendly territory.

They found nothing.

Or almost nothing—some stashes of rockets and rifle cartridges, a few rifles and machine guns, but no soldiers. At first, they didn't even find bodies. Later, some troops managed to dig up 100 bodies, and some other troops caught a handful of prisoners. The 30,000 men in Operation Pegasus had launched the army's Sunday punch, and it landed in a vacuum. The American planes had dropped 90,000 tons of bombs—a greater tonnage than landed in all of Europe during 1942 and 1943—around this little plateau. The only visible effect was a lot of churned up dirt.

What of the tunnel-busting bombs? There were no tunnels. What of the trenches and saps that had the world's press comparing Khe Sanh with Dien Bien Phu? There were trenches, all right, just as the aerial photos had shown them. Douglas Robinson of the *New York Times* described them:

> Some of the zigzag trenches come within a few feet of the barbed wire on the edge of the mined no man's land that separated the marines from their attackers by about 30 yards.
>
> However, the trenches are only 14 to 20 inches deep and wide enough for just one man at a time to crawl toward the Marine positions.

Not exactly the sort of thing Vauban used to use. Not the sort of thing anyone who intended to launch a serious assault would use. Ideal, though, for anyone who wanted to give the impression of serious siege works to aerial observers.

It began to occur to many people that Westmoreland may have fallen for the biggest con since the Greeks sold the Trojans a wooden horse. Westmoreland didn't think so.

"We took 220 killed at Khe Sanh and about 800 wounded and evacuated. The enemy by my count has suffered at least 15,000 dead in this area," he said. As there were few bodies, Westmoreland's count depended on something other than the traditional "body count."

The official U.S. Air Force history of the battle throws some light on the general's new way of counting.

> The enemy's losses around Khe Sanh cannot, of course, be confirmed since no actual body count was possible. General Westmoreland's Systems Analysis Office prepared four mathematical models from which its technicians concluded that the total enemy killed and wounded numbered between 49 and 65 percent of the force that began the siege—between 9,800 and 13,000 men. The generally cited estimate, 10,000, is half the number of North Vietnamese troops believed committed at the outset of the operation.

Assuming the unprovable—that there were 20,000 NVA troops there in the first place—the technique is interesting.

Long before Pegasus, though, the public had begun losing confidence in leaders who talked about holding flanks in a flankless war and counted non-existent bodies by computer.

After Tet, public confidence in Johnson's handling of the war dropped from a 58 percent approval rating to 35 percent. It continued to drop. Even before the poll-takers released their results, the politicians began demonstrating that the administration's Vietnam policy was bankrupt. Eugene McCarthy, a presidential hopeful who was given little more chance than the Greenback Party candidate, gathered a large, enthusiastic and surprisingly well-financed organization. The newspapers talked about "Gene's kids," but most of McCarthy's followers were well beyond college—and draft—age. The charismatic Robert Kennedy, the late president's brother, after supporting Johnson reluctantly, began to show signs of wanting to run as a peace candidate. In the Republican camp, Richard Nixon, considered a shoo-in for his party's nomination, pledged "new leadership" in Washington to end the war.

Even within the administration, Tet took its toll. Westmoreland wanted to ask Johnson to mobilize the reserves and give him another 206,756 men. Ambassador Ellsworth Bunker tried to talk him out of it. He told the general that nobody in Washington believed either of them anymore. Westmoreland asked anyhow. Clark Clifford, the new secretary of defense, described the reaction in Washington:

> Tet had a very substantial impact on me as it had on others. As I recall, it was said in 1967 that we could see 'light at the end of the tunnel.' General Westmoreland said he thought it entirely possible that we could begin to bring American boys home in 1968. Tet changed all that. The fact that the enemy could mount a simultaneous offensive against so many cities, towns and hamlets at one time and that the effect of such an offensive, even though blunted militarily, could result in our military asking for an additional number of troops, amounting to over two hundred thousand, changed the complexion entirely.
>
> After Tet, I assure you, there was no suggestion that we could see any 'light at the end of the tunnel,' nor was there any thought of sending any American boys home. The whole thrust was exactly the reverse.

Johnson remained determined to fight in Vietnam, but he wasn't going to send over another 200,000 troops. He pulled Westmoreland out of Vietnam and kicked him upstairs to be army chief of staff.

In the New Hampshire Democratic primary, in late March, McCarthy came within 300 votes of beating Johnson. When the write-in votes were counted, it turned out that McCarthy had actually beaten Johnson. Kennedy entered the race.

In Washington, Dean Rusk, the most die-hard of hawks, began circulating among senior administration officials a proposal to suspend indefinitely the bombing of North Vietnam as a preliminary to opening negotiations. Clark Clifford, another one-time enthusiastic hawk, supported the idea.

Clifford had asked the CIA for an assessment of the situation in Vietnam. One CIA paper, delivered March 1, answered a series of questions by Clifford. One answer was:

> Q. What is the likely course of events in South Vietnam over the next 10 months, assuming no change in U.S. policy or force levels?
> A. . . . It is manifestly impossible for the Communists to drive U.S. forces out of the country. It is equally out of the question for U.S./G.V.N. forces to clear South Vietnam of Communist forces. (Pentagon P. 599)

After a meeting of Johnson's advisors, Dean Acheson, the original hawk, summed up the feelings of the majority, "We can no longer do the job we set out to do in the time we have left and we must begin to take steps to disengage."

On March 31, Johnson announced that he would not run for another term. The Defense Department historian whose work form the core of the "Pentagon Papers," summed up the situation.

> In March of 1968, the choice had become clear-cut. The price for military victory had grown vastly, and there was no assurance that it would not grow again in the future. There were also strong indications that large and growing elements of the American public had begun to believe that the cost had already reached unacceptable levels and would strongly protest a large increase in that cost.
>
> The political reality which faced President Johnson was that 'more of the same' in South Vietnam, with an increased commitment of American lives and money and its conseqent impact on the country, accompanied by no guarantee of military victory in the near future, had become unacceptable to these elements of the American public. The optimistic military reports of progress in the war no longer rang true after the shock of the Tet offensive.

With his announcement that he would not run again, Johnson added that he was limiting the bombing of the North and hoped to begin peace talks. The talks began in May. For the rest of the year, the war continued in spurts, which most observers thought mirrored the talks.

Hubert Humphrey, the vice president, was nominated by the Democratic party, largely because of the influence Johnson was able to exert in party circles. Forced to defend the administration's policy, Humphrey, whatever his personal inclinations might have been, became the "war candidate." Nixon was the "peace candidate." After Nixon's election, peace talks were expanded to include the Viet Cong as well as North Vietnam.

While Johnson was still in office, he began withdrawing American troops from Vietnam. Withdrawals began in June, 1968, the same month in which the United States, without publicity or fanfare, dismantled and abandoned the base at Khe Sanh. Under Nixon, troop withdrawals continued steadily.

Nixon's war policy included a show of belligerence, provocative adventures like the invasion of Cambodia and an enormous amount of aerial bombardment. The policy kept the vociferous but diminishing American hawks happy while the president continued to pull ground troops out of Vietnam. Nixon estimated correctly that self-interest played at least as big a part in the peace movement as idealism. The last U.S. combat troops left Vietnam August 11, 1972. It was hardly a surprise. The course of the war had been obvious ever since the Tet Offensive.

On October 26, 1972, the government of North Vietnam announced that secret peace talks with the United States had reached a tentative agreement. Twelve days later, Nixon was overwhelmingly reelected.

A peace pact was formally signed January 27, 1973.

Two years later, North Vietnamese forces took over all of South Vietnam, and the remaining American civilians in the country were whisked out by helicopter from the roof of the U. S. embassy. A steady stream of Vietnamese refugees, the so-called boat people, began. And in neighboring Cambodia, the Khmer Rouge, Cambodian communists under Pol Pot, began one of the proportionately bloodiest purges (two million killed out of an estimated eight to nine million population) in history. Vietnam invaded Cambodia, and the United States, incredibly, seemed to side with the bloody Pol Pot.

The United States was totally out of Vietnam. Because of the United States victory over Giap's Tet Offensive, the country lost a war for the first time in its history. It was a war that nobody really wanted. Nothing that went on in Vietnam could affect the United States. Further, the fighting in South Vietnam was civil war. North Vietnam had not invaded the country, as North Korea had invaded South Korea.

President John Kennedy, anxious to demonstrate that he was not "soft on Communism" and fascinated with covert action and with the notion that a small number of elite troops like the army's Special Forces ("Green Berets") could have a powerful impact, sent military advisers and CIA agents to Vietnam. As the war continued to go badly for the South, President Lyndon Johnson, whose real interest was fighting poverty, feared that he would be the first American president to lose a war. An attack by North Vietnamese torpedo boats on American destroyers in the Tonkin Gulf was reported. Whether the attack ever really happened is disputed, but Congress passed the Tonkin Gulf Resolution and American combat troops were sent to South Vietnam. North Vietnam sent in its own troops, and the United States became a participant in a full-scale war.

Even after the United States got out of Vietnam, the effects of Vietnam were not out of the United States. The Tet Offensive's exposure of official lying had created a new inclination to skepticism in the American body politic. No official was so high as to be above suspicion.

On October 10, 1973, for the first time in history, a vice president of the United States was tried and convicted of a felony. Before the Tet Offensive, it's unlikely that anyone would have seriously looked into the charges against Spiro Agnew.

It's even less likely that the complicated corruption called "Watergate" would have reached the public eye if this Tet-born skepticism had never developed. Never, before Richard Nixon, had a United States president been forced to resign under threat of impeachment.

If this skepticism about official pronouncements and officials continues, and if it keeps the country from again drifting into a useless and wasteful war to satisfy the egos of individual leaders, the fatal victory at Tet, 1968, will not be an unalloyed disaster.

Notes

1. The Absolute Masterpiece

THE BEST SOURCES FOR HANNIBAL, CANNAE AND ROME AT THIS PERIOD ARE THE CLASSICAL historians, Polybius, Livy and Plutarch. This is not the ideal situation, because all look at the war from the point of view of the Roman aristocracy. Unfortunately, there are no extant writings by Carthaginian historians or lower class Romans. The versions used here are the two-volume translation of *The Histories of Polybius* translated from the text of F. Hultsch by Evelyn Shuckburgh in 1962 by the Indiana University Press, Penguin Books' 1965 translation (by Aubrey de Selincourt) of Livy's *The War with Hannibal* and Modern Library's revised version (by Arthur Hugh Clough) of John Dryden's translation of *Plutarch's Lives*. The author, remembering the frustrations of his student years trying to find references cited by the traditional "books" (actually scrolls) gives citations in the modern manner, by page numbers.

Several modern works have also been helpful. Among them are B. H. Warmington's *Carthage*, Harold Lamb's *Hannibal*, and Sir Gavin de Beer's *Hannibal*.

3   "Infantry was the decisive arm. . . ." All figures are from Polybius, *The Histories*, Indiana University Press, Bloomington: 1962, page 264 (III, 107), 269 (III, 113), 273 (III, 117)
4   "And the Romans were better armed. . . ." Polybius, pages 476–8
4   "'What's the matter, Gisco? . . .'" Plutarch, *Plutarch's Lives*, Random House, New York, page 223
4   "Next to the Celtic . . ." The Libyans were trained as phalangites, When armed "in the Roman manner," they would select the Roman weapons that fitted the tactics they knew. So they carried the long spear, or *hasta*, rather than the *pilum*.
6   "The Senate, though . . ." This was the first time in Roman history that two consular armies were combined. Considering the obvious difficulties of command, the desire to hobble Varro must have been strong.
10   "At the beginning of the battle . . ." A head wound severe enough to have this effect would have knocked Paulus unconscious. A leg wound would have unhorsed him immediately. A blow on the corselet would have been absorbed by the solid bronze corselet. The wound described is about the only kind that would have weakened the consul as Livy relates.
10   "'You don't have much time . . .'" Livy, page 148
12   "The Celts hurled their pila . . ." The Celts would have had to dismount for effective shock action in this pre-stirrup age. And shock action was what the situation called for. Evidence of this dismounted attack may be found in the large number of hamstrung Roman bodies found on the field.
12   "'My men still have plenty of energy,'" Livy, page 151; Plutarch, page 224
13   "He used up most of his time . . ." Hannibal's post-Cannae score: counsuls killed—Marcus Claudius Marcellus and Titus Quintus Crispinus; generals killed—Tiberius Sempronius Gracchus, Fulvus Centumalus and Marcus Sentius Penula; armies annihilated—one led by Marcellus, one led by Penula, one led by Centumalus and one led by Gnaeus Fulvius. Many other officers and smaller units were also wiped out.

2. Who's Afraid of the Big Bad Hun?

Perhaps the best overall view of the period discussed in this chapter is contained in the first volume of J. B. Bury's classic *History of the Later Roman Empire*. Bury also covers the wars and invasions of this period in his more compact *The Invasion of Europe by the Barbarians*. C. D. Gordon's *The Age of Attila* is invaluable for anyone interested in the Roman Empire during the chaotic fifth century. Gordon has collected most of the existing fragments of works by fifth century writers that deal with contemporary events. Many writings of authors like Olympiodorus, Priscus, Malchus and Joannes Antiochenes are published in English for the first time in this volume. Priscus, who spent time at Attila's court, is a particularly valuable reference. The first volume of George Vernadsky's *Ancient Russia* provides much detail on such shadowy (to Westerners) peoples as the Alans, Antes, Sarmatians and Huns. *The Myth of Rome's Fall* by Richard Mansfield Haywood is also helpful, especially because it demolishes the the old saws about the Roman Empire having succumbed to excessive luxury, Christianity or a combination of both. Major General J. F. C. Fuller's *A Military History of the Western World*, is valuable on Hunnish tactics, coming, as it does, from a modern master of mobile warfare.

16   " 'Those men . . .' " Priscus, fragment 10, quoted in Gordon, page 58
16   "In 35 B.C. . . . ." Khan seems to have been originally a gutteral pronunciation of Han, the name of the great Chinese dynasty that fought and ultimately drove off the Western Huns. It is related to the Turkish Han, a prince. The same thing happened to Caesar, originally a Roman name. It became a Roman title, then a German (kaiser) and Russian (tsar) title.
17   "The westernmost . . ." The colors were: gold, center; red, south; black, north; blue, east; and white, west. This has led to some confusion among Europeans, all the way back to the Romans, who thought the White Huns were Caucasian. No one, however, has thought that the Blue Turks were Martians or that the Golden Horde was richer than any other Mongol power. When the Turks settled in Anatolia, they named the Black Sea, which was north of their empire, and the Red Sea, which was south.
17   " 'Almost all the Halani . . .' " Ammianus Marcellinus XXXI, 2, 21, quoted in Vernadsky, Vol. 1, page 90
17   "Alanic nobles . . ." The invention of the stirrup is obscure and controversial. John Beeler (*Warfare in Feudal Europe 730–1200*, page 9) writes of "the introduction of the stirrup in the early eighth century." William H. McNeill (*The Pursuit of Power*, page 20) says "Stirrups, apparently, were invented only around the turn of the fifth-sixth centuries A.D . . ." But R. Ewart Oakeshott (The Archaeology of Weapons, page 85) maintains, "There is evidence both literary and pictorial to show that they [stirrups] originated in the East as early as the fourth century B.C., and were an essential item in the military equipment of a conquering race at the very beginning of the Christian era. In the sculptures of the great Buddhist Stupa at Sanchi we find carvings of the second century before Christ where horsemen appear riding with stirrup loops, and similarly on a copper vessel of rather later date from northern India. Then from south Russia comes a magnificent jug made of electrum. . . . It is of Greek workmanship of the fourth century B.C. . . . made for the Scythian market. One horse's saddle is clearly furnished with stirrups or stirrup loops."
         Finally, it is difficult to explain the Roman defeat at Adrianople unless the Goths used a radically new type of cavalry attack, made possible by the stirrup.
17   " 'They are almost glued . . .' " Ammianus Marcellinus, quoted in Vernadsky, page 128
17   "According to Ammianus . . ." Ammianus Marcellinus, quoted in Vernadsky, page 128
18   "The Goths fled west . . ." In their flight, the Ostrogoths met and defeated a Slavic-Alanic people, the Antes, whose nobles were related to Alans. Vithimir, the Ostrogoth king, crucified the king of the Antes and seventy of his nobles. The Alans in the Hunnish horde got the Huns' permission to revenge their relatives. United (by the Huns) for the first time in decades, the Alans attacked and defeated the Ostrogoths and sent the

survivors to the Hunnish king as slaves. The king, knowing the value of warriors, incorporated the Goths into his army. Vernadsky, pages 130–31.

19   "That Roman said . . ." Priscus, who left the unflattering description of the Huns quoted above, accompanied the ambassador. He left a memorable picture of Attila (Priscus, fragments 1 and 8, quoted in Gordon, pages 61 and 95):

> He was a man born to shake the races of the world, a terror to all lands, who in some way or other frightened everyone by the dread report noised abroad about him, for he was haughty in his carriage, casting his eyes about him on all sides so that the proud man's power was to be seen in the very movements of his body. A lover of war, he was personally most restrained in action, most impressive in counsel, gracious to suppliants, and generous to those to whom he had once given his trust. He was short of stature with a broad chest, massive head and small eyes. His beard was thin and sprinkled with gray, his nose flat and his complexion swarthy, showing thus the signs of his origin.
>
> . . . While sumptuous food had been prepared—served on silver plates—for all the other barbarians and us, for Attila there was nothing but meat on a wooden trencher. He showed himself temperate in other way, too, for gold and silver goblets were offered to the men at the feast, but his mug was of wood. His dress, too, was plain, having care for nothing other than to be clean, nor was the sword by his side, nor the clasps of his barbarian boots, nor the bridle of his horse, like those of the other Scythians, adorned with gold or gems or anything of high price.

20   "Although they were called barbarians . . ." A century before the invasions, an Arian bishop named Ulfilas translated the Bible into Gothic, using the Gothic script.

20   "The next day . . ." The Franks were a coalition of Western German tribes who adopted the name Frank (Free). The Alemanni somewhat exaggerated the extent of their coalition by taking the name Alemanni (All Men).

22   "Aëtius, who has been . . ." For a glimpse of the canonization process, see Fuller, page 291

23   "The real Huns . . ." The Slavs mentioned here are Antes, a Slavic group ruled by Iranian Alans.

23   "On a plain . . ." See Bury, *Later Roman Empire*, Vol. I, page 293, for a discussion of the location.

24   "Seek swift victory . . ." Jordanes XXXIX, 108, quoted in Fuller, Volume I, page 295

27   "Attila had had . . ." Although drowning in his own blood sound suspiciously like legend, evidence indicates that Attila died of natural causes. He definitely was not, as Roman rumor had it, murdered by Idilco. The killing of Attila by his queen, however, is a feature of the Niebelungenlied. Those who imply, like General Fuller (Vol. I, page 301) that the Attila (Etzel) of the Niebelungenlied was some kind of monster, have apparently never read that German epic. In it, Attila is a kind of well-meaning stranger manipulated by conniving Germans.

27   "A few years after Chalons . . ." The circumstances of Aëtius's murder are typical of the last days of the Roman Empire of the West. A certain Petronius Maximus hated Aëtius and yearned to replace him. He conspired with one of the emperor's most trusted servants. The servant, Heraclius, told Valentinian that Aëtius was planning to kill him. After Valentinian killed Aëtius, Petronius approached him with the suggestion that the new strongman of the empire could be Petronius Maximus. When Valentinian laughed at the suggestion, Maximus persuaded two of Aëtius's Hunnish bodyguards that it was dishonorable to allow their master's murderer to live. Shortly afterwards, while Valentinian was at archery practice, the two Huns killed him. Maximus then made himself emperor and forced Valentinian's widow, Eudoxia, to marry him. Eudoxia found him so repulsive she wrote to Gaiseric, the Vandal king, asking him to rescue her.

Gaiseric sailed to Rome and sacked it so thoroughly his people's name became a synonym for wanton destroyers in many languages. Gaiseric took Eudoxia and her daughters captive, then married one of the daughters. When the Vandals arrived, Maximus tried to flee, and a Roman mob tore him to pieces. Bury, *Later Roman Empire*, Vol. I, pages 298–300 and 323–6

3. What Happened at Hattin

There are many books on the crusades, but the most comprehensive are probably Sir Steven Runciman's three-volume *History of the Crusades* and the six-volume *A History of the Crusades* edited by Kenneth M. Setton. Among the many popular histories, Harold Lamb's *The Crusades*—really two earlier books, *Iron Men and Saints* and *The Flame of Islam*, in one volume—is unique in its combination of old-time story-telling and meticulous scholarship. One of the best one-volume histories is Regine Pernoud's *The Crusades* which presents the story largely through the eyes of contemporaries, Christian and Moslem. Amin Maalouf's *The Crusades Through Arab Eyes* gives Western readers both a look at the conflict from the Moslem point of view and valuable background on the politics and internal affairs of the Moslem countries. A couple of fairly short books, Malcolm Billings' *The Cross and the Crescent*, and Ernle Bradford's *The Sword and the Scimitar*, are useful because they include much of the latest scholarship.

In *Crusade, Commerce and Culture*, Aziz S. Atiya presents the crusades as part of a much longer struggle between Europe and the Near East, beginning in classical times and extending into the modern world. Particularly interesting are the European attempts to continue the crusades lasting into the fifteenth century. These including attacking the Turks in Asia Minor and Eastern Europe and the Moslems in various parts of North Africa, from Morocco to Egypt. They also included overland expeditions to the Far East, during the heydey of the Mongol Empire and attempts to enlist the Mongols in a joint attack on Islam. One aim of Columbus's voyage was to renew contact with the Great Khan, which had been cut off by the Moslems of Central Asia.

Carlo Cipolla in *Guns, Sails and Empires* discusses the technological developments, inspired by the failure of the crusades, which resulted in the maritime outflanking of the Islamic powers.

Of the many books on arms and armor of the time, Sir Ralph Payne-Gallwey's *The Crossbow* is outstanding. It is based on the reproduction and use of medieval crossbows and siege engines.

31   "The decade of 1020 . . ." Billings, page 19
31   "The pope and the German emperor . . ." Charlemagne founded what came to be called the Holy Roman Empire, but to him it was the renewal of the Western Roman Empire. Otto the Great again restored the Western Empire. By this time, it included all the German principalities and a part of Italy. The Eastern Empire didn't recognize the new emperors as being truly Roman, however. Eventually, the western empire came to be called the Holy Roman Empire of the German People and the eastern empire was called the Byzantine Empire or, sometimes, the empire of the Greeks.
32   "'A grave report . . .'" Billings, page 18
32   "'You oppressors of orphans . . .'", Billings, pages 18–19
33   "'A German count . . .'" Billings, pages 16–17
33   "'The men from the North . . .'" quoted in Montross, *War through the Ages*, page 94
36   "The Franks responded . . ." The famous Turkish flight bows were adapted from weapons carried by the Ottoman Janissaries, an infantry corps. They were developed in the seventeenth and eighteenth century when the bow was long obsolete in the Turkish Army. See Payne-Gallwey's *Treatise on Turkish and Other Oriental Bows* in the appendix to The Crossbow. For information on the crusader crossbows, see Payne-Gallwey, pages 62–9.
36   "Most of the Turks wore . . ." H. Russell Robinson, *Oriental Armour*, pages 53–60

36   "'I have seen soldiers . . .'" Beha ed-Din Ibn Shedad, Saladin's friend and companion, quoted in Pernoud *The Crusades*, page 18
36   "'The Turks came upon us . . .'" quoted in Billings, page 40
36   "'We pursued . . .'" Billings, pages 40–1
37   "A few stayed . . ." "Latin" was the name the Eastern Rite Christians gave to the crusaders and their states.
40   "Each time, the crossbowmen . . ." Payne-Gallwey, pages 73–6
41   "The crusaders' coordination . . ." Beha ed-Din Ibn Shedad wrote: "The Franks kept
42   the same order whether they were marching or fighting; they never left the main body of the army, no matter what attempt was made to draw them out of the ranks." Pernoud, *op. cit.* page 18
42   "'I was beside my father . . .'" Ibn al Athir in *The Sum of World History* quoted in Pernoud *The Crusades* page 167
42   "'Remind the king . . .'" Beha ed-Din Ibn Shedad quoted in Lamb *The Crusades*, page 315
43   "If the ransom . . ." When Richard the Lionhearted attempted to arrange a prisoner exchange with Saladin, he learned that the sultan had none of the knights captured at Hattin. Those that had not been released had been killed. Richard killed prisoners, too. When the Moslems would not or could not carry out the terms he laid down for the surrender of Acre, he killed the entire garrison.
43   "Unlike Saladin . . ." After Saladin recaptured Jaffa, Richard waded ashore from a galley, leading 80 knights and 200 foot soldiers plus some unarmored sailors. He drove the sultan's whole army out of the city. Marching south along the coast, he improved the basic Crusader infantry-cavalry formation into a system all of Saladin's horse archers couldn't even slow down.
43   "The triumph of the horse archer . . ." The Europeans tried horse archers, but found that in their wet, heavily wooded homeland they weren't very useful. They concentrated on developing stronger crossbows and developed new longbow tactics. That led to a new kind of plate armor and, consequently, a quantum jump in metal-working skills. Plate armor led to a practical use for the gunpowder the Moslems had scorned— muskets, which could penetrate the heaviest armor a man could carry.

4. The Blind Leading the Blind

Strangely, the Fourth Crusade, the most shameful of that long series of wars, is the best documented. Geoffroy de Villehardouin told the whole story from the leadership point of view in his narrative translated (by M. R. B. Shaw) as *The Conquest of Constantinople*. It appears in *Chronicles of the Crusades*, Penguin, Harmondsworth, Middlesex, England.

The other narrative of this war is by Robert de Clari, an ordinary knight—not a leader— who took part. Also titled *The Conquest of Constantinople*, it provides the viewpoint of a fighter in the ranks. Translated with an introduction and notes by Edgar Holmes McNeal, it was copyrighted by Columbia University Press in 1936 and 1964 and published by W. W. Norton, Inc., New York: 1969

An excellent history of this particular crusade, using all available modern sources, is *The Sundered Cross: The Story of the Fourth Crusade*, by Ernle Bradford.

46   "'I can assure you . . .'" Villehardouin, pages 58–59.
47   "'He who had possessed so much . . .'" Beha ed-Din quoted in Lamb, page 315
48   "Venice was a city-state and a republic . . ." For a description of the city-state's unique system of government, see Toynbee, Arnold (ed.) *Cities of Destiny*, J. R. Hale's chapter on Venice, pages 48–67
49   "'that no Venetian should be so bold . . .'" Clari, page 38.
     "'You shall not depart . . .'" Clari, page 40.
51   "'Firstly, if God permits . . .'" Villehardouin, page 50
52   "'Here is your natural lord . . .'" Villehardouin, page 64, Clari, page 80

52 "Other sailors tightened . . ." see Payne-Gallwey, *The Crossbow*, pages 249–319 and pages 5–19 in the appendix for details on the operation of pre-gunpowder siege engines.
54 "'Put me ashore . . .'" Villehardouin, page 71
54 "'It looked as if the whole plain . . .'" Villehardouin, page 72
54 "In this emergency . . ." Clari, page 72
57 "'We were in very grave danger . . .'" Villehardouin, page 89

5. Mephistopheles and the Snow King

One of the very best books on the campaigns of Gustavus and Wallenstein is Sir Basil H. Liddell Hart's *Great Captains Unveiled*. For the Thirty Years War as a whole, C. V. Wedgwood's *The Thirty Years War* is an excellent one-volume history of that complicated event. David Chandler's *The Art of War on Land* is excellent on both the equipment and organizations of the opposing armies and also on the Battle of Lützen itself. Lynn Montross's *War Through the Ages* also does a good job of explaining Gustavus's military reforms. *War and Rural Life in the Early Modern Low Countries* by Myron P. Gutmann provides a good picture of the impact of war on civilians during this period, although the war in Germany was longer, more intense and even more brutal than in the Low Countries.

There are, of course, many books that cover this subject. Some of them, though, become more hagiography than history when they discuss Gustavus Adolphus.

63 "'Give the peasantry . . .'" Liddell Hart, page 171
64 "Not the least of these . . ." Charlemagne claimed that his domain was the restoration of the Roman Empire of the West, just as Otto said that what came to be called the Holy Roman Empire was the restoration of Charlemagne's empire.
67 "Born to the throne . . ." The Swedish army kept up its strength by a modern-style conscription and was backed by trained reservists.
67 "'Gustavus was . . .'" Wedgwood, page 322
67 "At the same time, the reader wonders . . ." English speakers are often surprised to learn that in Germany, Wallenstein is widely regarded as a national hero—and not just by Catholics. Schiller's tragedy, *Wallenstein*, celebrates the Friedlander's life. Schiller wrote of his hero, "Germany turns ever to Wallenstein as she turns to no other leader of the Thirty Years War . . . such faithfulness is not without reason. Wallenstein's wildest schemes were always built upon the foundation of Germany's unity. . . . During the long dreary years of confusion which were to follow, it was something to think of the last supremely able man whose life had been spent battling against the great evils of the land, against the spirit of religious intolerance, and the spirit of division." (Quoted in Liddell Hart, page 203.)
67 "But each used plunder . . ." Of Gustavus, Wedgwood says (page 266), "When, for political or strategic reasons, he wished to ruin a country, his men, released from the customary restraint, made up with interest for the opportunities they had been forced to miss."

These "opportunities" were primarily murder and rape. Robbery, called "requisitions," was standard operating procedure. As Wedgwood puts it (page 321) "He plundered as no man had plundered before in that conflict, because he plundered to destroy the resources of his enemies. 'Your Grace would not recognize our poor Bavaria,' wrote Maximilian to his brother. "Villages and convents had gone up in flames, priests, monks and burghers had been tortured and killed at Fuerstenfeld, at Diessen, at Benedicktbeueren, in the Ettal."

68 "'Now you have . . .'" Liddell Hart, pages 112–3
68 "'We have been obliged . . .'" Montross, page 267
68 "The infantry was divided . . ." At that time: earlier there had been more pikemen than musketeers.

69 "The Swedish King's musketeers . . ." Pratt, Fletcher, *The Battles that Changed History*, Doubleday, Garden City, N.Y.: 1956, page 167; Peterson, Harold L., *The Treasury of the Gun*, Ridge Press, New York: 1962, page 68. It may be doubted that all Gustavus's infantry had wheel locks after he had been in Germany a while. Gustavus recruited native troops and foreign mercenaries heavily and must have had difficulty in keeping them all supplied with these expensive weapons. But his musketeers seem to have been able to fire two or three times faster than those of any other general, so a good number of them must have carried wheel locks all through the fighting. Some may also have carried guns with the Swedish lock, an ancestor of the flintlock.

70 "Although it's often cited . . ." Wedgwood, page 278–80

71 "Also, the Swedish musketeers . . ." Wedgwood says the Swedes were five ranks deep, but the first two ranks fired simultaneously. Their advantage over Tilly's musketeers is the same.

72 " 'Should the war last longer . . .' " Wedgwood, page 322

72 " 'The King of Sweden is hard to content.' " Wedgwood, page 302

72 " 'If I become emperor . . .' " Wedgwood, page 302

73 "He dictated . . ." Liddel Hart, pages 189–90; Wedgwood, page 306

74 "This time, Gustavus . . ." Liddell Hart, pages 145–7

74 "That left Wallenstein . . ." Chandler, page 122

76 " 'Swedes!' he shouted . . ." Pratt, page 178

76 "In what the British military commentator . . ." Liddell Hart page 197

77 "Some estimate that Germany . . ." Estimates range from three-quarters to one third of the German population—a lot of people in any case.

6. "My Enemies, Not My Children"

Vincent Cronin's *Louis XIV*, Olivier Bernier's *Louis XIV: A Royal Life*, and John B. Wolfe's *Louis XIV* provided much of the information on the Sun King himself.

The Great Marlborough and his Dutchess by Virginia Cowles provided valuable information on Louis' greatest military opponent.

Lynn Montross in *War Through the Ages* celebrates that bombastic, larger-than-life genius, Claude-Louis-Hector Villars, a soldier too often ignored by history.

The Sieur de Vauban is a prominent subject in any military history covering either the seventeenth century or fortification. Ian V. Hogg's *Fortress* describes his techniques of both siege and fortification neatly and concisely.

81 " 'My dominant passion . . .' " Cronin, page 189

82 "Although he never said . . ." Cronin, page 79

82 " 'With a little patience . . .' " Wolfe, page 221

86 " '. . . the ninth of this month . . .' " Wolfe page 429

88 " 'Gentlemen . . .' " Cronin, page 311

88 "To the new king . . ." Cronin, page 311

92 "Finally, he said . . ." Bernier, page 318. Another translation is, "If I must fight, I will fight my enemies, not my children."

92 " 'I can say . . .' " Wolfe, page 565

92 " 'I am humble . . .' " Wolfe, page 565

95 "He fell from his horse . . ." Montross, page 366

95 " 'If it please God . . .' " Montross, page 366

95 " 'I am infinitely miserable . . .' " Cronin, page 323

96 " 'You are a man of war' . . ." Cronin, page 330

96 "He ordered Villars . . ." Cronin, page 333

96 " 'Gentlemen,' he told his staff . . ." Cronin, page 334

97 " 'Soon you will be king . . .' " Wolfe, page 618

7. A Different Kind of War

A large number of good books are concerned with the French and Indian War (known in Canada as one of the series of "American Wars") and many are concerned solely with Braddock's defeat. The principal sources for this chapter were Walter O'Meara's *Guns at the Forks*, Allan Eckert's *Wilderness Empire, Braddock at the Monongahela* by Paul E. Kopperman, *Battle for a Continent* by Harrison Bird, *The French and Indian War* by Col. Russell P. "Red" Reeder, Jr., *Empire of Fortune* by Francis Jennings and, by no means least, *The Autobiography of Benjamin Franklin* in *Franklin: Writings*. Each of these books presents somewhat different aspects of the Braddock campaign.

The O'Meara book is noteworthy for its detail about the battle and about George Washington's activities the previous year. Eckert's sweeping narrative concentrates on what happened on the frontier during 1755 and includes strong portraits of such famous frontiersmen as Sir William Johnson and Lieutenant Charles de Langlade. Jennings gives the Indians' side of the story as well as defending the Colony of Pennsylvania against slanders originating with the proprietor, Thomas Penn. Kopperman, in *Braddock at the Monongahela* presents and analyzes British and French eyewitness accounts, some of them previously unpublished.

101 "At Pickawillany, a town . . ." Unemakemi was the son of a Piankeshaw woman who had been accepted into the Miami Nation. He had been raised a Miami, but he used his Piankeshaw ancestry to gain followers from that nation, too.

101 "There was a fight . . ." There are several accounts of what happened, but none are totally reliable. There is some evidence that Jumonville was tomahawked after he had surrendered by a Mingo chief accompanying Washington. See Jennings, pages 67–70

102 "He did know that two Delawares . . ." What they actually heard remains a mystery to this day. There were no British troops in the area. See Eckert, page 249

102 "Washington had to sign . . ." Washington's friend, Captain Jacob Van Broom translated the agreement, telling the colonel that "l'assassinat" meant "the death" rather than "the murder."

103 "He needed colonial troops . . ." Braddock had several conferences with Indian chiefs, but they refused to lend him warriors—probably because he told them he was not, as British Indian agents led them to believe, fighting to preserve the Indians' land for them. Later, some Indians did join him, but they left when he sent their women away on the grounds that they were disrupting discipline in his army—a curious charge, because his troops had their own female camp followers who followed the army right into the ambush.

103 "Franklin later . . ." Franklin, pages 1440–1

104 "There were a million and a quarter . . ." Leckie, Robert, *The Wars of America*, page 40

104 "'Captain,' Langlade said . . ." Eckert. page 180

106 "'Elder Brother . . .'" Eckert, pages 190–1

107 "'I have seen the English . . .'" Eckert, page 288

107 "The next morning . . ." Eckert, pages 289–90

107 "When everyone was ready . . ." Eckert, page 290

108 "There were better roads . . ." Waitley, Douglas, *Roads of Destiny*, Page 40. Also, O'Meara, page 125

108 "Suddenly, . . . a painted man . . ." Eckert, page 292

109 "Captain Jean Dumas . . ." Eckert, page 293; O'Meara, page 144

110 "Lieutanant Henry Gladwin . . ." Eckert, page 296

110 "Braddock stood in the stirrups . . .'" Eckert, page 297

110 "Then a bullet . . ." For many years there were rumors that Braddock had been killed by one of his own men. One man even boasted of having fired the fatal shot. The stories are probably untrue, but their persistance is a testimony to Braddock's unpopularity in the colonies. See Kopperman, pages 137–40

111 "'We shall better know . . .'" Eckert, page 307

111   "Of the 1,459 men engaged . . ." O'Meara, page 148. See also Morison, Samuel Elliot,
        The Oxford History of the American People, page 163. Morison gives the total casualties
        as 977.
112   "But these mightiest of warriors . . ." They were extremely helpful at Niagara and a few
        other places, but it is unlikely that their aid was ever essential.
113   "'Delivered from a neighbor . . .'" Leckie, page 80

8. Regulars and Rabble

More books have been written on the beginning of the Revolution than anyone is likely to
finish. Considering its importance, that is not surprising. Since all these books use essentially
the same sources, there is wide agreement on the facts. Works that proved particularly helpful
in the preparation of this chapter include Richard Ketchum's *The Battle For Bunker Hill*; Louis
Birnbaum's *Red Dawn at Lexington*; George Athan Billias's collection of essays about *George
Washington's Opponents*; Francis Russell's *Lexington, Concord and Bunker Hill*; Thomas
Fleming's *Now We Are Enemies*; John Bakeless's *Turncoats, Traitors and Heroes*; Curt Johnson's
Battles of the American Revolution; R. Ernest and Trevor N. Dupuy's *Compact History of the
Revolutionary War*; Robert Middlekauff's *The Glorious Cause*; Benjamin Franklin's *Autobiogra-
phy*; Donald Barr Chidsey's *The Siege of Boston*, Henry B. Carrington's *Battles of the American
Revolution*; Michael Pearson's *Those Damned Rebels*, and William P. Cummings and Hugh
Rankin's *The Fate of a Nation*. The last two are particularly interesting, as they are British.
Cumming and Rankin also tell the story primarily through contemporary documents.

114   "'Since you left me . . .'" John Shy in *Thomas Gage, Weak Link of Empire* in Billias's
        George Washington's Opponents, page 21–2.
116   "'Civil government is near its end . . .'" Billias, page 24
116   "Troops continued to arrive. . . ." Fleming, page 44
117   "In the past . . ." Franklin, page 608
118   "On February 24, 1775 . . ." For a full account of Gage's remarkable spies, see Bakeless,
        pages 37–67
119   "'Stand your ground . . .'" Leckie, page 100. But Leckie confuses the militia commander,
        Captain John Parker, a veteran of Rogers' Rangers, with his cousin, Jonas.
119   "'Lay down your arms . . .'" Leckie, page 100
119   "'Fire, by God . . .'" Leckie, page 101
119   "'Soldiers, soldiers . . .'" Leckie, page 101
120   "'One British soldier . . .'" Leckie, page 101
120   "Some 400 militiamen . . ." Leckie, page 101
120   "'Will you let them burn . . .'" Johnson, page 34
121   "'God damn it . . .'" Leckie, page 103
121   "'Fire, fellow soliders . . .'" Leckie, page 103
122   "Of the total . . ." Leckie, page 106
126   "'I shall take no . . .'" Leckie, page 116
127   "'I shall not desire . . .'" Ketchum, page 120
129   "'An incessant stream of fire . . .'" Ketchum, page 122
129   "Standing by the battery . . ." Johnson, page 48
130   "'Most of our grenadiers . . .'" Ketchum, pages 122–3
130   "'A choice party of . . .'" Ketchum, page 207
130   "'The light infantry being . . .'" Ketchum, page 123
131   "One of the rebels . . ." Ketchum, page 130
132   "'They looked too handsome . . .'" Ketchum, page 130
132   "Another rebel . . ." Ketchum, page 130
132   "'But they fought . . .'" Ketchum, page 133
132   "John Burgoyne . . ." Ketchum, page 137
132   "And Henry Clinton . . ." Ketchum, page 139
132   "The entire British Army . . ." Young, Peter, *The American Revolution* in *History of the
        British Army*, edited by Peter Young and J. P. Lawford, page 84

133   "Economic warfare . . ." Kennedy, Paul, *The Rise and Fall of the Great Powers*, pages
        76–90
133   "Much of it was scantily . . ." Kennedy, pages 93 and 99. Two million is probably a low
        estimate. The population was about 2 million in 1750 and 4 million in 1800. According
        to Paul Kennedy it was doubling every 30 years.
134   "In reply, George . . ." Morison, Samuel Elliot, *The Oxford History of the American
        People*, page 218
134   "At Breed's Hill . . ." Fleming, page 329; Leckie, page 121
134   " 'If I could . . .' " Fleming, page 331

9. "You Got Into Our Inwards"

As with the Revolution, there are piles of good books on all phases of the American Civil War.
Concerning Chickamauga, one of the most easily available, detailed and readable is Glenn
Tucker's *Chickamauga: Bloody Battle in the West*. Fairfax Downey's *Storming of the Gateway* is
excellent on Chickamauga's aftermath, the rout of the Confederates at Chattanooga. Robert V.
Bruce's *Lincoln and the Tools of War* is very helpful on equipment of the era. Of the many
standard histories of the war, Allan Nevins' multi-volume The War for the Union was very
helpful. *Battlecry of Freedom*, James McPherson's one-volume history of the war, gives a good
summary of the political background. The one-volume *Ordeal by Fire*, Fletcher Pratt's mostly-
military history of the war is in a class by itself for sheer readability. It also offers many original
insights.

140   "Although Vicksburg's loss . . ." Strategically, the capture of Vicksburg was much more
        important than Gettysburg. But even Vicksburg was far from decisive. Many level-
        headed Confederates, such as General Lafayette McLaws, thought the loss of Vicks-
        burg would help their cause by making more men available in the far more important
        sectors east of the Mississippi.
142   "No unit in either army . . ." The Lightning Brigade was sometimes called the Hatchet
        Brigade, because they carried light axes to carry out the pioneering tasks Rosecrans
        often assigned them.
142   "Wilder threw in a bonus . . ." There is some controversy as to whether Wilder's men
        carried Spencer rifles or Spencer carbines. Wilder's men were mounted infantry, which
        always dismounted to fight, so they probably carried the longer rifle, an infantry
        weapon, rather than the carbine, a cavalry weapon.
143   "They had to be brave . . ." In Camp Douglas, a POW camp set on a swampy plain near
        Chicago, 750 interned Confederates died of starvation and disease in three months.
        During one stormy period, 30 men froze to death. None of this was considered to be
        out of the ordinary. See Nevins, Vol. III, page 379
144   "As one of Bragg's officers said . . ." Tucker, page 66
144   "That night . . ." Pratt, page 246
146   "The troops continued to rush forward . . ." Bruce, page 101
146   "When these two enormous shotguns . . ." Downey, page 39; Tucker, page 163
147   "Bragg uttered . . ." Tucker, page 228
147   " 'Tell General Wood . . .' " Pratt, page 250
149   "Dana had been sent . . ." Tucker, pages 52–4
150   "Fix bayonets . . ." Pratt, page 252
151   "Bragg had suffered . . ." Tucker, page 388
152   " 'Stop, men! . . .' " Pratt, page 260
152   "The statistics for the battle . . ." Downey, page 195
152   " 'No satisfactory excuse . . .' " Downey, page 224
152   " 'After Chickamauga . . .' " Pratt, page 283

10. Rabble and Regulars

Oliver Ransford's *The Battle of Majuba Hill* is the best easily-available book on the almost-
forgotten (except in South Africa) Anglo-Boer war of 1881. *The Scramble for Africa*, Thomas

Pakenham's history of the European colonization and decolonization of Africa is also very good. It necessarily has less detail than the Ransford book. It looks at the war from a British, rather than, as with Ransford's book, a South African point of view. Thomas Fortescue Carter's *A Narrative of the Boer War* is hard to find.

Commando by Denys Reitz is the story of a South African soldier in the better-known war at the turn of the century. Although the equipment had changed and the Afrikaners had a few professional artillerymen, their military organization was much the same as it was twenty years previous. Donald R. Morris's, *The Washing of the Spears*, a history of the Zulu nation, provided valuable background to the 1881 war.

Another book by Pakenham, *The Boer War*, Rayne Kruger's *Good-bye Dolly Gray*, and Stuart Cloete's *Against These Three* provided information on the aftermath of Majuba, as well as, in Cloete's case, profiles of the principal Afrikaner leaders.

154 "She shouted at the first sentry . . ." Ransford, page 88
154 " 'It might just be mountain goats . . .' " Ransford, page 89
154 "The burghers broke camp . . ." There is one story that Mrs. Joubert single-handedly stopped a rout by shouting, "There are Englishmen now on the mountain; you must bring them down." But it seems unlikely.
156 "The Transvalers elected . . ." Ransford, pages 22–4
156 " 'I have orders . . .' " Ransford, page 27
157 "Usually, the men . . ." Reitz, page 21
158 "In U. S. Army tests . . ." Smith and Smith, *Small Arms of the World*, page 50
158 "From the end of the Napoleonic Wars . . ." Kruger, page 62.
158 "At the time Anstruther's . . ." Bond, Brian, *Colonial Wars and Punitive Expeditions* in Young, Peter and Lawford, J. P. *History of the British Army*, page 175
159 "One sentence from . . ." Ransford, page 50
163 "Thomas F. Carter . . ." Carter, Thomas Fortescue, A *Narrative of the Boer War*, page 438
163 "Of the 365 British troops . . ." Ransford, pages 108–9
164 "Because gold had been discovered . . ." Cloete, page 103
165 "At their peak . . ." Kruger, page 438
165 "Because the British . . ." Kruger, page 439

11. The Bee's Sting

The best generally available book on the murder of Archduke Franz Ferdinand and Duchess Sophie is Joachim Remak's *Sarajevo*. Remak bases the book on just about all available sources and stays completely impartial. *Archduke of Sarajevo*, by Gordon Brook-Shepherd is an excellent biography of the ill-fated royal heir. Rebecca West's extravagantly praised *Black Lamb and Grey Falcon* is very long on words and very short on coherent information. Modern readers unfamiliar with the amount of propaganda produced during and just before World War II are apt to be shocked by the quantity and blatantness of this book's bias. A reader of *Black Lamb and Grey Falcon* might get the impression that all Austrians are totally evil, all Croats are Austrian stooges, all Slavic Moslems are permeated with Oriental weirdness, and Serbs are the only real Slavs.

For anyone interested in what had been Yugoslavia, *Land Without Justice* by Milovan Djilas is invaluable. Here is a picture by an insider, a former vice president of Yugoslavia, of a world far from modern America—a land of partisan warfare against Turks, against Austrians, against Moslems, against Christians of slightly different faiths and against neighboring clans with the same language and religion. Djilas grew up in the turbulent Yugoslavia between the wars, became a communist, fought the Nazis in World War II, rose high in the government. Eventually, Tito imprisoned him. Through it all, he retained the doomed dream of Dimitrijević the Bee.

Robert St. John's *From the Land of Silent People* is an excellent account of the Nazi conquest of Yugoslavia. Fred Singleton's *Twentieth Century Yugoslavia* and Lovett F. Edwards' *Yugoslavia* were both helpful.

166– In Serbo-Croatian, s is pronounced like the s in sink; š, like the sh in shift; č, like the
177   ts in mats; ć, like the ch in change; č, like the ch in arch—a bit lighter than ć; ž, like
      the French j; j, like the y in yell; nj, like n as in neutral, g, like the g in go; dj, like the g
      in george; lj, like the li in million.
160   "Franz Ferdinand wanted to make . . ." Remak, pages 25–7; Brook-Shepherd, pages
      146–7
167   "The conspirators started a whispering . . ." West, on page 550 effectively demolishes
      the charges against Queen Draga. But because she was to a considerable extent
      ignorant of the activities and influence of the Black Hand, she can't explain how the
      stories gained currency.
167   "'Although there was nothing despotic . . .'" Remak, page 52
168   "Again, Bogicević: . . ." Remak, page 52
170   "In a rare moment of candor . . ." Remak, pages 56–7
171   "He once told a friend . . ." Remak, pages 10–11; Brook-Shepherd, page 99
174   "'Mr. Mayor . . .'" Remak, page 130; Brook-Shepherd, page 248
174   "'Our hearts are filled . . .'" Remak, page 130
174   "'As long as the archduke . . .'" Remak, pages 134–5; Brook-Shepherd, page 249
174   "'No, Franz . . ." Remak, page 135
174   "'What's this? . . .'" Remak, page 137
175   "'For heaven's sake . . .'" Remak, page 140; Brook-Shepherd, page 251
175   "'Sophie dear . . .'" Remak, page 140; Brook-Shepherd, page 251
175   "'It is nothing . . .'" Remak, page 141; Brook-Shepherd, page 251
176   "At the execution . . ." Remak, page 253–4
176   "The government had stationed . . ." Robert St. John, a war correspondent, wondered
      why there were no Yugoslav fighter planes opposing the German Stukas when the
      invasion began. Then he learned that General Dušan Simović, commander of the air
      force and effective head of the government, had to borrow the illegal short-wave radio
      of the British air attache to contact his troops. Traitors had cut all the telephone and
      telegraph lines between the capital and the outside world.

12. Easter Egg

One of the best books on the fighting in Dublin is *The Easter Rebellion* by Max Caulfield.
Dublin 1916, edited by Roger McHugh is very valuable: it include many accounts of the events
by participants and other contemporaries. Another valuable volume is *The Making of 1916:
Studies in the History of the Rising*, edited by Kevin B. Nowlan and published by the Irish
government Stationery Office in Dublin. Peter de Rosa's massive bestseller (in Ireland) *Rebels*,
has a great deal on the personalities of the rebels and on Casement's gun-running expedition.
Winding the Clock: O'Rahilly and the 1916 Rising, Aodogan O' Rahilly's biography of his
father, one of the genuine heroes of the rebellion, is well worth reading. William Irwin
Thompson's *The Imagination of an Insurrection: Dublin, Easter 1916*, traces the growth of
the Irish literary revival that had so much to do with the development of nationalism.

In Ireland, the Rising is still the subject of much scholarly inquiry and dispute. C.
Desmond Greaves' *1916 As History: The Myth of the Blood Sacrifice* gives a rather Marxist-
flavored analysis. *Revising the Rising*, edited by Mairin Ni Dhonnchadha and Theo Dorgan, is a
collection of eight essays analyzing the rebellion from eight points of view.

George Dangerfield's *The Damnable Question: One Hundred and Twenty Years of Anglo-
Irish Conflict* neatly covers the area specified in its title, putting 1916 in historial perspective.
Cecil Woodham-Smith's superb *The Great Hunger* covers the Irish potato famine of the mid-
nineteenth century in great detail and makes it obvious why this was a major driving force
behind the revolution. *Paddy's Lament* by Thomas Gallagher, which looks at the famine more
from an American point of view, is also useful. So were a couple of standard histories of
Ireland, *The Story of Ireland* by Maire and Conor Cruise O'Brien and *The Course of Irish
History*, edited by T. W. Moody and F. X. Martin.

178   "The Irish Volunteers . . ." This weapon, the Mauser Model 1871, has been called the
      Howth Mauser in Ireland ever since 1914, when a shipment, purchased in Germany
      before the outbreak of World War I, was landed at the Irish town of Howth.
180   "There was a time . . ." England had claimed Ireland ever since Henry II in the twelfth
      century, and the English managed to enforce their rule fairly consistently over a portion
      of the country around Dublin. It was not until the Tudors, however, that the English
      made a serious attempt to destroy the rule of the native kings.
180   "They rose again . . ." The Protestants of Ulster were descendants of English and
      Lowland Scots who were "planted" there by successive British governments. They
      were not, of course, the only Protestants in Ireland. Protestants were distributed all
      through the island, and, during the penal laws period, they controlled every means of
      producing wealth. Because they controlled Irish business, Protestants were especially
      incensed by what they considered unfair advantages to British industry. This led not
      only to the 1798 uprising, but to heavy immigration of the "Scotch-Irish" to America
      and to strongly pro-American feeling among Irish Protestants during the American
      Revolution.
180   "During what was known as . . ." O'Brien, page 73
180   " 'There never was a country . . .' " Woodham-Smith, page 20
180   "Ireland presented . . ." Caulfield, page 18
182   "He urged . . ." Dangerfield, page 129
185   " 'We've used your name . . .' " Dangerfield, page 172
185   " 'Volunteers have been . . .' " Dangerfield, page 172
185   " 'Owing to the very critical . . .' " Lieberson, Gordon (editor) *The Irish Uprising*, CBS
      Records, New York: 1966. Page 29
185   "The Dublin rebels . . ." de Rosa, pages 296, 323
185   "In a half-whisper . . ." Caulfied, page 8
185   "Because I helped . . ." The quote is from W. B. Yeats poem, *The O'Rahilly*, a more
      poetic version of what he really said: "Well, I've helped to wind up the clock, so I might
      as well hear it strike." Caulfield, page 10
187   "In Dublin . . ." Dangerfield, page 188
187   " 'Go back, boys . . .' " Caulfield, page 90
188   " 'I shot him! . . .' " Caulfield, pages 87–8
190   "They detailed 200 men . . ." Sinn Fein ("ourselves alone" in Gaelic) was a political party
      advocating separation from Britain by non-violent means. This would be done by
      building parallel institutions in every sphere of activity—an Irish parliament, Irish banks,
      Irish courts, an Irish stock market, etc. The British knew there was a philosophical
      movement behind the Irish Volunteers. Because of the secrecy the Irish Republican
      Brotherhood was able to enforce, Sinn Fein was the only movement that was visible. In
      the same period, the Austrians made the same mistake when they ascribed to *Narodna
      Odbrana* the activities of the Black Hand.
191   " 'If he is not free tonight . . .' " Coffey, Thomas M., *Agony at Easter*, pages 72–3
192   "Then their commander . . ." Caulfield, page 211
195   "The British were later to make much . . ." Before the 1880s, large caliber lead bullets
      of the type used by the Howth Mauser were the only kind fired from military rifles.
      The United States last used these bullets less than 20 years before the Easter Rising,
      in the Spanish American War and the following Philippine Wars. The Hague Convention
      outlawed them along with dumdum (from the British arsenal at Dumdum, Bengal)
      bullets—jacketed bullets with a soft point, like modern hunting bullets. To improve the
      wounding ability of full jacketed bullets, as well as to flatten the trajectories of their
      service ammunition, Germany and then the United States adopted the "spitzer" bullet—
      a pointed projectile with a tendency to turn end-over-end when it encouters resistance.
      Britain increased the tendency of its bullets to tumble by making them with a compound
      core—fiber or aluminum at the tip and lead at the base—inside the metal jacket. For a
      quote from the British *Small Arms Manual*, 1929 edition, see Sharpe, Philip B.,

Complete Guide to Handloading, Funk and Wagnalls Company, New York: 1953. Pages
        123–4
196   "'Every bullet clanged . . .'" Caulfield, page 337
197   "More than 3,000 . . ." Hayes-McCoy, G. A., *A Military History of the 1916 Rising,* in
        The Making of 1916, page 303
198   "The British colonel . . ." Caulfield, pages 371–2
198   "Britannia's sons . . ." The line is from an Irish rebel ballad, *The Foggy Dew*
199   "'They all will forget . . .'" Dangerfield, page 218

13. A Single Miscalculation

The most important source for this chapter was the late Gordon Prange's *At Dawn We Slept.*
His second book, *Dec. 7, 1941,* is also most valuable. It gives more details about the actual
attack and less on the background. The citations below are from *At Dawn We Slept.* Dr.
Prange spent 37 years researching the book—looking at all available documents and interview-
ing survivors on both sides. H. P. Willmott's *Pearl Harbor* is an excellent short account of the
battle which also summarizes Japan's economic condition before and after Pearl Harbor.
Willmott also contributed the naval portion of Octopus Books Ltd.'s *Weapons & Warfare of the
Twentieth Century.*

   The Two Ocean War, Samuel Eliot Morison's one-volume history of the U.S. Navy in
World War II, includes, of course, a section of the raid on Pearl Harbor. More important, it
covers the largely forgotten role of U.S. submarines in the war. British writers like Willmott,
perhaps because of their experience with the German U-boats, tend to concentrate on what
American submarines did to Japanese merchant shipping—with, compared with the German
effort, small losses. Most of them forget the submarines' enormous role in destroying the
Japanese Navy.

   Most of the controversy about Pearl Harbor concerns allegedly ignored warnings derived
from code intercepts. The late Admiral Edwin T. Layton's *And I Was There,* coming, as it
does, from the Pacific Fleet's intelligence officer, is a powerful indictment of the mishandling
of information in Washington. The title of *Betrayal at Pearl Harbor: How Churchill Lured
Roosevelt into WWII* is more sensational than the contents. The book is by James Rusbridger,
a writer on intelligence matters, and Eric Nave, an Australian who worked as a Japanese code
breaker for the British Navy in World War II. It's full of the esoterica of code-breaking and
explains why codes are not "broken" in one fell swoop but are gradually deciphered (with
setbacks as keys are changed).

   Like most writers on the subject, Rusbridger and Nave somewhat overrate the importance
of code breaking. For example, they state that Yamamoto's decision to bomb Pearl Harbor was
triggered by the discovery in December 1940 of a British cabinet decision not to send naval
units to protect Singapore if threatened by the Japanese. Yamamoto, according to *Betrayal,*
had Southeast Asia as his main objective and was unwilling to divide the fleet in order to attack
Pearl until he learned British ships wouldn't intervene. Actually, Yamamoto had been brooding
about Pearl Harbor half a year before. Pearl Harbor and the U.S. Pacific Fleet was his main
objective. He was so set on that objective he was ready to resign because the Naval General
Staff wanted to take half of his carriers for the Southern Operation. As for British intervention,
he knew the British could do little in late 1940. And when the British did send a carrier,
Repulse, and a battleship, *Prince of Wales,* to Southeast Asia soon after Pearl Harbor, the
Japanese promptly sank them.

   Betrayal is valuable for revealing that the British and probably the Americans were
deciphering the Japanese "JN 25" code before Pearl Harbor. It also presents evidence of
Churchill's duplicity—particularly in how he got the "Purple" code machine from the U.S. while
withholding the "Enigma" machine from the Americans. Perhaps it's most valuable for the way
it details how agencies of the United States, United Kingdom, Australian and New Zealand
governments are still trying to hide details of code intercepts because they would embarass
officials who were in office fifty years previously. And they do this on the grounds of "national
security."

 Samurai by Saburo Sakai, with Martin Caidin and Fred Saito, and *Zero* by Masatake Okumiya and Jiro Horikoshi, again with Martin Caidin, present the Pacific war from the Japanese point of view. Both are valuable. *The Atlas of Maritime History* by Richard Natkiel and Antony Preston covers Pearl Harbor superficially and includes dumb errors ("Oahu, biggest of the Hawaiian Islands"). It does, however, summarize most of the Pacific war rather neatly.

200 "'If we are ordered . . .'" Layton, page 72. This translation is probably truer to Yamamoto's tone than the bookish version most often seen. The same extract from Konoye's memoirs appears in Prange (page 10) as:
  "If I am told to fight regardless of the consequences, I shall run wild for the first six months or a year, but I have utterly no confidence for the second or third year. The Tripartite Pact has been concluded, and we cannot help it. Now that the situation has come to this pass, I hope you will endeavor to avoid a Japanese-American war."

200 "And even the Pact's . . ." For instance, the Germans wanted Japan to attack the U.S.S.R. The Japanese resisted, because, while they were not averse to attacking the Russians, that didn't have the priority the oil in Southeast Asia had. See Prange, page 175 and page 478

201 "In 1941 . . ." Willmott in *The Navies Rebuild* in *Weapons & Warfare in the Twentieth Century*, page 200

202 "One difference . . ." Japan was a parliamentary democracy, sort of. More than a thousand years of tradition, though, had conditioned people to obeying those placed above them and continuing to accept such pre-Meiji-Restoration institutions as the "thought police."

203 "Should hostilities . . ." Prange, page 11

204 "Yamamoto, however . . ." Q—Where does a 600-pound gorilla sit? A—Anywhere he wants to.

204 "One was Rear Admiral . . ." Despite reports to the contrary, the air-minded Yamamoto never piloted a plane.

205 "As he worked . . ." Prange, page 21

205 "In protesting . . ." Prange, pages 21–6

207 "The Americans had broken . . ." Modern codes are immensely complicated. Reading them is something like the work scholars had to do reading Babylonian cuneiform in the last century. Admiral Layton said that in early 1942, U.S. intelligence people understood perhaps 10 percent of what was sent under the Japanese "JN 25" naval code.

208 "Stimson saw no need . . ." Prange, page 131

208 "'Since Germany . . .'" Prange, page 129

208 "Even after the Pearl Harbor . . ." Prange, page 558

209 "Rear Admiral Patrick N. L. Bellinger . . ." Prange, pages 91–2

209 "'Marshall 'indicated . . .'" Prange, page 121

209 "In a memo . . ." Prange, pages 122–3

210 "Marshall concluded . . ." Prange, page 123

210 "Nisei or Isei . . ." Nisei are persons of Japanese ancestry born in the United States and therefore U.S. citizens. Isei are immigrants from Japan.

212 "In view of the present . . ." Prange, page 443

213 "'Japanese! Man your stations!' . . ." Prange, page 506

214 "On the fleet . . ." The Hawaiian Air Force was the name of the U.S. Army Air Forces unit in Hawaii.

214 "As the first crewman started . . ." Prange, page 514

216 "Sands emptied . . ." Prange, pages 532–3

216 "They had sunk or crippled . . ." Prange, pages 539–40

217 "And its location . . ." Prange, page 527

217 "On January 7, 1941 . . ." Prange, page 16

218 "Before the war . . ." Willmott, *Pearl Harbor*, pages 65–6

218 "Of the 8,000,000 tons . . ." Morison, page 511

14. The Year of the Monkey

The most important sources for this chapter were newspapers and magazines—specifically, the *New York Times*, *Time* and *Newsweek* issues for the complete years of 1963 through 1968. *The New York Times* publication of *The Pentagon Papers*, by Neil Sheehan, Hedrick Smith, E. W. Kenworthy and Fox Butterfield provided most valuable behind-the-scenes information.

For the history of Vietnam and other background information, *Viet Nam, History Documents and Opinions on a Major World Crisis*, edited by Marvin E. Gettleman, was extremely helpful. So were *Fire in the Lake* by Frances Fitzgerald and *Last Reflections on a War* by Bernard Fall. For the earlier war, especially at Dien Bien Phu, Fall's *Hell in a Very Small Place* is excellent. His *The Two Viet-Nams* is excellent background for both wars.

Several biographies, Neil Sheehan's *A Bright Shining Lie: John Paul Vann and America in Vietnam*, Cecil B. Currey's *Edward Lansdale: The Unquiet American*, Merle Miller's *Lyndon: An Oral Biography*, and Doris Kearns' *Lyndon Johnson and the American Dream*, were helpful. Miller's book was especially worthwhile because he interviewed and quotes leading participants in the U.S. policy decisions.

Two books approaching the subject from opposite directions had very useful information. Bernard C. Nalty's *Air Power and the Fight for Khe Sanh*, was published by the Office of Air Force History and is a very official view of that "siege." Michael Herr's *Dispatches* is a very personal view of the war by a correspondent who became unabashedly anti-war.

221   "The photographer's assistant . . ." His real name was Nguyen That Thanh. He was the son of a minor mandarin. Because he had dropped out of school and taken menial jobs, Nguyen changed his name to avoid disgracing his family. Nguyen Ai Quoc means Nguyen the Patriot.

221   "When the uprising was crushed . . ." Fall, *Last Reflections*, page 70. See also Dangerfield, George, *The Damnable Question*, page 309.

221   "When Giap, also in exile . . ." Viet Nam, meaning South Viets or Land of the South Viets is the ancient name of the country. The French called it Annam, and it, with Cochin China, Tonkin, Cambodia and Laos, formed what was called French Indochina. In ancient times, Cochin China and Tonkin had been parts of Viet Nam.

221   "He had also taken . . ." "Ho Who Englightens."

222   "As for Vietnam . . ." Gettleman, pages 152–3

223   "In January, 1961 . . ." Marchetti, Victor and Marks, John D., *The CIA and the Cult of Intelligence*, also Currey, page 212 and pages 216–39

224   "First, up to that time . . ." Viet Cong, meaning Vietnamese Communists, is a nickname that became the most widely used term for the South Vietnamese guerrillas.

224   "By 1966 . . ." Fitzgerald, page 356

224   "By the end of the year . . ." Fitzgerald, page 406, 456

225   "President Johnson had set . . ." Fitzgerald, page 456

225   "'Whereas in 1965 . . .'" Nalty, page 3

225   "Its next attack . . ." The attacks had begun before Westmoreland's statement. Right after Operation Junction City, in fact.

226   "On January 17, Westmoreland told . . ." *New York Times*, January 18, 1968

226   "On January 25, Westmoreland's headquarters . . ." *New York Times*, January 26, 1968

226   "Within a short distance . . ." *Time*, February 2, 1968, page 25

227   "Actually, according to Michael Herr . . ." Herr, page 101

228   "Some of the Vietnamese . . ." They were usually called the C-10 Sapper Battalion. "Sapper," a European term for military engineer, apparently was unknown to someone in the Saigon Public Information Office, who thought it was a unique Viet Cong word for shock troops. Some of the Viet Cong shock troops did, in fact, operate as combat engineers. But they were usually used as infantry.

229   "During the fighting . . ." *New York Times*, February 4, 1968

230   "It was during the fighting . . ." Fitzgerald, page 525

230   "According to American intelligence . . ." *Newsweek*, March 11, 1968, page 65

231 "United States forces . . ." Dillin, John, *Vietnam—the War* in *Colliers Encyclopedia Year Book* covering the year 1968, page 609
231 "In Washington, an unnamed official . . ." *Newsweek*, February 19, 1968, page 33
231 "In Saigon . . ." *Newsweek*, February 19, 1968, page 33
231 "Further, according to *Newsweek's* . . ." *Newsweek*, February 12, 1968, page 32
231 "Robert Shaplen . . ." *The New Yorker*, March 14, 1968, *Letter from Saigon* by Robert Shaplen, page 114
232 "According to *Time* . . ." *Time*, March 1, 1968, page 4
232 "This was a month . . ." Fitzgerald, page 519
232 "A little later . . ." Newsweek, March 18, 1968, page 26
233 "Douglas Robinson . . ." *New York Times*, April 10, 1968
233 " 'We took 220 killed . . .' " *Time*, April 12, 1968, page 30
233 "The Official U.S. Air Force . . ." Nalty, page 103
234 "Clark Clifford . . ." Miller, page 501
235 " 'Q. What is the likely . . . ?' " Pentagon Papers, page 599
235 "After a meeting of Johnson's . . ." Sheehan, page 722
235 " 'In March of 1968, the . . .' " Pentagon Papers, page 611–12
237 "Whether the attack ever happened . . ." John White, a former naval officer, reported that a sonar man on one of the destroyers told him there were no torpedo boats. White later tried to find the sonar man but the man he found could not remember saying such a thing. White and his story were ridiculed. In 1992, with the aid of Admiral James Stockdale, White discovered that he had been confused about the destroyer his informant was on, not about what he was told. He found the right sonar man, who confirmed what White had reported.

Bibliography

Books

Adcock, F. E., *The Greek and Macedonian Art of War*, University of California Press, Berkeley: 1962

Ashley, Maurice, *The Age of Absolutism 1648–1775*, G. & C. Merriam Company, Springfield, Mass.: 1974

Ashmore, Harry S. and Baggs, William C., *Mission to Hanoi*, G. P. Putnam's Sons, New York: 1968

Atiya, Aziz S., *Crusade, Commerce and Culture*, Indiana University Press, Science Editions, New York: 1966

Bakeless, John, *Turncoats, Traitors and Heroes*, J. P. Lippincott Co., Philadelphia: 1959

Baldwin, Marshall W. (ed.), *A History of the Crusades, Volume One, The First Hundred Years*, University of Wisconsin Press, Madison: 1969

Baynes, N. H. and Moss, H. St. L. B., *Byzantium*, Oxford University Press, Oxford: 1961

Beeler, John, *Warfare in Feudal Europe 730–1200*, Cornell University Press, Ithaca: 1972

Beer, Sir Gavin de, *Hannibal: Challenging Rome's Supremacy*, Viking Press, New York: 1969

Bernier, Olivier, *Louis XIV: A Royal Life*, Doubleday, New York: 1987

Billias, George Athan (ed.), *George Washington's Opponents: British Generals and Admirals in the American Revolution*, William Morrow and Company, Inc., New York: 1969

Billings, Malcolm: *The Cross and the Crescent*, Sterling Publishing Company, Inc., New York: 1988

Bird, Harrison, *Battle for a Continent: The French and Indian War 1754–1763*, Oxford University Press, New York: 1965

Birnbaum, Louis, *Red Dawn at Lexington*, Houghton Mifflin Company, Boston: 1986

Bloch, Marc, *Feudal Society* (two volumes), University of Chicago Press, Chicago: 1968

257

Bradford, Ernle, *The Sword and the Scimitar*, G. P. Putnam's Sons, New York: 1974

Bradford, Ernle, *The Sundered Cross: The Story of the Fourth Crusade*, Prentice-Hall, Inc., Englewood Cliffs, N.J.: 1967

Brocklemann, Carl, *History of the Islamic Peoples*, Capricorn Books, New York: 1960

Brook-Shepherd, Gordon, *Archduke of Sarajevo: The Romance and Tragedy of Franz Ferdinand of Austria*, Little, Brown and Company, Boston: 1984

Brown, R. Allen (ed.), *Castles: A History and Guide*, Blandford Press, Ltd., Poole, England: 1980

Bruce, Robert V., *Lincoln and the Tools of War*, Bobbs-Merrill, Indianapolis: 1956

Bury, J. B., *History of the Later Roman Empire from the Death of Theodosius I to the Death of Justinian* (in two volumes), Dover Publications, Inc., New York: 1958

Bury, J. B., *The Invasion of Europe by the Barbarians*, W. W. Norton & Co., Inc., New York: 1967

Cannon, John and Griffiths, Ralph, *The Oxford Illustrated History of the British Monarchy*, Oxford University Press, New York: 1988

Carrington, Henry B., *Battles of the American Revolution 1775–1781*, Promontory Press, New York

Carter, Thomas Fortescue, *A Narrative of the Boer War*, Cape Town: 1896

Casson, Lionel, *The Ancient Mariners*, Funk & Wagnalls, New York: 1959

Caulfied, Max, *The Easter Rebellion*, Holt, Rinehart and Winston, New York: 1963

Chandler, David (ed.), *The Dictionary of Battles*, Henry Holt and Company, New York: 1987

Chandler, David, *The Art of Warfare on Land*, Hamlyn Publishing Group, Ltd., New York: 1974

Chidsey, Donald Barr, *The Siege of Boston: An On-the-scene Account of the Beginning of the American Revolution*, Crown Publishers, Inc., New York: 1966

Churchill, Winston S., *My Early Life: A Roving Commission*, Charles Scribner's Sons, New York: 1958

Cipolla, Carlo M., *Guns, Sails and Empires*, Funk & Wagnalls, New York: 1965

Clari, Robert of, *The Conquest of Constantinople*, W. W. Norton & Co., New York: 1969

Clark, Sir George, *Early Modern Europe*, Oxford University Press, New York: 1960

Clausewitz, Carl von, *On War*, Princeton University Press, Princeton: 1989

Cleator, P. E., *Weapons of War*, Thomas Y. Crowell Company, New York: 1967

Cloete, Stuart, *Against These Three*, Houghton Mifflin Co., Boston: 1943

Coffey, Thomas M., *Agony at Easter*, Penguin, Baltimore: 1971

Cowles, Virginia, *The Great Marlborough and His Dutchess*, Macmillan Publishing Company, New York: 1983

Creasy, Sir Edward and Mitchell, Lt. Col. Joseph B., *Twenty Decisive Battles of the World*, The Macmillan Company, New York: 1964

Creel, Herrlee Glessner, *The Birth of China*, Frederick Unger Publishing Company, New York: 1961

Cronin, Vincent, *Louis XIV*, Houghton Mifflin Company, Boston: 1965

Cumming, William P. and Rankin, Hugh, *The Fate of a Nation: The American Revolution Through Contemporary Eyes*, Phaidon Press Limited, London: 1975

Currey, Cecil B., *Edward Lansdale: The Unquiet American*, Houghton Mifflin Company, Boston: 1988

Dangerfield, George, *The Damnable Question*, Little, Brown and Co., Boston: 1976

Davis, Richard Harding, *Notes of a War Correspondent*, Charles Scribner's Sons, New York: 1911

Dawson, Christopher, *The Making of Europe*, Meridian Books, New York: 1959

Delbruck, Hans, *History of the Art of War*, Vol. I–IV, University of Nebraska Press, Lincoln, Neb.: 1990

de Rosa, Peter, *Rebels: The Irish Rising of 1916*, Corgi Books, London: 1991

Derry, T. K. and Williams, Trevor I., *A Short History of Technology*, Oxford University Press, New York: 1961

Dillin, John, *Vietnam—The War*, article in *Colliers Encyclopedia Year Book for 1968*, Crowell Collier Educational Corporation, New York: 1969

Djilas, Milovan, *Land Without Justice*, Harcourt, Brace and Company, New York: 1958

Downey, Fairfax, *Storming of the Gateway*, David McKay Co., Inc., New York: 1960

Duckett, Eleanor Shipley: *The Gateway to the Middle Ages: France & Britain*, Ann Arbor Paperbacks, University of Michigan Press, Ann Arbor, Michigan: 1964

Duggan, Alfred, *The Story of the Crusades*, Pantheon Books, New York: 1966

Dunan, Marcel (ed.), *LaRousse Encyclopedia of Ancient and Medieval History*, Harper and Row, New York: 1963

Dunnigan, James F. and Nofi, Albert A., *Dirty Little Secrets: Military Information You're Not Supposed to Know*, William Morrow and Company, Inc., New York: 1990

Dupuy, R. Ernest and Trevor N., *The Compact History of the Revolutionary War*, Hawthorn Books, Inc., New York: 1963

Eckert, Allan W., *Wilderness Empire: A Narrative*, Little, Brown and Company, Boston: 1969

Edge, David and Paddock, John Miles, *Arms and Armor of the Medieval Knight*, Crescent Books, New York: 1988

Edwards, Lovett F., *Yugoslavia*, Hastings House, New York: 1971

Effros, William G. (ed.), *Quotations Vietnam: 1945–1970*, Random House, New York: 1970

Ellis, Chris and Chamberlain, Peter, *Fighting Vehicles*, Hamlyn, London: 1972

Ellis, John, *The Social History of the Machine Gun*, Pantheon Books, New York: 1975

Fall, Bernard B., *Hell in a Very Small Place*, J. B. Lippincott Company, Philadelphia: 1967

Fall, Bernard B., *The Two Viet-Nams: A Poltical and Military Analysis*, Frederick A. Praeger, Inc., New York: 1967

Fall, Bernard B., *Last Reflections on a War*, Doubleday & Company, Garden City, New York: 1967

Falls, Cyril, *A Hundred Years of War*, Collier Books, New York: 1962

Fitzgerald, Frances, *Fire in the Lake*, Random House, New York: 1972

Fleming, Thomas J., *Now We Are Enemies*, St. Martin's Press, New York: 1960

Franklin, Benjamin, *Franklin: Writings*, The Library of America, New York: 1987

Fuller, J. F. C., *A Military History of the Western World*, Vol. 1, Minerva Press, Funk & Wagnalls, New York: 1967

Fuller, Maj. Gen. J. F. C., *The Conduct of War 1789–1961*, Rutgers University Press, New Brunswick, New Jersey: 1961

Gallagher, Thomas, *Paddy's Lament: Ireland 1846–1847, Prelude to Hatred*, Harcourt Brace Jovanovich, Publishers, New York: 1982

Gettleman, Marvin E. (ed.), *Vietnam: History, Documents, and Opinions on a Major World Crisis*, Fawcett Publications, Inc., Greenwich, Connecticut: 1965

Goodrich, L. Carrington, *A Short History of the Chinese People*, Harper & Row, New York: 1963

Gordon, C. D., *The Age of Attila: Fifth Century Byzantium and the Barbarians*, The University of Michigan Press, Ann Arbor: 1966

Grant, Michael, *Dawn of the Middle Ages*, Bonanza Books, New York: 1986

Greaves, C. Desmond, *1916 As History: The Myth of the Blood Sacrifice*, The Fulcrum Press, Dublin: 1991

Greene, T. N. (ed.), *The Guerrilla—and How to Fight Him*, Praeger, New York: 1962

Grousset, Rene, *The Rise and Splendour of the Chinese Empire*, University of California Press, Berkeley: 1959

Guevara, Ernesto (Che), *Guerrilla Warfare*, Random House, New York: 1961

Guerdan, Rene, *Byzantium*, Capricorn Books, New York: 1962

Gutmann, Myron P., *War and Rural Life in the Early Modern Low Countries*, Princeton University Press, Princeton: 1980

Hammel, Eric, *Khe Sanh: Siege in the Clouds, An Oral History*, Crown Publishers, New York: 1989

Hargreaves, Reginald, *Beyond the Rubicon: A History of Early Rome*, New American Library, New York: 1967

Harvey, Frank, *Air War—Vietnam*, Bantam Books, New York: 1968

Hatton, Ragnhild, *Europe in the Age of Louis XIV*, Harcourt, Brace & World, Inc., New York: 1969

Haywood, Richard Mansfield, *The Myth of Rome's Fall*, Thomas Y. Crowell Co., New York: 1962

Halle, Armin, *Tanks: An Illustrated History of Fighting Vehicles*, New York Graphic Society, Greenwich, CT: 1971

Herr, Michael, *Dispatches*, Alfred A. Knopf, New York: 1977

Hogg, Ian V., *Fortress: A History of Military Defence*, St. Martin's Press, New York: 1975

Holmes, Urban Tigner, Jr., *Daily Living in the Twelfth Century*, University of Wisconsin Press, Madison: 1966

Jennings, Francis, *Empire of Fortune: Crowns, Colonies & Tribes in the Seven Years War in America*, W. W. Norton & Company, New York: 1988

Jobe, Joseph (ed.), *Guns: An Illustrated History of Artillery*, New York Graphic Society, Greenwich, CT: 1971

Johnson, Curt, *Battles of the American Revolution*, Rand McNally Co., New York: 1975

Kearns, Doris, *Lyndon Johnson and the American Dream*, Harper & Row, New York: 1976

Keegan, John, *The Illustrated Face of Battle*, Viking Penguin, Inc., New York: 1989

Keegan, John, *The Mask of Command*, Viking Penguin, Inc., New York: 1987

Keegan, John and Wheatcroft, Andrew, *Who's Who in Military History*, William Morrow & Co., Inc., New York: 1976

Kennedy, Frances H., (ed.), *The Civil War Battlefield Guide*, Houghton Mifflin Company, Boston: 1990

Kennedy, Paul, *The Rise and Fall of the Great Powers*, Random House, New York: 1987

Ketchum, Richard M., *The Battle for Bunker Hill*, Doubleday & Company, Garden City, New York: 1962

Kirk, George E., *A Short History of the Middle East: From the Rise of Islam to Modern Times*, Frederick A. Praeger, New York: 1959

Kopperman, Paul E., *Braddock at the Monongahela*, University of Pittsburgh Press, Pittsburgh: 1977

Kruger, Rayne, *Goodbye Dolly Gray*, J. P. Lippincott, Co., Philadelphia and New York: 1960

Lamb, Harold, *Charlemagne*, Bantam Books, New York: 1958

Lamb, Harold, *Genghis Khan: Emperor of All Men*, Bantam Books, New York: 1953

Lamb, Harold, *Hannibal*, Bantam Books, New York: 1960

Lamb, Harold, *The Crusades*, Bantam Books, Inc., New York: 1960

Layton, Rear Admiral Edwin T., with Pineau, Captain Roger and Costello, John, *And I Was There: Pearl Harbor and Midway—Breaking the Secrets*, William Morrow and Company, Inc., New York: 1985

Leckie, Robert, *The Wars of America*, Harper and Row, New York: 1968

Levenson, Joseph R. (ed.), *European Expansion and the Counter-Example of Asia, 1300–1600*, Prentice-Hall, Inc., Englewood Cliffs, New Jersey: 1967

Lieberson, Gordon (ed.), *The Irish Uprising*, CBS Records, New York: 1966

Liddell Hart, Basil H., *Great Captains Unveiled*, Little, Brown and Company, Boston: 1928

Liddell Hart, B. H., *Sherman, Frederick A.*, Praeger, New York: 1960

Liddell Hart, Basil H., *Strategy*, Frederick A. Praeger, New York: 1960

Liddell Hart, Basil H., *The Real War 1914–1918*, Little, Brown and Co., Boston: 1930

Lindsay, Merrill, *The New England Gun: The First Two Hundred Years*, The David McKay Company, New York: 1975

Livermore, Thomas Leonard, *Numbers and Losses in the Civil War in America*, University of Indiana Press, Bloomington: 1957

Livy (Aubrey de Selincourt, trans.), *The War with Hannibal*, Penguin Books, Baltimore: 1965

Lyon, Bryce, *The Origins of the Middle Ages: Pirenne's Challenge to Gibbon*, W. W. Norton, Inc., New York: 1972

Maalouf, Amin (Jon Rotschild, Trs.), *The Crusades Through Arab Eyes*, Schocken Books, New York: 1985

McEvedy, Colin, *The Penguin Atlas of Ancient History*, Viking Penguin, New York: 1967

McEvedy, Colin, *The Penguin Atlas of Medieval History*, Viking Penguin, New York: 1967

McGarvey, Patrick J., *CIA: The Myth and the Madness*, Penguin Books, Inc., Baltimore: 1972

McHugh, Roger, *Dublin 1916*, Hawthorn Books, Inc., New York: 1966

McNeill, William H., *The Pursuit of Power*, The University of Chicago Press, Chicago: 1982

McPherson, James M., *Battle Cry of Freedom: The Civil War Era*, Ballantine Books, New York: 1989

Marchetti, Victor and Marks, John D., *The CIA and the Cult of Intelligence*, Dell Publishing Company, New York: 1975

Marshall, S. L. A., *World War I*, American Heritage Publishing Co., New York: 1964

Manchester, William, *A World Lit Only by Fire: The Medieval Mind and the Renaissance*, Little, Brown & Company, Boston: 1992

Mao Tse-tung on Guerrilla Warfare, Frederick A. Praeger, Inc., New York: 1962

Melegari, Vezio, *Great Military Sieges*, Exeter Books, New York: 1981

Middlekauff, Robert, *The Glorious Cause: The American Revolution, 1763–1789*, Oxford University Press, New York: 1982

Miller, Merle, *Lyndon: An Oral Biography*, G. P. Putnam's Sons, New York: 1980

Millis, Walter, *Arms and Men: A Study of American Military History*, New American Library, New York: 1958

Montross, Lynn, *War Through the Ages*, Harper & Row, New York: 1960

Moody, T. W. and Martin, F. X. (eds.) *The Course of Irish History*, Mercier Press, Cork: 1978

Morison, Samuel Eliot, *The Two-Ocean War*, Little, Brown and Company, Boston: 1963

Morison, Samuel Eliot, *The Oxford History of the American People*, Oxford University Press, New York: 1965

Morris, Donald R., *The Washing of the Spears: The Rise and Fall of the Zulu Nation*, Simon and Schuster, New York: 1969

Morris, Eric; Johnson, Curt; Chant, Christopher, and Willmott, H. P., *Weapons & Warfare in the Twentieth Century*, Octopus Books Ltd., Hong Kong: 1975

Morrison, Sean, *Armor*, Thomas Y. Crowell Co., New York: 1963

Moss, H. St. L. B., *The Birth of the Middle Ages, 395–814*, Oxford University Press, New York: 1967

Nalty, Bernard C., *Air Power and the Fight for Khe Sanh*, Office of Air Force History, U. S. Air Force, Washington: 1973

Natkiel, Richard and Preston, Anthony, *Atlas of Maritime History*, Facts on File, Inc., New York: 1986

Nevins, Allan, *The War for the Union*, Charles Scribner's Sons, New York: 1971

Ni Dhonnchadha, Mairin and Dorgan, Theo (eds.), *Revising the Rising*, Field Day, Derry: 1991

Nickel, Helmut, *Warriors and Worthies*, Atheneum, New York: 1971

Norman, A. V. P. and Pottinger, Don, *English Weapons and Warfare 449–1660*, Dorset Press, New York: 1985

Nowlan, Kevin B. (ed.), *The Making of 1916: Studies in the History of the Rising*, Stationery Office, Dublin: 1969

Oakeshott, R. Ewart, *The Archaeology of Weapons*, Frederick A. Praeger, New York: 1960

O Broin, Leon, *Dublin Castle and the 1916 Rising*, New York University Press, New York: 1971

O'Brien, Conor Cruise, *Passion & Cunning: Essays on Nationalism, Terrorism and Revolution*, Simon and Schuster, New York: 1988

O'Brien, Conor Cruise, *States of Ireland*, Random House, New York: 1972

O'Brien, Conor Cruise and Maire, *The Story of Ireland*, Viking Press, New York: 1972

Okumiya, Masatake and Horikoshi, Jiro (with Martin Caidin), *Zero*, Ballantine Books, New York: 1957

Oman, Sir Charles, *The Art of War in the Middle Ages*, Cornell University Press, Ithaca: 1960

O'Meara, Walter, *Guns at the Forks*, Prentice-Hall, Inc., Englewood Cliffs, New Jersey: 1965

O'Rahilly, Aodogan, *Winding the Clock: O'Rahilly and the 1916 Rising*, Lilliput Press, Ltd., Dublin: 1991

Osanka, Franklin Mark (ed.), *Modern Guerrilla Warfare*, Macmillan, New York: 1962

O'Toole, G. J. A., *Honorable Treachery: A History of U. S. Intelligence, Espionage and Covert Action from the American Revolution to the C.I.A.*, The Atlantic Monthly Press, New York: 1991

Pakenham, Thomas, *The Boer War*, Random House, New York: 1979

Pakenham, Thomas, *The Scramble for Africa: The White Man's Conquest of the Dark Continent from 1876 to 1912*, Random House, New York: 1991

Payne-Gallwey, Sir Ralph, *The Crossbow*, The Holland Press, Ltd., London: 1986

Pearse, Padraic H., *O'Donovan Rossa's Address at Graveside*, Office of Public Works, Dublin: 1990

Pearson, Michael, *Those Damned Rebels: The American Revolution As Seen Through British Eyes*, G. P. Putnam's Sons, New York: 1972

Pernoud, Regine (ed.), *The Crusades*, G. P. Putnam's Sons, New York: 1962

Peterson, Harold L., *Arms and Armor in Colonial America*, 1526–1783, Bramhall House, New York: 1956

Peterson, Harold L., *The Book of the Continental Soldier*, Promontory Press, Stackpole Co., Harrisburg, Pa.: 1968

Peterson, Harold L., *Round Shot and Rammers: An Introduction to Muzzle-loading Land Artillery in the United States*, Bonanza Books, New York: 1959

Peterson, Harold L., *The Treasury of the Gun*, Ridge Press, New York: 1962

Phillips, E. D., *The Royal Hordes: Nomad Peoples of the Steppes*, McGraw-Hill, New York: 1965

Plutarch (John Dryden trans.), *Plutarch's Lives*, The Modern Library, Random House, New York

Polybius (F. Hultsch-Evelyn S. Shuckburgh trans.) *The Histories of Polybius*, two volumes, Indiana University Press, Bloomington: 1962

Pope, Dudley, *Guns*, Hamlyn Publishing Group, Ltd., London: 1965

Prange, Gordon W., *At Dawn We Slept: The Untold Story of Pearl Harbor*, McGraw-Hill Book Company, New York: 1981

Prange, Gordon W., *Dec. 7, 1941: The Day the Japanese Attacked Pearl Harbor*, Wings Books, New York: 1991

Prange, Gordon W., *God's Samurai: Lead Pilot at Pearl Harbor*, Brassey's (U.S.), Inc., New York: 1990

Pratt, Fletcher, *Ordeal by Fire*, William Sloane Associates, New York: 1948

Pratt, Fletcher, *The Battles That Changed History*, Doubleday, Garden City, New York: 1956

Prawdin, Michael, *The Mongol Empire: Its Rise and Legacy*, The Free Press, New York: 1967

Preston, Richard A., Wise, Sydney F. and Werner, Herman O., *Men in Arms*, Fredrick A. Praeger, New York: 1962

Ransford, Oliver, *The Battle of Majuba Hill: The First Boer War*, Thomas Y. Crowell Company, New York: 1967

Raskin, Marcus G. and Fall, Bernard B. (eds.), *The Vietnam Reader: Articles and Documents on American Foreign Policy and the Viet-Nam Crisis*, Random House, New York: 1965

Reeder, Russell P., Jr., *The French and Indian War*, Thomas Nelson, Inc., Nashville, Tenn.: 1972

Reid, William, *Weapons Through the Ages*, Crescent Books, Crown Publishers, New York: 1986

Reitz, Deneys, *Commando: A Boer Journal of the Boer War*, Faber & Faber, Ltd., London: 1968

Remak, Joachim, *Sarajevo*, Criterion Books, Inc., New York: 1959

Robinson, H. Russell, *Oriental Armour*, Walker & Co., New York: 1967

Rodgers, W. L., *Naval Warfare Under Oars*, United States Naval Institute, Annapolis: 1967

Ropp, Theodore, *War in the Modern World*, Collier Books, New York: 1962

Runciman, Sir Steven, *Byzantine Civilization*, World Publishing Company, Cleveland: 1961

Runciman, Sir Steven, *History of the Crusades* (three volumes), Cambridge University Press, Cambridge: 1951–1954

Rusbridger, James and Nave, Eric, *Betrayal at Pearl Harbor: How Churchill Lured Roosevelt into WWII*, Summit Books, New York: 1991

Russell, Francis, *Lexington, Concord and Bunker Hill*, American Heritage Publishing Co., New York: 1963

Sakai, Saburo (with Martin Caidin and Fred Saito), *Samurai!* Ballantine Books, New York: 1967

St. John, Robert, *From the Land of Silent People*, Doubleday, Doran and Co., Garden City, N.Y.: 1942

Schoenbrun, David, *Vietnam: How We Got In, How to Get Out*, Atheneum, New York: 1961

Seymour, Charles, *The Diplomatic Background of the War*, 1870–1914, Yale University Press, New Haven: 1923

Sharpe, Philip B., *Complete Guide to Handloading* (Third Edition, Second Revision), Funk & Wagnalls Company, New York: 1953

Sheehan, Neil, *A Bright Shining Lie: John Paul Vann and America in Vietnam*, Random House, New York: 1988

Sheehan, Neil and Smith, Hedrick; Kenworthy, E. W.; and Butterfield, Fox, *The Pentagon Papers*, New York Times, New York: 1971

Showalter, Dennis E., *Tannenberg: Clash of Empires*, Archon Books, Hamden, CT: 1991

Singleton, Fred, *Twentieth Century Yugoslavia*, Columbia University Press, New York: 1976

Smith, W. H. B. and Smith, Joseph, *Small Arms of the World*, tenth ed., Stackpole Books, Harrisburg, Pa.: 1973

Snodgrass, A. M., *Arms and Armour of the Greeks*, Cornell University Press, Ithaca, New York: 1967

Southern, R. W., *The Making of the Middle Ages*, Yale University Press, New Haven: 1962

Stillman, P. Gordon B., *Heroes of the Middle Ages*, Bartlett Hoffman, Inc., New Haven: 1960

Stone, George Cameron, *A Glossary of the Construction, Decoration and Use of Arms and Armor in All Countries and at All Times*, Jack Brussel, New York: 1961

Sun Tzu, *The Art of War*, Oxford University Press, New York: 1971

Tarassuk, Leon and Blair, Claude, (eds.), *The Complete Encyclopedia of Arms and Weapons*, Bonanza Books, Crown Publishers, Inc., New York: 1982

Thayer, Charles W., *Guerrilla*, Harper & Row, New York: 1963

Thompson, William Irwin, *The Imagination of an Insurrection: Dublin, Easter 1916, A Study of an Ideological Movement*, Harper and Row, New York: 1972

Toynbee, Arnold (ed.), *Cities of Destiny*, McGraw-Hill Book Company, New York: 1968

Toynbee, Arnold, *War and Civilization*, Oxford University Press, New York: 1950

Tuchman, Barbara, *The Guns of August*, Dell Publishing Co., New York: 1963

Tucker, Glenn, *Chickamauga: Bloody Battle in the West*, Bobbs-Merrill, Indianapolis: 1956

Tunis, Edwin, *Weapons*, World Publishing Co., Cleveland: 1954

Vasiliev, A. A., *History of the Byzantine Empire* (two volumes), University of Wisconsin Press, Madison: 1964

Vernadsky, George, *Ancient Russia* (Vol. I), Yale University Press, New Haven: 1969

Villehardouin, Geoffrey de, *The Conquest of Constantinople* (M. R. B. Shaw, translator) in *Chronicles of the Crusades*, Penguin, Harmondsworth, Middlesex, England: 1970

Vlahos, Olivia, *Far Eastern Beginnings*, Viking Press, New York: 1976

Waitley, Douglas, *Roads of Destiny*, Harper and Row, New York: 1968

Wallace-Hadrill, J. M., *The Barbarian West: The Early Middle Ages*, Harper & Row, New York: 1962

Warmington, B. H., *Carthage*, Penguin Books, Harmondsworth, Middlesex, England: 1964

Wedgwood, C. V., *The Thirty Years War*, Doubleday & Company, Garden City, New York: 1961

West, Rebecca, *Black Lamb and Grey Falcon: A Journey Through Yugoslavia*, Penguin, Harmondsworth, Middlesex, England: 1984

Wilkinson, Frederick, *Arms and Armor*, Grosset & Dunlap, Inc., New York: 1971

Wilkinson, Frederick, *Edged Weapons*, Doubleday & Company, Inc., Garden City, New York: 1970

Willmott, H. P., *Pearl Harbor*, W. H. Smith Publishers, Inc., New York: 1990

Willmott, Ned and Pimlott, John, *Strategy and Tactics of War*, Marshall Cavandish, Ltd., London: 1983

Wolf, John B., *Louis XIV*, W. W. Norton & Company, Inc., New York: 1974

Woodham-Smith, Cecil, CBE, *The Great Hunger*, Harper and Row, New York: 1962

Young, Peter (ed.), *Great Battles of the World*, Bookthrift Publications, New York: 1978

Young, Peter and Lawford, J. P., *History of the British Army*, G. P. Putnam's Sons, New York: 1970

Young, Peter, *The Machinery of War*, Crescent Books, New York: 1978

Magazines

Newsweek, every issue for the years 1963 through 1968

New Yorker, March 14, 1968

Time, every issue for the years 1963 through 1968

Newspapers

New York Times, every issue for the years 1963 through 1968

Index